Creative Learning in the Early Years

Taking a fresh look at the role of creativity within the early years, this accessible guide explores what is meant by creativity and considers how creative skills, behaviours, and thinking can be identified and fostered in the individual child. Underpinned by the latest research and policy, chapters illustrate how creative attitudes can be adopted in all subject areas and opportunities for creativity maximised.

Creative Learning in the Early Years acknowledges the power of creative processes in helping children reach their full potential in the early years and beyond. Photocopiable work tools enable the reader to plan, observe, assess, and record progress as they develop playful and creative approaches, whilst practical advice and demonstrable examples are easily integrated into existing practice. Topics addressed include:

- Recognising and encouraging creative tendencies

- Stimulating the child's imagination

- Developing adult creativity and self-awareness

- Creating enabling environments and creative spaces

- Using documentation and planning to inspire creativity

An exciting and accessible guide which encourages exploration, experimentation, reflection, and development, *Creative Learning in the Early Years* will support current and future early years practitioners as they discover the rich opportunities opened by creative practice.

Ruksana Mohammed is Senior Lecturer for PGCE Primary, MA and BA Early Childhood Studies and Programme Leader for Early Years Initial Teacher Training at the University of East London, UK.

Creative Learning in the Early Years

Nurturing the Characteristics of Creativity

Ruksana Mohammed   2018

Routledge
Taylor & Francis Group

LONDON AND NEW YORK

First published 2018
by Routledge
2 Park Square, Milton Park, Abingdon, Oxon OX14 4RN

and by Routledge
711 Third Avenue, New York, NY 10017

Routledge is an imprint of the Taylor & Francis Group, an informa business

British Library Cataloguing-in-Publication Data
A catalogue record for this book is available from the British Library

Library of Congress Cataloging-in-Publication Data
Names: Mohammed, Ruksana, author.
Title: Creative learning in the early years : nurturing the characteristics of creativity / Ruksana Mohammed.
Description: Abingdon, Oxon ; New York, NY : Routledge, 2018.
Identifiers: LCCN 2018001324 (print) | LCCN 2018016074 (ebook) |
   ISBN 9781315206400 (eb) | ISBN 9781138635395 (hbk) |
   ISBN 9781138635401 (pbk) | ISBN 9781315206400 (ebk)
Subjects: LCSH: Creative thinking—Study and teaching (Early childhood) |
   Creative ability in children.
Classification: LCC LB1062 (ebook) | LCC LB1062 .M58 2018 (print) |
   DDC 370.15/7—dc23
LC record available at https://lccn.loc.gov/2018001324

ISBN: 978-1-138-63539-5 (hbk)
ISBN: 978-1-138-63540-1 (pbk)
ISBN: 978-1-315-20640-0 (ebk)

Typeset in Melior
by Apex CoVantage, LLC

For my Bubba.

Contents

Figures and tables

Figure

Table

Acknowledgements

Thank you to all the children, practitioners, educators, teachers, leaders, managers, lecturers, students, and parents whose creativity never ceases to amaze me. Your many possibilities have made this book a possibility.

Thank you to my family, for being here by my side, and choosing to be my supporters and cheerleaders. Your many insights and discussions in our often-dysfunctional unit helped sow the creative seeds of my success today. You truly are my tribe!

About the author

Ruksana Mohammed is a Senior Lecturer in higher education, with a career of 20 years in educating children, practitioners, teachers, educators, and students in the early years. Her background is predominately in early years education and practice, which she has an undeniable passion for. Ruksana has worked with young children, families, and professionals and uses this experience and knowledge in her teaching and training to educate all those who have an interest in the education of young children. She still maintains a key involvement with early years settings, schools, and early years practitioners. Ruksana's educational interests include, of course, creativity, play, the early years curriculum, leadership and the early years workforce, student identities in teaching and learning, and the arts.

Preface

**ELVES AND THE SHOEMAKER (FAVOURITE TALES) –
OBSERVATION OF A STUDENT TEACHER**

I'm on a busy train making my way to a primary school. I have an observation of a student on a teacher training programme. She sent me her lesson plan the night before and I was excitedly reading it whilst sandwiched between two huge men in the morning rush hour. Based on a story, it was a science lesson for children in Reception. Children had been introduced to the story two weeks earlier and the planning incorporated the themes set for the term.

For this particular lesson, children were to explore the properties of shoes and then plan and design their own to make the following week. There I was, imagining a range of shoes and children busy exploring them, then various materials laid out for them to touch and feel during the design process: a stimulation of all the senses, and to get the ideas flowing! After all, many learning experiences are initiated, developed and assimilated through the senses, right? Children would have to think about materials suitable for their shoe design, try them on, think about weather resistance – oh, how exciting indeed!

So I got in, settled myself into a chair, and started to record. As the lesson unfolded, I could see all the thoughts I had on the train slowly popping as if pricked by a needle. No real shoes, just laminated cards with pictures of shoes – pop! No real materials on the tables, just paper and pencils – pop! I don't even want to comment on the disruptive behaviour that I witnessed – pop! I know this isn't appropriate, but I just sat there wishing the lesson would end. It was the longest 40 minutes of my life. I looked at the drained faces of the children, and then remember writing on the observation feedback form for the student, 'were you teaching creatively?' 'were children engaging with the content in flexible and innovative ways?' When providing verbal feedback to the trainee, her response was 'but it was not an art lesson . . .' And this ultimately was the driving force behind the writing of this book!

This short story is not placing blame on the student teacher; after all, she is learning, and in her training programme, the concept of creativity is not explored. But what it does highlight is that the role of creativity in practice, and its mere process, is still unclear to the many adults working, or about to work, with children today. It is commonly associated with the arts only. I wrote this book because I believe in the importance of creativity in children's learning – especially in this rapidly changing world.

Creativity is not just confined to the arts; in fact, it has a much broader place in the curriculum. Yet it is through elements of art that the youngest child can express their creativity – i.e. ideas in drawings, visible thinking in sculptures, and making connections in constructions. Creativity is also not just about preparing children for the economy, which the literature heavily advocates, and rightly so, but also significantly supports with developing children as individuals. This, then, makes the role of early years practice not just about imparting knowledge and facts, but also about fostering creative thinking and creative behaviours as well as building creative identities. It is about encouraging children to learn and apply creative thinking processes in all that they do, with the overall aim of supporting them to be creative regardless of when and where it may be used.

This book draws on my own experiences, first and foremost, as an early years practitioner, where I have observed many times creative abilities of children that have left me in awe and wonder. I draw on my experience as an educator and the many interactions I have had with adults that work with children, as well as the many creative moments I have had the pleasure of witnessing in early years settings, primary schools, and universities, as well as in many lectures and seminars. This book intends to support creativity in children's learning by giving examples of it in action. For example, literature tells us to foster creative attitudes, skills, and experiences in teaching and learning, but *what exactly are these? How are they visible? And how can they inform early years practice?* This book intends for you, the reader, to visualise creativity through practical approaches with the use of work tools, practice stories, case studies, activities, research notes, reflective thinking, and other tasks to engage with. It is hoped that this book will excite you, as it did me when I was writing it. Most of all, it is hoped that it will support you in capturing the creativity of children which enables them to learn, and to capture your own in order to teach.

Introduction

Decades of literature and research support the power of creativity. Predominately studied by psychologists as a phenomenon, and only available in the very rare 'and only available in rare individuals', it was the education discipline that advocated its inherent role in children's everyday lives. A landmark 1999 report by the National Advisory Committee on Creative and Cultural Education (NACCCE), *All Our Futures*, was the key driving force, urging educational systems to change by embedding creativity in the curriculum. This was so that creative individuals, with curious minds, can evolve for the futures to come. The report went on to define creativity as 'imagination, fashioned so as to produce outcomes which are original and of value' (p. 29). This provided the foundation for a range of educational policy innovations in England across all phases of education, from the early years through to higher education. Creativity, then, was here to stay, and it has become a much-debated subject in the academic research field over the last 20 years or so for its place in teaching and learning.

In present times, the rise of modern technology and changes in the economy towards global innovation have seen creativity as critical to survival through generative problem-identification and problem-solving across life (Craft and Hall, 2015, p. 7). Creativity is now seen to contribute to inventiveness, innovation, and social and cultural change, as well as political development and economic progression. It is regarded as a skill set, a characteristic, with education having a key role in its cultivation. In early years education, the manifestation of creativity is at its highest, and this is where it has the potential to be nurtured and developed the most. By developing the skills they need to perform in the work place and wider society as entrepreneurs and citizens here, children are more likely to succeed in adult life.

Continual research in early years education acknowledges that, as far as young children are concerned, the creative process is as important as its products (Craft, 2010, p. 33). The early years curriculum framework, Early Years Foundation Stage (EYFS), supports a play-based pedagogic approach and advocates the centrality of the Characteristics of Effective Teaching and Learning (CoETL), which are fundamental to the development of every child as a lifelong learner (Pascal and

Bertram, 2017a). It is the early years practitioner's responsibility to support the development of these skills through playful and creative approaches. Yet, since the NACCCE Report in 1999, despite what is known about creative learning, I still witness children turn from enthused learners to goal and standard conformers, and not by choice. I still observe children in the early years being given 'worksheets' to determine what knowledge they may hold, or to follow dotted lines to create a letter of the alphabet. I still watch a child cut out a caterpillar from a ready-made sheet that has even been coloured in for them by the computer, and then pin it together exactly as the one just shown on the carpet session by the adult. And I still sit and ask myself, *where is the creativity in that?* Yet, I'm also told to hang out and learn from 3-year-olds, because they are the real experts in creativity. *So, where is it going wrong?*

Well, so much has changed at all levels of education since *All Our Futures* – socially, politically, and economically. These changes, at whatever level they occur, always filter down to impact the youngest children. Those working in early years education face daily pressures and frustrations such as qualification overhauls, funding cuts, redundancies, lack of resources, changing policy, and a curriculum that focuses on the outdated belief that concentrating on literacy and numeracy will strengthen early years practice. This places creativity on the fringes, rather than at the centre, of adult thinking for children's learning and quickly drains away any creativity in both children and adults alike. However, it is also true that many adults undervalue and underestimate the role of creativity in the learning process of children. This is mainly because they don't understand it, don't know what it is, or associate it with the arts only, which then prevents them from fostering it, regardless of what informs them of creativity's importance. Sir Ken Robinson famously argued during his celebrated TedTalk that we don't grow into creativity; it is present in early childhood and we are educated out of it – *but how? and why?*

From an alternative perspective, there is innovative early years practice that exists which not only allows for 'teaching creatively', but also 'creative learning'. There are early years practitioners, teachers, nursery nurses, and nursery managers who all place importance on making a difference to early childhood learning by using creative processes. They seek innovative ways to shape the curriculum by testing challenges and barriers daily. It is the people who work on a daily basis with young children who have the biggest influence on their learning, and therefore need the most support to get it right – especially during times of change. It is hoped that this book sets out to achieve this for you. Early years practitioners need to capture the creativity of children to enable them to learn; it is about the here and now, the being and becoming. This book is designed to support this process by encouraging practitioners to rethink and develop their skills set, practical approaches, and understanding of creativity. It aims to help contextualise creative early years approaches which directly support and extend children's progression, and raises awareness of how and why creative approaches in all aspects of early years practice can develop all areas of early learning and, in turn, the creative child.

Who is this book for?

The terms 'early years practitioner' and 'creative adult' are used throughout this book to describe practitioners, managers, teachers, students, early years professionals, support staff, parents, graduates, tutors, lecturers, and all those that have an interest in the teaching and learning of young children, whatever their qualification route or training experience. This book is designed for adults who are keen to support creativity by incorporating approaches in their daily work with children and other adults. Although the book focuses on the early years, it is intended for the contents to be adapted and used across the early years and primary sector, and even beyond!

How to use the book

If this book sounds like more work on top of an already busy agenda, fear not! This book not only offers a discussion of the issues involved in creativity, but for those reading, it also offers useful ideas and strategies to adapt and apply to existing practice. The book is intended to provide creative approaches that work, approaches that are worth thinking about, and approaches that can be explored and experimented with. For this reason, this book has been designed to give you a sense of a 'guide', with easy to read chapters, which can be used to navigate your way through its contents. It is hoped that you can use this to reflect on and support you in your early years practice.

This book deliberately prioritises approaches over theoretical discussions, although everything written has been informed by theory, research, experience, and knowledge to ensure it is intellectually stimulating and at the same time accessible. It is hoped that practitioners reading this book take it as practical steps to infuse their teaching and learning with passion and creativity! How far you go, and how much you get involved, depends on how you will use this book. It can be all or any of the following:

1) As an overview on the use of creativity in the early years.

2) As a key piece of reading for examining creativity in your studies – *what it is? How is it used? How it will support what you are writing?*

3) As a starting point for all the coming creative possibilities in early years practice and lifelong learning (highly recommended!).

Summary of chapters

Chapter 1 gives a contextual overview of the role of creativity in children's education through its past, present, and future. Although governments place emphasis on creativity for the economy, they do so in principle, while continually moving early years towards a formalised and structured approach. The chapter argues that education should prepare children for the future, but that the use of creativity is in the here and now, and the being and becoming, for which early years practitioners need to advocate.

Chapter 2 analyses the interpretation of creativity through its key definition and key concepts that explain it. Though creativity is as ever difficult to define, this chapter attempts to identify a more early years friendly definition associated with creative processes, creative behaviours, and creative thinking. This chapter introduces the concept of 'creativity's characteristics', which children exhibit and should be nurtured by the early years practitioner.

Chapter 3 provides a holistic understanding of the creative child in *what* they learn and *how* they learn. The chapter explores the EYFS Characteristics of Effective Teaching and Learning and their inherent role in creativity's characteristics, as identified in Chapter 2. The chapter explores how children can be observed to approach their learning in ways which makes it unique to them and a factor in exhibiting creativity's characteristics. It pays homage to the role of play in all children say and do and its undeniable presence in creativity.

Chapter 4 explores the role of imagination in creativity through the area of the EYFS Being Imaginative. The concept of possibility thinking is reinforced, and various approaches to stimulate young children's imaginations are provided with planning prompts. This includes stories, imaginative play, the use of humour, and much more.

Chapter 5 is dedicated to the early years practitioner in exploring and understanding their own creativity as the 'creative adult'. It provides an understanding of the misunderstandings and creative blocks adults face when viewing creativity as part of their roles. The chapter provides various practices and strategies for the practitioner to use to invite creativity into their lives and to develop themselves for early years practice.

Chapter 6 discusses the notion of the creative curriculum, and although it acknowledges the EYFS as a play-based framework, it advocates that this is only one part of a broad and balanced curriculum and is open to interpretation. The chapter provides approaches to constructing a creative curriculum, around the EYFS, in which holistic experiences, pedagogical approaches, and identification of the creative skills and characteristics that children should develop are key features.

Chapter 7 analyses the differing planning approaches in the early years as a tool to devising opportunities for creativity to be nurtured. It offers a discussion for those settings that use documentation and therefore advises on good practice. However, the chapter advocates early years friendly planning in the form of cross-curricular, emergent, and the very recent 'in the moment' planning. These are key to capturing and extending children's creative learning as and when it happens. The chapter explores formative assessment methods in the form of observations to identify creative learning and characteristics as important steps to help them materialise.

Chapter 8 explores the environment in nurturing, stimulating, and supporting creativity through 'creative spaces'. It asks early years practitioners to study their environments, both indoors and outdoors, and how they may hinder the nurturing of creativity. It goes onto provide approaches for how to go about planning quality spaces with key features that allow the creative process to unfold.

Chapter 9 is all about creative approaches needed to teach creatively within creative spaces. It provides good practice and ideas to inform early years practitioners' approaches to creativity-rich sessions, activities, experiences, processes, and much more so that children's opportunities for creative learning are maximised.

Chapter 10 explores reflection, reflexivity, and reflective practice for practitioners to develop their work with children through continuous professional inquiry. It moves away from the cognitive tools of reflection, although it identifies thinking as a vital aspect, and offers creative practices that can enhance a practitioner's self-awareness for teaching creatively and creative learning.

The Appendix includes the photocopiable work tools referenced in the chapters. Completing these will bolster self-reflection, analysis, and creativity, and will help you track progress.

On the next page, you will find a 'book map' which sets out what is included within each chapter and its purpose. This will be helpful for you to navigate your way through the many tasks and stories and consolidate what you read.

 REFLECT

Now that you have a general sense of what this book is about, think about how you will use it by answering the following:

1) Why are you interested in creativity?

2) What is your role in the use of creative approaches in children's learning?

3) How far can you embed creative approaches? In a group, a whole class, a setting, a phase group?

4) Identify three goals you wish to achieve by the end of reading this book.

Book Map

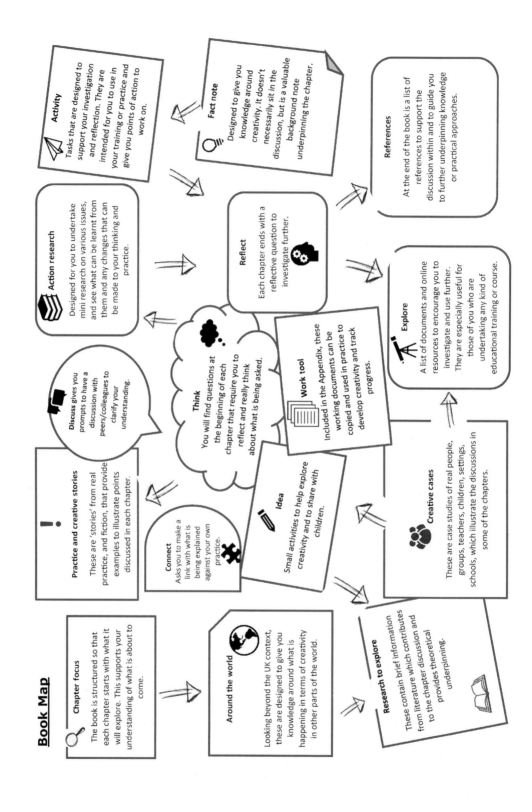

Chapter focus

The book is structured so that each chapter starts with what it will explore. This supports your understanding of what is about to come.

Around the world

Looking beyond the UK context, these are designed to give you knowledge around what is happening in terms of creativity in other parts of the world.

Research to explore

These contain brief information from literature which contributes to the chapter discussion and provides theoretical underpinning.

Practice and creative stories

These are 'stories' from real practice, and fiction, that provide examples to illustrate points discussed in each chapter.

Connect

Asks you to make a link with what is being explained against your own practice.

Discuss gives you prompts to have a discussion with peers/colleagues to clarify your understanding.

Think

You will find questions at the beginning of each chapter that require you to reflect and really think about what is being asked.

Idea

Small activities to help explore creativity and to share with children.

Work tool

Included in the Appendix, these working documents can be copied and used in practice to develop creativity and track progress.

Creative cases

These are case studies of real people, groups, teachers, children, settings, schools, which illustrate the discussions in some of the chapters.

Action research

Designed for you to undertake mini research on various issues, and see what can be learnt from them and any changes that can be made to your thinking and practice.

Reflect

Each chapter ends with a reflective question to investigate further.

Explore

A list of documents and online resources to encourage you to investigate and use further. They are especially useful for those of you who are undertaking any kind of educational training or course.

Activity

Tasks that are designed to support your investigation and reflection. They are intended for you to use in your training or practice and give you points of action to work on.

Fact note

Designed to give you knowledge around creativity. It doesn't necessarily sit in the discussion, but is a valuable background note underpinning the chapter.

References

At the end of the book is a list of references to support the discussion within and to guide you to further underpinning knowledge or practical approaches.

Creativity and education

THINK

What is the purpose of education?

What are we preparing children for?

Why should you be concerned with creativity?

CHAPTER FOCUS

■ A history of creativity in education and the factory model

■ The link of creativity to economic development towards the fourth revolution

■ Creativity in educational aims as a twenty-first-century skill and the creativity crisis

■ Creativity and early years education

■ Bold beginnings

■ Advocating for creativity in the early years

This chapter is not intended to bombard you with information about a political stance on creativity and education, or generate another explanation for it, but is rather to give you enough grounding to understand its importance and in turn what it means for the early years. There is a vast amount of literature advocating the role of creativity for education and future economic success; these are available through the references provided within this book for you to explore at your own convenience. However, this chapter brings to the forefront a continuing case for creativity in the early years.

The concept of creativity has always been popular in educational thought and over the years has become an essential aim for education. It was recognised in the 1950s that education should prioritise the development of creativity, but it was not until the late 1990s that greater emphasis started to be placed upon it and what it meant for education. In the UK alone, a number of studies made an attempt to link the essential role of creativity in learning to the early years and primary class-rooms. These studies were closely followed by the 1999 report *All Our Futures*, led by Sir Ken Robinson, then Professor of Education at the University of Warwick. His report argued that creativity should be set alongside literacy and numeracy as a strategic priority at all levels of education and made a case for a national strategy for culture and creativity in education.

The report recommended new priorities, which included a much stronger emphasis on creativity and a new balance of teaching and the curriculum between learning knowledge and skills and having the freedom to innovate and experiment. However, regardless of the varying literature advocating for and explaining the place of creativity in children's learning, there are still issues as to how educators perceive it, how creativity is visible in practice, and the approaches that should be taken to foster it within educational contexts – the key question being *what does creativity look like?* Many of these issues arise from the historical roots of our education system, which very much continue to echo in our present.

 FACT NOTE
THE SPUTNIK SHOCK

On October 4, 1957, the Soviet Union beat the United Kingdom and United States to the launch of the first satellite to orbit the Earth. It was known as Sputnik 1. It is claimed that the US, UK, and other Western countries lost what was known as the 'space race'. For this very reason, education systems came under scrutiny, as the loss was attributed to, and judged to be the results of, defects and the **'lack of creativity'** in education.

 DISCUSS

With peers/colleagues the link of creativity to education. What patterns emerge?

Back to the past . . .

Over the last 200 years, the UK has lived through what can be defined as three industrial revolutions. The first, between 1760 and 1840, involved a transition to new manufacturing processes, including going from hand production methods to machines, new chemical manufacturing and iron production processes, efficiency of water, increase of steam power, the development of machine tools, and, of course, the rise of the factory system. The second industrial revolution involved the widespread introduction of steel to the UK, electrification of factories, and the introduction of mass production and the production line. The third revolution took place towards the latter half of the twentieth century and saw industry make the switch from mechanical and analogue electronic technology to digital electronics. It was the latter, in fact, that marked the beginning of what is known as the 'information age' that we currently live in.

Buried under rules and regulations, our education system was designed during the first industrial revolution to train us to be good workers and follow instructions for the benefit of the economy. It was regarded as the 'factory model' of education, assembling masses of children (raw material) to be processed by teachers (workers) in a centrally located school (factory) (Toffler, 1970). Creativity didn't have a place; it didn't exist. Even today, the echoes of the factory model are still present. Pink (2006) illustrates this well; he defines education progression through past economic development, but also advocates that it really is time for a much-needed change:

1) **Agricultural age** (farmers) – education was for the very few and was class-bound, i.e. for the rich only. The structure of schooling at that time mirrored monasteries and army life.

 RESEARCH TO EXPLORE

■ 1995–1996 Wood and Jeffery explored teacher creativity.

■ Later, the renowned Anna Craft (1996, 1998, 2000, 2001, 2005) focused on how to nourish the creative teacher and on the essential role of creativity in early childhood.

■ Fryer (1996) went on to study teachers' attitudes towards creativity in their daily professional work.

■ Beetlestone (1998) focused on creativity's place in the early years environment of the classroom.

2) **Industrial age** (factory workers) – a basic level of education was required by production workers; creativity and thinking were not required. The curriculum was modelled on the factory metaphor, with children divided into year groups; knowledge divided into subjects; and progression made through school batches. This still exists today.

3) **Information age** (knowledge workers) – an age we currently live in. Governments view education as a product and a personal investment. Hierarchal approaches to education exist in the form of league tables, with private schools for the rich and mainstream schools for the working class and the poor.

4) **Conceptual age** (creators and empathisers) – an age one needs to prepare for. Pink (2006) believes that to survive in the economy to come, it is not the factory model masses that are needed, but the creators and empathisers that education should be working towards developing.

As well as the current information age, one can say that we are in fact living in a 'digitalised age'; therefore, Pink's conceptual age could be moving towards an age beyond our imagination, an almost 'imaginative age'. So *how prepared are we for this?* Or, more importantly, *how prepared are children for an age we cannot foresee?* We can only imagine!

> ### ✸ CONNECT
>
> Where can you observe the 'factory model' of education present in the early years?

In 2007, Howard Gardner further provided a case for a change in education by identifying what are known as the five different minds. Gardner believes that these will be increasingly important in our future in order for us to thrive in the eras to come, and that these need to be developed through education.

1) The **disciplined** mind – developed through education to support individuals becoming 'experts' in one area of specialism or discipline. One could say that our current teaching of subjects in education represents the beginnings of catering for this type of mind. However, times have changed and there is a need to become interdisciplinary, or multi-disciplinary, in order to gain expertise in multiple disciplines and keep them going.

2) The **synthesising** mind – being able to synthesise huge amounts of information. This includes a wide range of sources and experiences, making decisions about what is important, and combining and communicating information in a meaningful way. Within the synthesising mind will be an area of expertise (discipline), though, which will then know the trusted sources of information within that area and be able to keep an overview of it and see the big picture.

3) The **creating** mind – what this book is really all about. It is the mind that develops new ideas, practices, and experiences, solves problems, innovates, provides fresh thinking and perspectives, and engages in creativity. A mind that adapts to the changing world. However, both the disciplined and synthesising mind play a role within the creating mind, as new and innovative developments in

disciplines cannot occur without the ability to be knowledgeable in areas and synthesise the information from it in order to create.

4) The **respectful** mind – 'responding sympathetically and constructively to differences among groups; seeking to understand and work with those who are different; extending beyond mere tolerance and political correctness' (Gardner, 2007, p. 157). This mind welcomes social contact, tries to form links, and avoids making judgements. This mind is vital in exploring diverse experiences across communities and cultures in order to embed them further in changing disciplines and creating.

5) The **ethical** mind – considers sophisticated moral issues in an abstract way. Decisions, behaviour, and beliefs of those around you can influence the development of this mind and provide role models for it.

There seems to be a harmonious rhythm needed across all five minds in order for them to function and develop. A disciplined mind is needed to be able to synthesise; creativity involves synthesis, and needs to draw on the disciplined mind for knowledge – although a very disciplined mind is less likely to be creative, and a highly synthesising mind may not lead to creativity (Johnston et al., 2018, p. 145). A balance is thus required where education should be developing all five minds equally.

Use!

 ACTIVITY

Taking each of Gardner's Five Minds, list under each how early years education is currently developing them in children.

Can you see connections across the minds? Make this visible by highlighting or drawing arrows.

Is there more emphasis on particular minds than others? Why could this be?

Seventeen countries in the Organisation for Economic Cooperation and Development (OECD), a forum made up of governments, identified creativity as a core competency, so valuable for the next generation that it requires major restructure of national and international educational programmes (Ananiadou and Claro, 2009). Settings and schools were thus viewed as the place for the encouragement and development of creativity, because apparently they can do so more efficiently and can develop it en masse (Shaheen, 2010, p. 166). The echoes of the factory model are still very much alive today.

Use!

It is frustrating that many aspects of our education system have not changed for over a hundred years, especially since both Pink and Gardner have provided sensible insights into a bigger picture relating to the role of education and the future.

So Robinsons work side lined ?? UK Gov

However, despite this, in 2006, the Leitch Review of Skills (HMSO, 2006) continued to focus political attention upon numeracy and literacy, maintaining a line of continuity in UK education policy highlighting the acquiring of 'essential knowledge'. In 2011, Sir Ken Robinson was asked to reflect on the current challenges around creativity in education, and his own assessment of the UK government's response to his work is that it was 'marginalised' by a government in thrall to more basic issues of numeracy and literacy. In 2015, he continued his advocacy for creativity in education to prepare children for a world we cannot envisage, a shape-shifting world, so that when they get stuck with something they've never seen before, instead of just remembering and following instructions (per the factory model), they choose instead to think (Robinson, 2015) (as creators and empathisers do, using the disciplined, synthesising, creative mind). This makes a crucial link between thinking and creativity, but also brings the past to an end as we step into another era or, rather, revolution.

ViP
Use!

AROUND THE WORLD
SINGAPORE AND SOUTH KOREA

Singapore and South Korea are two good examples of countries emphasising **creativity** in their curriculum. South Korea expects its schools to **foster creativity** as part of quality learning, with almost 10% of its time devoted to projects and other activities that do this.

Singapore's outcomes for education include **critical and inventive thinking** as well as social and emotional competencies. The goal is that by the end of secondary school, children are expected to be resilient in the face of adversity and **innovative** and **enterprising** as well as able to **think critically** and **communicate persuasively**.

CREATIVE CASE
CREATIVITY AND THE GENERATIONS

Name: Ruksana Mohammed   **Role**: Senior Lecturer in Higher Education
Location: London

I recall the exact moment the temperature changed in my teaching. I was speaking to an audience of 100 students. I was relating my experiences on building a career through the early years degree programme. Every time I threw out phrases like 'paying your dues' and 'playing the game', the students stared at me blankly. I made references to songs and movies from my time – blank! This was not the reaction I had come to expect from early twenty-somethings. Usually they took notes on how they could get ahead in the programme as quickly as possible. I would soon learn, however, that a new type of cohort had come on the scene, and I noticed a pattern which seem to be linked to the generations, as it affected all the people born and living at the same time. And it made me think about those children in their early years right now.

Baby Boomers, 1946–1964: people born in the immediate years after World War II, when there was – thanks to soldiers returning home – a significant spike in births. Baby boomers in Britain were the first to be born in free NHS hospitals. Technology is a difficult concept for them to grasp, and they are currently being blamed for Brexit. A very small amount of our student cohort is from this generation, though academic staff are more so.

Generation X, 1965–1979: regarded as the generation that worked hard and played hard. Generation X are very industrious. They were paid by the government to go to university and are said to be the last generation able to afford home ownership and mortgages. Generation X created the internet by taking progressive late-boomers Bill Gates and Steve Jobs under their wing and showing them what they could do with their stuff. They had a dot com boom (and a couple of busts). Gen X walked around with phones the size of rucksacks and sent the first halting text messages. They are adaptable and still occupy university as learners; however, more and more of them are becoming academic staff who are now teaching Gen Y and Z.

Generation Y (also known as Millennials), 1980–1995: the largest generation since the Boomers and born between the advent of the Walkman and the founding of Google. The members of Gen Y are unsurprisingly shaped by technology and raised on the internet. They are comfortable sharing their entire life online; 'Let me take a selfie' is their catchphrase, or 'let's Snapchat this lesson'. Known as independent problem-solvers and ambitious self-starters, they want support but do not want to be told what to do or how to do it. They expect instant gratification and immediate feedback; however, they also know that they must keep learning to be marketable – hence why many undertake more than one job. They move quickly from one thing to another and are not as independent as Gen X as they still have parents' support. Over half of our student cohort is made up of Millennials.

Generation Z, 1996–2010: sometimes referred to as iGen, they were born into a world in which the internet, social media, and mobile technology always existed. Too young to remember 9/11, they have grown up in a world blighted by financial, economic, and environmental turmoil, and they want to make a change. They have echoes of Gen Y in them in terms of online lives, but can be described as the 'first tribe of true digital natives' or 'screenagers'. Generation Z is beginning to appear in further and higher education, and they're bringing their new technology and big ideas with them. The question is, *how prepared is the higher education discipline for them?*

Generation Alpha, 2011–2025: at present the youngest within this generation are new-borns, and the eldest are 6. *How will social, political, and economic changes affect them?* The evolution of each generation indicates the influence of technology, which then highlights that innovation and creativity are forerunners in the survival of generations to come. Research indicates that the early years set the foundations for later learning and life; this is also true for creativity. *If Gen Alpha is not exploring and cultivating their creativity right now, then what could this mean for their education, their employment, their survival, but most of all, their lives?*

The fourth revolution

There is no denying that the link of creativity to education is made through economic competitiveness or, rather, survival. As an evolving economy in the UK, we are ever changing and, as always, face an uncertain future. We are currently standing on the brink of a technological revolution that will fundamentally alter the way we live, work, and relate to one another. We are dealing with the interface between creativity, culture, economics, and technology in a contemporary world dominated by images, sounds, texts, and symbols. Known as the tech and robot age, the fourth revolution is upon us at an extremely evolving rate. From desktop files, we have moved to the cloud, Dropbox, and apps – *whatever next?* The inevitable expansion of robotics, artificial intelligence, and automation is poised to wipe out more jobs than it creates, an almost double-edged sword. For example, a Tesla Motor car, currently being controlled by a smart phone, may be ready to drive itself (yes, itself!) across America in late 2018. In the UK, Amazon is testing its drone delivery fleet, removing the need for humans to drive and deliver to your doorstep. In Italy, pasta-making factories are increasingly replacing human labour with robotic machines. In a globalised world, such things are quickly evolving and disrupting every industry in the country and across the world, which can then have a domino effect upon society, security, the environment, the economy, politics, and, above all, education.

 RESEARCH TO EXPLORE
RISE OF THE ROBOTS

A report commissioned by The Sutton Trust (2017) warns that 15 million jobs in the UK could disappear due to technology. The rise of robotics is taking away traditional ladders of opportunity in the workplace, affecting those from poorer backgrounds who usually do these jobs. The report states that only 29% of people believe that today's youth will have a better quality of life than their parents, down from 42% in 2003.

Unlike previous industrial revolutions that created employment, Industrial Revolution 4.0 will reduce it. Sir Peter Lampi, Chairman of the Sutton Trust, calls for young people from low and moderate-income backgrounds to be equipped with essential life skills – is **creativity** one of them?

So why bother with creativity, then? Well, technology's past may also be a hopeful indicator of its future. With the previous three industrial revolutions, when new technology came in, some jobs disappeared, but new ones were created. Don't forget, robots and drones still need someone to operate them! The fourth revolution has the potential to raise global income levels and improve the quality of life for populations around the world. But at the same time, it can also yield greater inequalities amongst us (Schwab, 2016). Traditional good grades then may no longer suffice to equip children with the skills needed to fuel innovation-driven economic growth, much less 'how to learn' and survive in the present and coming era. This is, then, about altering the education paradigm, where children can develop skills in creativity, just as much as in mathematics and literacy, so that they can adapt to the emerging, shape-shifting world. It is not that we did not know that this was going to happen; nearly two decades ago, Kessler (2000) emphasised that it was essential for education to create a climate, and the skills, for fostering creativity. This is so that a generation of young people can visualise new solutions to not only the problems of today, but also tomorrow's workforce, social fabric, and the environment. This is just as relevant today, as creativity becomes a critical twenty-first-century skill 'essential for survival' (Xanthoudaki, 2015, p. 248). Educational aims across the world have confirmed this; the idea is for children to open up their minds to what is possible, take risks and opportunities, and create as well as solve problems and become better creative and imaginative thinkers and doers – all for the possible survival of the economy.

Various educational disciplines have identified creativity as important for the evolution of their specialism in the future, yet again for the economy. In education and psychology, the term 'creativity' is widely used; however, in other disciplines, terms closely associated with creativity are common. For example, in economics the terms 'entrepreneurship' and 'enterprise' are used, whereas in sociology it is 'innovation'. In the business world, importance is placed on creativity as a much-needed concept to remain competitive in a global economy, and the terms 'entrepreneurship' and 'innovation' represent this. The thinking is that creativity sits at the heart of innovation, and innovation is a growth driver, and therefore becomes an economic imperative (Seifter and Buswick, 2005). However, this book argues that yes, the purpose of education may be economic towards the fourth revolution – but it is personal, too. Personal to the child as they grow up and survive in an ever-changing, uncertain world and go through what is known as life.

ACTION RESEARCH

The terms 'innovation', 'enterprise', and 'entrepreneurship' are closely associated with creativity. Research these terms within their disciplines and answer the following:

■ How do these terms associate themselves with creativity?

■ How do they link with education?

■ What other terms do various disciplines use to describe creativity?

Paul Collard, Chief Executive of Creativity, Culture, and Education, has stated that 'in the modern workplace, what you know matters far less than what you can do with what you know. Your creative capacity is far more important than academic knowledge' (Be Open, 2017) – although I argue that knowledge is vital for creativity to develop. Smart policy-makers worldwide are aware of the importance of fostering a creative economy, and have an appreciation that in our post-industrial world, it is now ideas that drive economic success. So, whereas in the past economic success may have come from money and machinery, today it comes from idea-led groups and individuals in diverse sectors, not just within the arts. In 2016, Enrique Avogadro, the Secretary of Culture and Creativity for Argentina, highlighted a key characteristic of this new age being 'a young creative population'. Yet, there still exists in education the reinforcement of the historic divide between knowledge and creativity, and echoes of the factory system in wanting to develop creativity en masse.

The creativity crisis

Regardless of what is known about creativity in research, the fourth revolution, educational aims, and creativity's recognition as a twenty-first-century skill, we are still experiencing what is referred to as the 'creativity crisis' (Bronson and Merryman, 2010; Starko, 2014). We must be, because 20 years later we are still having the same discussion. Education has become so test-driven, with an emphasis on output and 'economy readiness', that creativity is being extinguished in children and adults alike. There is no denying that the government places importance on encouraging creativity in settings and schools, but this mainly occurs through investing in the arts and creative industries. Although there is a widespread notion that the curriculum should be delivered through creative approaches, the actual use of it is the opposite of this, a concern that it is being used by educators in too linear and prescriptive a manner, which in turn hinders creativity. And of course, this filters into the early years as there is an emphasis on 'school readiness', which then encourages a formal, top-down approach. Settings and schools continue to use formal methods, tests, and checklists as the determining approaches of children's progression of knowledge. Gruelling inspections and monitoring of the curriculum further add to this. Testing and standards come at the expense of children's ability to question, problem solve, and innovate (Starko, 2014, p. 5).

Although educational aims speak of developing skills, knowledge, and attitudes through the fostering of creativity, these are not specifically stated, nor is it indicated how they are visible in practice, or even how they can be approached. It is also apparent that there is a dilemma in terms of what is required by the educational leaders of each country for the economy, and what the realities are of the educational context that we are faced with. On the one hand, there is a push for academic standards, and on the other, a push for economic relevance. This suggests a political misunderstanding about the value and significance of creativity in children's education and, in turn, their lives, which of course filters down into every setting and classroom, and ultimately includes those educating children.

> **! STORY FROM PRACTICE**
> **● MA IN EDUCATION: SESSION ON CREATIVITY**
>
> A group of Year 1 teachers are studying for their master's degree in education and attend an evening class fortnightly at the school they work in. This particular term they are undertaking a unit titled 'Creativity and Imagination in Education'. After positively starting the class and discussing how important creativity is to children's education, they are then asked how they embed creativity in their teaching. The room falls silent. The teachers then discuss how they know creativity is important but don't have the time to think about it or incorporate it into their work. Some of the comments collected are as follows:
>
> 'It's easier in the early years'
>
> 'Too many standards to work with'
>
> 'We have to pull the children through to meet school targets, there's no time for it'
>
> 'Time limits what we can do, creativity is not one of them'
>
> 'Education is outcome driven, and doesn't allow for creativity'
>
> 'What we already do exhausts us to do anymore'

Early years education and creativity

At this point, you may be wondering what economy readiness has to do with present 3- and 4-year-olds. Well, research as early as 1974 in the early years has found that if creativity is not engaged with during the naturally creative childhood years, it is not something that can then be developed in later life (Marzollo and Lloyd). When children do not have the opportunity to engage with and experience their creativity early on, it will be an impossible task to get them to do so in later schooling years, further education, higher education, and, of course, in the world of work. This is why the early years are known as a vital period for laying the foundations for future learning. Engaging creativity in children in the early years essentially becomes an important milestone in the development of creative thinkers and innovators in adult life.

Until the 1980s, the early years, in most countries, largely focused on providing simple child minding (Tobin, Wu and Davidson, 1991). However, as discussed in the Introduction, the shifting of economies towards more knowledge-based needs (factory model) led to the awareness of the need to invest in young children and prepare them for formal education. Today, mounting evidence has deepened our understanding of what happens in the early years of a child's development, particularly that it has a profound impact on their capacity to succeed not only when they encounter formal education, but also beyond, into later life (Lombardi, 2013). Three strands of research combine to support the importance of the early years. From neuro-scientific research, we understand the criticality of early brain development; from social science research, we know that high quality programmes improve children's readiness for school and life; and from econometric research, we know that high quality early years programmes save society significant amounts of money over time (Kagan, 2012). Investment in the early years, then, contributes to creating the kinds of workforces that are going to be needed in the twenty-first century.

RESEARCH TO EXPLORE
EPPSE PROJECT

The Effective Pre-School, Primary and Secondary Education (EPPSE) project is a longitudinal study that was conducted between 1997 and 2014. It mapped the progress and development of 3,000 children in various pre-school settings. The key finding was the long-term cognitive and emotional impact of pre-school education (Waldron, 2017).

The children were followed throughout primary and secondary education, and it was concluded that the quality of early years education and care continued to influence children's learning through school. This then set children on a positive learning trajectory for life (Siraj-Blatchford, 2014).

In terms of the creativity agenda, the government did take on board much of what the research from the 1990s revealed, and as a result invested heavily in the early years. The 2008 Early Years Foundation Stage Framework (EYFS) was a result of this. The 2006 Roberts Review (DfES, 2006) fuelled this by mapping out a framework for creativity which included provision in the early years. The government's response to the review made a commitment to the early years, ensuring that creativity remained at the heart of the Foundation Stage and that creative practice was encouraged and rewarded. As Loughton and Teather (2010, p. 47) point out, 'promoting creativity and play in the early years is actually a first-class ticket to producing a creative, prosperous economy many years down the line'. This reinforces the role of creativity for the economy, but with the key point of starting by fostering and developing it in the early years. However, there is still a question as to whether this heavy investment in the early years was born out of genuine desire to meet children's present needs, or for future economic gain which sees education as developing creativity en masse? It seems very much the latter.

The 2008 EYFS emphasised a whole area of learning as 'creative development', where the role of imagination was central and children were to respond in a variety of ways to experiences, using media and materials, to express their ideas and feelings. In the 2012 update of the framework, areas of learning were renamed, with creative development becoming 'expressive arts and design'. Content was still the same, and creativity still existed, but this change of name emphasised the top-down approach of 'school readiness' by linking the EYFS areas of learning to the subject areas of the National Curriculum. The Tickell Review (2011) of the EYFS, however, did reinforce a role for creativity as imagination with an inherent role in expressive arts and design, and acknowledged critical and creative thinking together with active learning and play as characteristics of young children's engagement with the world around them. The renewed emphasis on the Characteristics of Effective Learning (which will be discussed in later chapters) still saw creativity and critical thinking as a core aspect of early years education, valuing it across the curriculum and balancing freedom with structure (Craft and Hall, 2015). The 2017 framework currently exists with this understanding, but how the EYFS is interpreted and implemented by early years practitioners is the key to this understanding.

Bold beginnings

In January 2017, Her Majesty's Chief Inspector (HMCI) commissioned an Ofsted-wide review of the curriculum. Its aim was to provide fresh insight into leaders' curriculum intentions, how these are implemented, and the impact on outcomes for children. In November 2017, the much-anticipated report for this was published, titled *Bold Beginnings*. The report highlights the Reception Year and the extent to which a school's curriculum for 4- and 5-year-olds prepares them for the rest of their education and beyond. Although the report acknowledges that a good early education is the foundation for later success, it classes children's Reception Year as a missed opportunity that can leave them exposed to all the 'painful and unnecessary consequences of falling behind their peers' (Ofsted, 2017, p. 4). The report was met with criticism from across the early years sector, as it moves away from the play-based pedagogy that the EYFS supports, making it look almost useless in the Reception context. *Bold Beginnings* continues to reinforce the mounting pressure of school readiness for Year 1.

The review, of course, only concentrated on math and literacy (no surprise there), and provided recommendations for these areas of learning. There is no mention of creativity, despite all we know about it so far, and despite the report illustrating that all other learning areas, including expressive arts and design, are where children are exceeding most in the expected category (Ofsted, 2017, p. 10). The findings of the review will be used to inform inspection policy, advise policy makers, and influence wider national thinking on the role and importance of the curriculum for Reception – *but what about the role of creativity within this?* The creativity crisis has thus been fuelled further by the historic emphasis on knowledge and math and literacy. However, creativity's existence in all areas of children's learning comes down to those interpreting these reports and, ultimately, to those working directly with the children.

The report highlighted one essential aspect to support this – that the schools visited understood that teaching has different purposes – but two-thirds of the staff confused what they were teaching (the curriculum) with how they thought they were supposed to teach it (the approaches). This seems to have stemmed from a misinterpretation of what the characteristics of effective learning required in terms of the curriculum provided. This can then lead to a misinterpretation of how creativity may be viewed by adults, i.e. as an area of learning rather than a holistic approach that underpins all areas of learning, including math and literacy – but also an adult lack of understanding of what creativity is and means for the children in the early years. The adult's understanding, therefore, is of vital importance.

 OBSERVE

Either a phonics, math, or literacy session in the early years. Where can you spot creativity within it?

Advocates for creativity

The government's education aim is about preparing children for society, for the economy, and to be flexible, innovative, and creative thinkers for the workplace, and for what is to come. Yet, this is thought to be achieved through religiously reinforcing math and literacy, and the continuing pressure of formalising the early years. It is agreed that we no longer live in a world where relying solely on logic, analysis, and problem-solving skills is sufficient. In today's rapidly changing environment, children need a new set of skills to cope with uncertainty and complexity, and creativity is very much a part of it. While this economic and regeneration driver is compelling, it is matched by an equal and moral imperative – the intrinsic importance of giving children creative experience, both to develop personal identity and confidence and to understand and prepare for a twenty-first-century society (The Roberts Review, 2006, p. 12). Therefore, adults in the early years, and beyond, need to understand creativity for children and their practice, and in turn advocate for it.

 DISCUSS

With peers/colleagues how they advocate for children on a day to day basis.

Though it is too often viewed merely as a political tool, advocacy can be so much more; it includes speaking for, supporting, or defending creativity in children's learning. Adults in the early years are everyday advocates for their children, families, communities, and the early education field as a whole (Riddle, 2016). This is where, more than ever, adults can sing in harmony about the benefits of high-quality creative teaching and learning. As advocates for the youngest children, you will agree that for us early years education is in the present, the here, the now, and not just about the future, about preparation for the economy. As parents, we want our children to be prepared for a world that we cannot envisage, but not at the cost of our children's childhood. The role of creativity is to engage children in learning, exploring, playing, and connecting with what they experience, and all the things that make up childhood as a right, with all the areas of learning interplaying equally in this. It is about fostering and developing creativity, regardless of where it may be used.

Early years education is what goes on between the practitioner and child in the actual learning environment, and it is here that creativity either begins its journey, or abruptly ends. Early years practitioners, to an extent, have control over what happens in their settings and how activities are planned and delivered for areas of learning; therefore, they are vital in planning for creative elements in their teaching – not only to teach creatively, but to teach *for* creativity. It is agreed that creativity can become difficult in a heavily regulated and accountable environment, where policies are constantly dictated. However, no education system exceeds the strength of its educator. Their ambition, professionalism, and knowledge are key variables in the process of education (Hunt, 2015). It doesn't matter how prescriptive the curriculum is or becomes; the real key to transforming education is the quality of teaching (Robinson and Aronica, 2015).

As advocates of creativity, early years practitioners are working towards a new era of knowledge and skills for children in which creativity is vital. Learners of all

Findings/Conclusion.

ages have been observed to come alive when their creativity is engaged, no matter the subject. They connect with content in more meaningful ways and find their way into many possibilities. Educators therefore need to bring a creative approach to all that they teach and offer so that children can learn to integrate their minds with their imaginations, for the here and now, for the being and becoming, which will then become a significant part of them throughout their lives. It is this advocacy for creativity, for bold beginnings, which is very much needed.

Five simple steps to advocate for creativity

1) **Speak up!** Share your experience and knowledge with parents, colleagues, students, and anyone willing to listen.

2) **Know your resources**: learn about creativity, use it in your work with children, link with others in the early years community and beyond. This book is a good starting point!

3) **Raise awareness**: participate in community events and celebrate children's creative expression and learning. Participate in meetings, discussions, and training outside the setting. Find out about your local early years events, forums etc., as well as online events, and participate in spreading the word! Think Twitter!

4) **Get involved with policy**: often, national reviews take place on policy initiatives impacting early years education. Find out about them and see where you can get involved, even if it is just a survey you complete.

5) **Vote with early years education in mind**: in local and national elections. It all matters as it filters down into the early years.

Next steps

 REFLECT

What knowledge and skills do you think are of vital importance for children to develop for the future?

How do you perceive the notion that creativity is a good thing for the economy, for society, and therefore for early years education?

 EXPLORE

Creativity Economy Report (2008): http://unctad.org/en/docs/ditc20082cer_en.pdf

■ The United Nations perspective on the topic of creativity.

Mind Shift, Sir Ken Robinson: Creativity Is in Everything, Especially Teaching (2015): ww2.kqed.org/mindshift/2015/04/22/sir-ken-robinson-creativity-is-in-everything-especially-teaching

■ An article by Sir Ken Robinson of the place of creativity.

Study: Stifling Creativity: https://blogs.adobe.com/conversations/2013/06/study-reveals-education-system-is-stifling-creativity-education.html

■ An international study on how education is stifling creativity.

All Our Futures (1999): http://sirkenrobinson.com/pdf/allourfutures.pdf

■ Makes recommendations on the creative and cultural development of young people through formal and informal education, which is still cited in all things creativity even today!

The Roberts Review: Nurturing Creativity in Young People (2006): www.creativetallis.com/uploads/2/2/8/7/2287089/nurturing-1.pdf

■ A framework for the development of creativity for children and young people.

World Economic Forum: These Are the World's Most Creative Countries (2015): www.weforum.org/agenda/2015/10/most-creative-countries-in-the-world/?utm_content=bufferb24c5&utm_medium=social&utm_source=twitter.com&utm_campaign=buffer

■ An article illustrating the most creative economies.

Tech tools

Ted2006, Do Schools Kill Creativity? www.ted.com/talks/ken_robinson_says_schools_kill_creativity

■ A video on Sir Ken Robinson's famous TedTalk.

Changing Education Paradigms (2010): www.ted.com/talks/ken_robinson_changing_education_paradigms

■ This is an animated talk where Sir Ken Robinson lays out the link between three troubling trends: rising drop-out rates, schools' dwindling stake in the arts, and ADHD. An important, timely talk for parents and teachers.

2 Defining creativity

THINK

What is creativity?

Where does it originate?

How can you spot creativity?

CHAPTER FOCUS

- Defining and understanding creativity

- Key threads in creativity's interpretation

- Defining creativity for the early years

- Creativity's characteristics

- Creative processes

- Creative thinking

Creativity is important in all aspects of children's learning and lives. So far, we have established that education must prioritise the development of creativity from the earliest years onwards. This then leads us to the question of, *what is creativity?* Adults often are heard to say 'it's something you are born with', 'it's for the right-brained people', or 'you've got to be a little weird and crazy to be creative, right?' Wrong! As much as this is interesting, they are just a few in a long line of myths and excuses. Creativity is so much more, which is what this chapter sets out to explore in order to give you at least an understanding of what it is and what it means for early years education.

! STORY FROM PRACTICE

For a very long time in the history of human thought, creativity was thought of as mysticism, magic, and incomprehensible. The ancient Greeks used to believe that creativity was bestowed upon you from a higher, otherworldly being. If you were suitable for acting on an idea, the gods would grant it to you and expect you to follow through. Muses would visit you if you begged for their gifts. The Romans believed that a creative muse was a spiritual guide that would visit those who were open to receiving them, in order to perform great works or feats.

Born out of the eighteenth-century Kantian notions of 'genius' and 'individual inspiration', there are those that believe creativity comes from getting an idea through a higher power that helps produce it – almost an act of a supreme being. And then there are those that think it is about new ideas and original products which are an inherent part of human characteristics (Ryhammar and Brolin, 1999, p. 260). There is also the notion of 'high' creativity, which assumes creativity is shown by exceptional people only, the Mozarts and Einsteins of the world. 'Ordinary' creativity implies everyday creativity that we all are capable of. For example, arranging a room, decorating a cake, choosing complementary clothing, and much more. And then there is creativity in 'domains', like high creativity; it can be assumed that people are creative in different disciplines, that they are talented in a particular area or field.

There is a great deal of research and literature on creativity – what it is and why it is important in education. When you start to explore, the lists and references are never-ending. However, what does quickly become apparent is that there is an almost vagueness surrounding creativity, a lack of a solid definition for it. In earlier times, this was not an issue, because creativity research was limited to creative personality and the creative thinking process. As the twentieth century progressed, a splintering of the research field took place, leading to a wide array of definitions for creativity. This is because one single definition is necessary and needed for concrete research into a concept, hence the need for creativity to be pinned down. In the history of creativity research, sometimes the emphasis has been on individual perspectives; sometimes its relevance has been on society. Creativity was mostly seen as a creative event, work, or action, or even as a creative product (Toivanena, Halkilahtib and Ruismäkic, 2013).

ACTION RESEARCH

When one explores definitions of creativity relevant to education, they predominately come from the 1990s, and sometimes from the 1980s. However, the definition of **creativity** has a long-standing history with roots in the 1930s, 1940s, and 1950s. Collate as many definitions of creativity as you can from the 1930s, 1940s, 1950s, 1980s, 1990s, and the present day and age.

■ What are the commonalities?

■ What has changed over time?

■ Which ones do you relate to and excite you?

■ Which ones are debatable and why?

The language used to discuss creativity is increasingly opaque and often incomprehensible to an adult attempting to nurture creativity in their environments. Joubert (2001, p. 29) has stated that creativity is an elusive concept to define, as it is interpreted in a variety of ways. Literature confirms this through the varied definitions it provides; the term creativity has preconceived notions, prejudices, and wishful thinking attached to it, and all we can do is try to understand this 'huge ball of stuff' (Root-Bernstein, 2016). Despite being tricky to pin down, it's often argued that 'you know creativity when you see it!' – *or do you?*

To define or not to define

The twenty-first-century, however, started with a new analysis of the concept of creativity and what it means in education. Anna Craft (2001) emphasised that the move towards empirical rather than theoretical studies of creativity in the early years of the twentieth century took place in four major traditions: psychoanalytic, cognitive, behaviourist, and humanistic. She suggested that, in education, the definitions of creativity that have had the most influence in the last 50 years have been those that marry creativity and imagination, and take an inclusive approach by suggesting that everyone has the potential for creativity as it is a fundamental aspect of human nature (Banaji, Burn and Buckingham, 2010). The NACCCE report, *All Our Futures*, was the forerunner in defining it.

All Our Futures suggests that we are all capable of creativity and that all learning involves elements of this. For this purpose, it coined the term 'democratic creativity', meaning the creativity of the ordinary person, recognising that all individuals (you, me, and, of course, the children) can be creative. The report goes on to define creativity as an 'imaginative activity fashioned so as to produce outcomes that are both original and of value' (p. 29). This reinforces Craft's earlier point regarding imagination playing a key role in creativity, something which will be explored in later chapters. It is interesting, however, that the definition speaks of 'outcomes', as it is argued that creative processes are as important as its products (Craft, 2010, p. 33), and an 'outcome' doesn't necessarily have to be of a concrete nature. Yet, it is the concrete outcome that is used to define a child's ability to achieve in education – for example, *where is the evidence of learning and progression?* Further, 'of value' is also interesting, as the question is, of value to whom? *The adult? The child? The educational aims? The economy?* These terms are all open to interpretation by individuals. Nonetheless, it was this landmark report that brought the educational importance of creativity to the forefront and gave many others a definition to explore, investigate, and filter into educational aims.

 ACTIVITY

In a group, introduce the word 'creativity'. What does it mean? Encourage the group to suggest words associated with it. Highlight key words as they are suggested and write them on a board. For example, 'original', 'new', 'useful', 'worthy', 'imaginative', 'engaging'. Once complete, discuss each word and what it really means for teaching and learning.

Ask each person to pick three words from those on the board, and then to create a definition for 'creativity' using them.

Although creativity is perceived in many ways, it must be understood that it is an ability that all humans possess to a greater or lesser extent. To live and progress, humans need to innovate and be creative – it's in our genes! As humans, we think, ponder, imagine, come up with ideas, predict, plan, and are highly capable of carrying out something new. So yes, we are all capable of being creative. *All Our Futures* continues to reinforce this by stating that 'all people are capable of creative achievement in some area of activity, provided that the conditions are right and they have acquired the relevant knowledge and skills' (1999, p. 5). Creativity can then be regarded as a human ability which begins with a foundation of knowledge and skills, learning an area or concept, and mastering a way of thinking, but in the right environment.

Key threads in creativity

Literature and research interpretation of creativity can be classed on a variety of levels: cognitively, intellectually, socially, economically, spiritually, and from the perspective of different disciplines. These interpretations come from a variety of subjects, as within the arts, but reaching beyond this in the sciences and humanities, affecting every discipline and numerous industries in its path. For example, in the Science, Technology, Engineering, and Mathematics (STEM) context, creativity is usually defined as the development of ideas and products that are original and useful. Further, it usually includes the examination and/ or combination of existing facts, ideas, and theories in original and useful ways. STEM uses creativity to develop and explore new problems and re-examine, re-articulate, or solve existing ones in novel ways. This highlights creativity as understood and described in many ways depending on the context in which it finds itself and ultimately functions. For each discipline, specialism, area, or expertise, creativity provides meaning in differing, multifaceted ways, which then aids in interpreting the processes of it, and how it is viewed and valued. The same can be said for education; how creativity is understood in the early years contrasts with how it is viewed in, say, Key Stage 2. The early years focuses on processes, whereas later years focus on outcome, a point we return to later in this chapter.

It is apparent, then, that creativity is a multi-dimensional and complex phenomenon. It is difficult to measure and one of the most difficult concepts to define (Kousoulas, 2010; McCammon et al., 2010; Sawyer, 2012). Nevertheless, it is possible to find some similarities in the various definitions and interpretations of creativity across most disciplines and, of course, in education, which keep reoccurring. These can be seen in the form of key features or characteristics associated with describing creativity; of these, the main ones are as follows:

Imaginative – this involves thinking and involves bringing about something that did not exist or was not known before, so it had to be imagined first. This can imply that the imagination first needs to be stimulated to lead to creativity.

 AROUND THE WORLD
WALLONIA, BELGIUM

In their report on approaches in a policy titled *Creative Little Scientists* (2015, p. 5), Belgium highlighted their definition of creativity as 'purposive imaginative activity generating outcomes that are original and valuable in relation to the learner'. They further highlight a definition in relation to science and mathematics as 'generat[ing] alternative ideas and strategies as an individual or community, and reason[ing] critically between these'.

Purposeful – creativity should have a purpose, an objective, an aim; it needs to be useful. However, what if the purpose is just pure pleasure or fun? Does it then have no place in a child's education?

Original – highlights that creativity is individual in some way, has a uniqueness of some kind. This requires looking at something like everyone else but thinking something different and coming up with ideas or products (process or outcome) that are new or unusual.

Novel – it is new, fresh, innovative, something not seen or heard before, unusual, or different.

Problem-solving – creativity surfaces when one is faced with a problem which they then solve, which could be original, novel, and purposeful. Knowledge and imagination are both applied here. However, *does creativity always emerge from a 'problem'?*

Product – creativity is an invention, a piece of art, theory, skill, or habit, a product of a result of something. However, it is known that creativity does not always manifest a certain concrete result. Even a creative idea can be a creative invention (Craft, 2005).

Of value – this implies that creativity has to be of value to meet its purpose. This term is open to interpretation, as discussed earlier.

These key threads in defining creativity demonstrate that it is made up of a number of components, features, or characteristics rather than being a concrete, pinned down definition which when stimulated leads to creativity. We therefore need to know what these features/characteristics mean for children's learning in the early years; as a result, many questions are raised for the adult, such as:

- 'What is meant by being creative in the early years?';

- 'Can creativity be learned?' 'Can creativity be taught?';

- 'How does creativity relate to the curriculum areas for learning?'; and

- 'How should practitioners in the early years help children to develop creativity?'

 **CONNECT**

How you may have used the above key words to define creativity personally or professionally?

Adults then need answers to the meaning of creativity in order to understand its relevance to early years education.

Defining creativity for the early years

Most theories of child development view children in their earliest years as highly creative, with a natural tendency to fantasise, experiment, and explore their environment (Sharp, 2004, p. 6). Children are said to have creative potential and be

> **❗ STORY FROM PRACTICE**
> ● EARLY YEARS INITIAL TEACHER TRAINING SESSION
>
> The session started with looking at attributes and characteristics of outstanding teachers. Many of the responses that were generated contained the word 'creativity', that adults working with children must be creative. Trainees were asked to explain further what they meant by this term.
>
> | | | | |
> |---|---|---|---|
> | Producing something | Getting somewhere | Use of imagination | |
> | Pupil-led | Learning through it | Discovery | Investigation |
> | Exploring ideas | Adapting thinking | Different approaches | |
> | Individual | Different representation of thoughts | Spontaneous | Debating |
> | Thinking outside the box | How it is discovered in each context | | |
> | Trying/Failing | Making it possible | Teaching through it | |
>
>

capable of creative expression (Hallet, 2016). Definitions of creativity have given us many features or characteristics that lead to it, including imagination, originality, productivity, problem-solving, novel thinking, and the ability to produce an outcome, or ideas, of value and worth. However, when applying this to the young child, these are concepts that are very broad in creativity, and hence in learning. They require mastering; they cannot just happen. For example, originality can be regarded as novel thinking, but *how does one reach originality? Or come up with something that is novel?*

An example of this can be, say, writing a poem. How can a child be creative in verbal poetry and come up with something original if they have never heard a poem? Have no information about it? Or the opportunity to explore it? How can they create a poem if they cannot string together grammatically correct sentences? Or have no opportunity to play with language in its many forms? Or, if they don't have much vocabulary to do so? Another example is painting. Children paint, but painting involves techniques – how to use tools such as the brush or sponge, mixing various materials, i.e. powder paint with glue to get a better consistency, and achieving different effects by splashing paint on, dabbing it, dotting it. These have to be learned, practiced, experimented with, tried another way in order to be mastered.

Let's go back to literacy. When children learn to write, how does it happen? They don't just pick up a pen one day and start writing; there are, yet again, a number of steps that they go through first. They need to imagine and make up stories in concrete forms, first by listening to them, taking part in imaginative play, and role-playing characters. Children need to scribble, draw, mark-make to convey messages, show they understand that these marks have meaning. They need to experience manipulating pencils, crayons, paint brushes, which will help in writing. They need to play with letters and sounds so they learn to be interested in and how to use them. These examples demonstrate that for creativity to occur, there is groundwork that needs to be done first – namely, developing knowledge, understanding, skills, and behaviours associated with processes in learning.

 ACTIVITY

As per the examples of poetry, painting, and writing, mind-map the processes of reaching the following terms associated with creativity. How do children get there?

- Originality

- Novel ideas

- Novel thinking

- Problem-solving

For the early years, then, a more recent definition for creativity has been provided by Pascal and Bertram (2017a, p. 1):

imaginative activity fashioned as to produce something (process or outcome) which is both original and of value.

This is like *All Our Futures*, but the emphasis here is on the *something*, which can be either 'process' or 'outcome'. This is because creativity in the early years places importance on the processes that children engage with in their learning environment, which are not necessarily outcome-based; the outcome is the child's choice to make. The earlier examples of poetry, painting, and writing all have processes entwined with how a child engages with reaching the outcome. Pascal and Bertram (2017a) have stated that they feel this definition could be applied to the whole range of learning areas and affordances for learning, and that it embraces a wide range of cognitive, emotional, and social/relational processes.

The concept of Craft's 'little c creativity' (2001, p. 45) can be applied here too. Little c defines children's creativity and creative learning, as it differs from adult's creativity due to its subjectivity. As stated earlier, adults in the early years see children as naturally creative, always open to new experiences, and with a tendency to be interested in everything new (Lin, 2011). Subjectivity, then, is an intrinsic characteristic of children's. The novelty in their creative ideas is not determined by outcome, but by the knowledge they hold (Kudryavtsev, 2011) and the processes they engage in. 'Imagination' is thus a relevant part of children's creativity. Children's creativity is always inventive but also mostly imaginative, where some aspects of the imagination may even be considered as an implicit part of creativity (Craft, 2005, p. 18).

In the context of early years education, the focus is therefore not on originality and products, but on the 'creative process' and the 'creative environment'. The concept of the creative process also defines 'creative behaviour' and 'creative thinking' as creative processes (Toivanena, Halkilahtib and Ruismäkic, 2013). During the creative process, children are constructing knowledge, learning, applying skills, using their imaginations, thinking creatively, and exhibiting creative behaviours in what they are doing and saying. It is this which then leads to the ability to be original, to produce something, or to reach an outcome while being creative. This implies that in addition to knowledge, there are certain attributes, skills, behaviours, and characteristics associated with creativity that need to be nurtured in young children – almost a need for stimulation of creativity to occur. Let's explore this.

○ FACT NOTE

Wolfgang Mozart (1756–1791) was an Austrian composer who created a string of operas, concertos, symphonies, and sonatas that profoundly shaped classical music. Mozart trained for 16 years before he produced an acknowledged piece of work. This reinforces **creativity** as a practice.

Creative habits of mind

During the process of creativity, it is noted that certain behaviours, characteristics, and dispositions to and for learning are exhibited by children and visible to the adults. An example to illustrate this can be found in the QCA framework of creative behaviours and the CCE 'creative habits of mind'.

In 2004, after undertaking a three-year research project, the QCA (Qualifications and Curriculum Authority) published *Creativity: Find It, Promote It*. The project outlined a number of creative behaviours associated with creativity that could be identified and promoted in Key Stages 1, 2, and 3. These were:

Questioning and challenging – creative pupils are curious, question and challenge, and don't always follow rules. They:

- Ask 'why?' 'how?' 'what if?'

- Ask unusual questions.

- Respond to ideas, questions, tasks, or problems in a surprising way

- Challenge conventions and their own and others' assumptions

- Think independently

Making connections and seeing relationships – creative pupils think laterally and make associations between things that are not usually connected. They:

- Recognise the significance of their knowledge and previous experience

- Use analogies and metaphors

- Generalise from information and experience, searching for trends and patterns

- Reinterpret and apply their learning in new contexts

- Communicate their ideas in novel or unexpected ways

Envisaging what might be – creative pupils speculate about possibilities. They:

- Imagine, seeing things in the mind's eye

- See possibilities, problems, and challenges

- Ask 'what if?'

- Visualise alternatives

- Look at and think about things differently and from different points of view

Exploring ideas, keeping options open – creative pupils explore possibilities, keep their options open, and learn to cope with the uncertainty that this brings. They:

- Play with ideas, experiment, try alternatives and fresh approaches

- Respond intuitively and trust their intuition

- Anticipate and overcome difficulties, following an idea through

 **CONNECT**

Have you observed these 'creative behaviours' in your work with children in the early years?

- Keep an open mind, adapting and modifying their ideas to achieve creative results

 Reflecting critically on ideas, actions, and outcomes – creative pupils are able to evaluate critically what they do. They:

- Review progress and ask 'is this a good . . .?' 'is this what is needed?'

- Invite feedback and incorporate this as needed

- Put forward constructive comments, ideas, explanations, and ways of doing things

- Make perceptive observations about originality and value

In 2011, Creativity, Culture and Education (CCE), an international foundation for creative learning, worked with the Centre for Real World Education at Winchester University to develop a language of creativity which adults could understand as a framework for assessing it (Spencer, Lucas and Claxton, 2012). This framework was in the form of 'Creative Habits of Mind' (CHoM), which identified creative skills and behaviours in children aged 5 years and up. It was advised that these skills and behaviours should be referenced in the planning and development of any teaching and learning approaches, with the aim of unlocking the creativity of children and young people. These skills and behaviours were defined as:

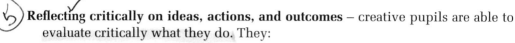

OBSERVE

A child or a group of children over a period of time. Where can you map the CHoMs in the observation?

Inquisitive	Wondering and questioning Exploring and investigating Challenging assumptions
Persistent	Tolerating uncertainty Sticking with difficulty Daring to be different
Imaginative	Playing with possibilities Making connections Using intuition
Disciplined	Crafting and improving Developing techniques Reflecting critically
Collaborative	Cooperating appropriately Giving and receiving feedback Sharing the 'product'

Both frameworks clearly demonstrate certain skills, behaviours, and characteristics associated with unlocking creativity, which are observable and identifiable by the adult and can thus be planned for. This means that in order for children to express their creativity capacities, they need a combination of these characteristics. These can then be classed as 'creativity's characteristics'; children's creative potential can then be achieved through the expression of such characteristics, and the practitioner can nurture them. It is no wonder that the EYFS advocates creating and thinking critically as a *characteristic of effective learning*. Figure 2.1 is a visible illustration for understanding this discussion. Creativity expert Robert Epstein (1996) further reinforces the idea that if children are helped to develop their creative competencies (creativity's characteristics), they will be better equipped for the world. The early years practitioner's role, then, is to pin down the many characteristics associated with creativity, rather than to pin down creativity itself, and foster and nurture these through creative processes, the environment, and approaches to teaching and learning; the goal is to ultimately raise its profile in children's learning and, in turn, in early years education.

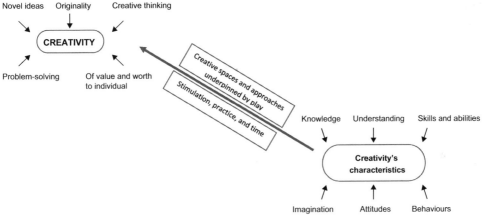

Figure 2.1 How creativity works

Creativity's characteristics

So, what are creativity's characteristics? How do they differ from the EYFS aspect of the characteristics of effective teaching and learning (CoETL)? Creativity's characteristics involve gaining and constructing knowledge, experimenting, playing, exploring, being active, questioning, using the imagination, generating ideas, making connections, thinking – and much more! They give children the ability to perceive things (whatever they may be) in new ways, to find new patterns or even hidden ones, to make or unpick connections, and to generate solutions or question existing ones (processes). They can also be about turning new and imaginative ideas into reality (outcomes). This should not come across as something new, because these are several features of learning that practitioners already work with in developing and nurturing in young children in the early years.

Creativity's characteristics do not differ from the CoETL. In fact, the CoETL are creativity's characteristics! Work Tool 1 is an amalgamation of what can be learnt about creative behaviours and skills from literature, such as the CHoMs, the QCA framework, and the CoETL from Development Matters (Early Education, 2012). The shaded aspects are the CoETL, which are an inherent part of nurturing creativity – these will be discussed in depth in the Chapter 3. Do note, Work Tool 1 is not designed to replace the EYFS CoETL, but rather to add to them. Creativity's characteristics can be developed in all aspects of the EYFS, and not just in obvious subjects like expressive arts and design. These help children learn better, whatever the learning may be. A focus on these can make learning more interesting, relevant, personal to the child, and engaging. Through stimulation, it motivates children to want to know more, apply what they already know and build on this, and take in information purposefully. Some children may already have some of creativity's characteristics in place, whereas others may need help, encouragement, and skill development in order to engage with them. This is because each individual has a different combination of abilities, personal traits, experiences, and knowledge that they will bring to the creative process at all times. This will determine the quality of engagement with their learning, and inform us that not all creative children are alike.

The creative process

When defining and applying creativity in the early years, there is an emphasis on the creative process, rather than the end goal for children. This is because children are acquiring, developing, and practicing creative behaviours and creative thinking that they need to be able to achieve a successful outcome; creative processes allow this to happen. A process is a series of steps, decisions, or tasks involved in the way learning, any learning, is completed. Processes are everywhere and in every aspect of life and work. For example, preparing breakfast, changing oil in a car, or placing an order are all processes. Similarly, processes exist in learning; they exist in creativity. The earlier examples of poetry, painting, and writing demonstrated processes in terms of how learning and mastering something are achieved.

 **DISCUSS**

With peers/colleagues how they use 'processes' in children's learning.

A creative process involves investigating something, exploring multiple viewpoints and options, generating and testing out ideas, developing, refining, and communicating solutions, and evaluating whether they have worked – all of which require creativity's characteristics to be engaged. The real magic to all of this is that it's a process that occurs so often in early years settings that it may not be thought of. If the right materials and environments are provided for children to use, this will often do much of the work for them; this is why ideas strike when they are least expected. Approaches should then embed processes in children's learning, with children able to use what they already know, build on it, and transfer it elsewhere, utilising creativity's characteristics. *So, what does this process look like?*

The following is an example that can be adapted or added to when thinking about creative processes in children's learning experiences. It should be read in conjunction with the section on creative thinking in this chapter.

Initiating – task/activity/discussion/observation initiated by the child or adult. This can be planned for or can just occur during children's play.

Exploring and gathering information – what is it the children need to do? And how will they go about it? Information can be in the form of books, images, resources, objects, people, visits, and much more. Children gather what may be needed or find out more. They explore the task at hand and find what's missing.

Connecting and experimenting – children see where all their exploring and gathering fit together and where they do not. They start seeing things that don't work and things that will. They notice when there are gaps in what they have, and look to problem solve this. They incorporate their surroundings into what they do.

Pulling it together – this can be regarded as creating, but not only in the form of a concrete product. It can be in the form of a discussion, observation by the adult, conveying ideas, or questioning. What is it that is expected during and after the process?

Feedback – provided by both child and adult. What process did the child follow? How did they achieve the outcome? What worked? What could they do with it?

 ACTIVITY

Look over a week's worth of plans for your setting. See if you can identify where the creative process discussed here is visible. What were children expected to do, and how?

Plan an activity or experience for a group of children which involves this process.

It is essential to note that children may not follow this process in a linear way, and this is not the expectation, either. This process is provided as a guide for the many possibilities children undertake during the creative process. You may find children moving in and out of each step, and it may also be essential for practitioners to provide ongoing feedback during the process, especially for those children that need adult reassurance constantly. However, it can be used as a tool against which to assess your planning – *are these processes available in what you have planned for both in children's learning and the environment? Can processes nurture, develop, and stimulate creativity's characteristics?* Creative processes also need a quality creative environment, as it is inseparable from its surroundings; Chapter 8 explores this in depth.

Creative thinking

How does a creative idea come to you? Where does it come from, and why does it occur? These are questions we – as humans – have been asking for centuries, primarily because the *process* continues to mystify us. We can do a lot of incredible things, but we just can't quite figure out what's going on in our brains when we happen upon a novel idea or stumble onto a solution for a problem. This is actually the effect of creative thinking during the creative process of learning, which we need to nurture and develop in children. There should be no surprise that 'thinking' has a crucial role in creativity; it has a crucial role in learning as a whole and is a vital characteristic in children's learning.

Creative thinking is a reoccurring concept associated with creative processes. When teaching young children, it is expected that what they think about what they learn. It is expected that they think about what they are learning. This thinking not only allows information to be taken in, but is vital in developing what is learnt – through thinking about it, understanding it, using it again elsewhere, and, of course, having an idea. However, how many of us have sat in a learning experience and not allowed what is being taught to go anywhere beyond the facilitator's mouth? Or, how many of us end up choosing the same children in group discussions to speak, not knowing if those who choose not to speak are actually thinking? Fumoto et al. (2012, p. 28) suggest that creative thinking is at the heart of all creativity, because it is within this that thought processes are activated and engaged with. Thoughts are where the birth pangs of creative ideas, solutions, and problem-solving occur.

In the early years, children's thinking is more visible than abstract; this is apparent in their mark-making, conversations, play, imaginative activities, and self-talk, as well as in the ideas they play with. For this reason, the concept of 'sustained shared thinking' (SST) is associated with children as a form of nurturing thinking. SST is defined as the result of two or more individuals (adults and children, child and child) working together in an intellectual way to solve a problem, clarify a concept, or evaluate activities (Siraj-Blatchford, 2007). It requires all participants to contribute to the thinking process, and vital to it is that thinking must be extended (Sylva et al., 2004). Siraj-Blatchford (2014) refers to this type of thinking as a 'cognitive dance' taking place, which can be fuelled through questioning from the early years practitioner. Veale (2014, adapted from Siraj-Blatchford, 2007) provides the following prompts to nurture SST in children:

- **Tuning in**: listening carefully to what is being said and what the child is doing.

- **Showing genuine interest**: giving their whole attention to the child.

- **Respecting children's own decisions and choices** by inviting children to elaborate – 'I really want to know more about this' – and engaging in the response.

- **Re-capping**: 'So you think that . . .'

- **Offering the adult's own experience:** 'I like to listen to music when I . . .'

- **Clarifying ideas:** 'Right, so you think that this stone will melt if I boil it?'

- **Suggesting:** 'You might like to try doing it this way.'

- **Using encouragement to further thinking:** 'You have really thought hard about where to put this door in the palace – where will you put the windows?'

- **Offering an alternative viewpoint:** 'Maybe Goldilocks wasn't naughty when she ate the porridge?'

- **Speculating:** 'Do you think the three bears would have liked Goldilocks to come to live with them as their friend?'

- **Asking open questions:** 'How did you . . .?' 'Why does this . . .?' 'What happens next?' 'What do you think?' 'I wonder what would happen if . . .?'

- **Using positive questioning:** 'I don't know, what do you think?' 'That's an interesting idea.' 'I like what you have done there.' 'What would happen if we did . . .?'

- **Making sense words:** 'I think', 'I agree', 'I imagine', 'I disagree', 'I like', 'I don't like', 'I wonder'.

 OBSERVE

An early years practitioner with children. How often do they use the SST prompts? How effective is it?

Creativity becomes more visible when adults try to be more attentive to children's cognitive processes rather than to the results children achieve in various fields of doing and understanding (Malaguzzi, 1993, p. 77). It is here that unlimited possibilities can be formed, leading to creative thinking.

The distinction between critical thinking and creative thinking must be drawn, as they have differing purposes. Critical thinking is the gathering and absorbing of information, whereas creative thinking is the transformation of this knowledge for generating new ideas (Simister, 2007). Creative thinking processes in learning allow for the management of ideas and making ideas a reality, with knowledge, understanding, and skills vital to the formation of new ideas (critical thinking). The concept of 'thinking outside the box', which is very often used to describe creativity, can only happen when one knows what is 'inside the box'.

 RESEARCH TO EXPLORE

YOUNG CHILDREN'S CREATIVE THINKING (RICHHART, CHURCH, AND MORRISON, 2011)

Two types of thinking are noted. Convergent thinking is about learning facts, following instructions, and solving problems with one right answer. Worksheets, colouring books, and templates used in the early years contribute to convergent thinking, which leads to surface learning.

Divergent thinking, on the other hand, generates different solutions and sees various possibilities in response to open-ended questions and problems; how many uses can you think of for a cup? Thinking in this way leads to deep and meaningful learning.

Creativity and divergent thinking are interrelated – you must be able to think divergently in order to be creative.

 FACT NOTE

HISTORY OF THE LIGHT BULB

The electric light, one of the everyday conveniences that most affect our lives, was not 'invented' in the traditional sense in 1879 by Thomas Alva Edison. He was neither the first nor the only person trying to invent an incandescent light bulb. In fact, some historians claim there were over 20 inventors of incandescent lamps prior to Edison's version. However, Edison is often credited with the invention because his version outstripped earlier versions because of a combination of factors. He refined what was already known and took this knowledge to develop a new idea.

Knowledge of previous information or ideas is vital to develop new ones, which is why gaining knowledge (and understanding it!) is just as vital for the creativity process to function. Allowing children to play with ideas in a concrete way can fuel creative and critical thinking – a characteristic of effective learning that will be discussed in Chapter 3 – as can the activation of their imagination. Children can make new connections and combinations of familiar ideas. They can generate new ideas by exploring existing ones and then go onto create new structures, leading to creative thinking.

Creativity is an inherent human ability and is made up of a number of components that can be achieved through the nurturing and stimulating of creative behaviours, creative skills, and creative thinking. Young children can develop this through creative processes and a creative environment provided by the early years practitioner. In Chapter 1, we made a strong survival case for creativity; however, as children develop skills for learning, life, and work, creativity not only helps them to understand their world, but also helps them to be sufficiently equipped to influence its shape and exercise control over their interactions with it (Education Scotland, 2013, p. 6). Originality, novel thinking, problem-solving, and the ability to produce an outcome of value and worth can only happen where children can apply, build, develop, and master creativity's characteristics.

Next steps

 REFLECT

This chapter has established that creativity is stimulated by several characteristics that take place in children's learning, which are nurtured through the environment and creative processes.

Taking Work Tool 1, can you map the CoETL to it further? Are there any other characteristics that you have observed in practice that you can note about it?

 EXPLORE

The standard definition of creativity, 2012: www.tandfonline.com/doi/full/10.1080/104 00419.2012.650092?src=recsys&

■ Focuses on issues around the definition of creativity.

Creativity Portal: http://creativityportal.org.uk/

■ A wealth of creative online teaching tools, CPD resources, inspiration, and examples of next and best practice allowing you to make connections and use your creative thinking skills.

Creativity, Culture and Education: www.creativitycultureeducation.org/

- An international foundation dedicated to unlocking the creativity of children and young people in and outside of formal education.

How creativity works – an interview: www.npr.org/2012/03/19/148777350/how-creativity-works-its-all-in-your-imagination

- Jonah Lehrer, a writer specialising in neuroscience, addresses 'how creativity works?' in this interview.

The Rhetorics of Creativity (2010): www.creativitycultureeducation.org/wp-content/uploads/rhetorics-of-creativity-2nd-edition-87.pdf

- A review of literature.

3 The creative child

 THINK

What are children actually doing when they are learning creatively?

Do children have a vision when they are learning?

CHAPTER FOCUS

- The need to understand children

- What and how do children learn

- Creativity as a characteristic of teaching and learning

- Creating and thinking critically

- Children's individual approaches to learning

- The essential role of play in creative learning

In the first three years of life, children's brains are far more active than those of university students (Ya̅nez, 2013). The idea that children begin to 'learn' when they reach Reception has been replaced by the understanding that learning in fact begins from birth. The process of learning and development, then, is continuous and culminates rapidly, which then makes it imperative not only to start developing creativity early, but also to ensure consistent support and scaffolding are in place for the child. It starts with understanding that all children are what I refer to as the 'creative child', and valuing the image of the creative child as someone who is born with creative abilities and is very capable of exhibiting them when given the opportunity to do so. The creative child is the real expert in creativity, because it is natural to them, and it is connected to all areas of the EYFS. Not all children are as creative as one another at the same time, but all show an ability to demonstrate it, and it is the creative adult's role to nurture this further. This chapter explores what makes up children's learning and, thus, the creative child.

ACTION RESEARCH

Research the theories relating to children's development and learning. Think about how these will be affected today by the current economic and political climate.

Discuss your ideas in a small group. How can this inform your work on creativity?

Understanding children

In ancient times and the middle ages, children were seen as 'mini adults'; discipline was harsh, children were considered servants or property, and at the age of 7, known as the 'age of reason', they were expected to work alongside adults. Until the twentieth century, little scientific attention was paid to studying how children develop and learn. Over time, however, a wealth of information emerged that identified early childhood as a separate and distinct phase of life with its own characteristics. As a result, many theories were developed to examine approaches and processes involved in teaching and learning against children's development. Psychologists, sociologists, biologists, and anthropologists all contributed to what is known about children's development today, which includes biological, cognitive, socioemotional, and sociocultural changes.

As educators of the young, it is important to understand the theory behind how children's knowledge, skills, experiences, and behaviours progress over time. This allows adults to support children's development and learning. However, as well as having knowledge of child development theory, there also needs to be a consideration of the latest research in the field of early years. This is because theoretical perspectives on children's learning and development have been tested time and time again, with the recognition that children learn differently, at different times and at different rates, in varying contexts and in different circumstances throughout their lives.

RESEARCH TO EXPLORE
NEUROSCIENCE

Emerging neuroscience research shows that at birth, babies' brains have around 100 billion neurons but only about a quarter of the connections – these are called synapses – have already been made between them. Therefore, quality experiences are more critical in the early years than at any other time for the development of healthy brains and well-rounded personalities. These **critical experiences include imaginative, creative, and cultural opportunities,** which can help children to build contexts, make meaning, and deepen understanding.

It is good practice to have knowledge of theories and how these are visible in a given setting, but this should not come at the expense of each child's individuality in terms of how they are taught and how they approach creative learning. It must be remembered that children's everyday life experiences create the conditions for their development (Fleer, 2015, p. 21). There needs to be an important balance between applying a general knowledge of child development and applying the particular knowledge gained by forming a relationship with each child and their family. This balance then becomes a route to understanding children and determining how best to support and foster their creative learning.

Adults can make decisions about children's learning based upon:

■ Child development and how children learn

■ The individual strengths, needs, interests, talents, approaches to learning, and characteristics of effective learning that children bring

■ Each child's family and community cultures

■ Research that ensures that adults know not only what and how to teach children, but why particular practices and strategies are effective

■ The knowledge and skills they hold on creativity and the many characteristics associated with it

 DISCUSS

With peers/colleagues what you all think makes up 'the creative child'.

We have come a long way in understanding children, and it is known that children develop a range of skills, knowledge, and understanding even before they start statutory schooling, at a speed that will never be repeated in their lives (Fisher, 2013, p. 1).

Children demonstrate emerging and evolving competencies and abilities cognitively, linguistically, physically, socially, and emotionally. Just through observing a child, we can learn so much about them. It is also apparent that no two children are the same; even given the same set of experiences, each child's abilities will differ from another's. However, there are some commonalities in how they approach their world.

In their earliest years, children have an appetite for discovery, creation, and connection. Children go through imaginative experiences which help them form awareness and knowledge of real things. It can be said that in the early years children are spontaneous, imaginative, full of joy, and possessed of a strong motivation to learn. They seem to strive for independence and are in the process of forming personal identities. Children are delighted with themselves and what they do: 'look at my painting', 'I can plant a seed'. This is very different from the growing dissatisfaction that appears as children progress through education; they become more self-critical as they learn to become uncreative. It can be said that formal education can inhibit some of the most prominent characteristics of young children (Fisher, 2013).

In children's everyday lives, they are making sense of the world around them through means they don't immediately relate to creativity. Observing, imitating, playing, talking with each other and adults, listening, being curious, questioning, exploring, discovering, and investigating are all ways in which children make sense of the world. These acts also serve a powerful purpose for unlocking creativity – creativity's characteristics – as they give children a perspective from which to build their ideas. When children seek to understand, and do so in a way that they comprehend, they are taking a step towards creativity by connecting the *what* with the *how* and the *why*.

Unfortunately, creativity in the setting can still be seen as potentially disruptive or as a kind of negative deviance (Beghetto, 2013). Although children are the real experts in creativity, they are not always ascribed the status of sole expertise by adults, and as a result, adults can dismiss unexpected and novel questions and ideas from children, or simply not pay attention to take them forward, which can then inhibit the creative process. When this happens, adults may view anything that doesn't easily fit into what they expect as irrelevant, surplus knowledge. This surplus, however, is filled with creative potential (Beghetto, 2013).

! STORY FROM PRACTICE

I heard a great story recently of a teacher who was teaching a drawing class with a group of 6-year-olds. There was a little girl in the back who hardly ever listened, hardly ever attended. But she was drawing and feverishly concentrating for about half an hour. The teacher went over to her and said, 'What are you drawing?' The girl said, 'I'm drawing a picture of God.' The teacher said, 'But nobody knows what God looks like.' The girl replied, 'They will in a minute.' Isn't that great? How many adults would do that? (Robinson, 2005, p. 3).

 **CONNECT**

What have you seen children do or say that demonstrates 'creative confidence'?

Young children have immense 'creative confidence', as per Sir Ken Robinson's story; however, adults may have a more difficult time appreciating the creative thinker unless the child demonstrates their creativity through the arts. This is because children are not only more likely to demonstrate the qualities of day-dreaming, wondering, and wanting to work with everyone, but also being alone, sharing bizarre thoughts and conflicting opinions, asking lots of questions, being overly energetic, not being able to sit still, and not conforming to adult expecta-tions – *sound familiar? Of course, it's near enough every child!* It is also true that children reach a point where they start to lose their creative confidence as a result of adult response, or lack thereof. Allowing children the opportunity to combine their unique personal insights and 'surplus' knowledge with the content being presented can result in new and meaningful understandings for the creative child, and give the adult a moment of awe and wonder.

Understanding that children are unique and very competent in making sense of the world provides an insight into exactly what and how the creative child learns. The EYFS is set on the principle that every child is a unique child who is constantly learning and who can be resilient, capable, confident, and self-assured (DfE, 2017). The creative child has the ability to think differently, as per Sir Ken Robinson's story above. This is something that must be appreciated and nurtured further, because we want different, we want individuality, we want a unique cre-ative child who is constantly learning.

 AROUND THE WORLD
REGGIO EMILIA, ITALY

The Reggio Approach establishes the image of the child as *strong, capable,* and *resilient* – rich with wonder and knowledge. Every child brings with them deep curiosity and poten-tial, and this innate curiosity drives their interest to understand the world and their place within it. Children question, hypothesise, predict, experiment, reflect on their discoveries, and revisit their projects to refine and clarify their understandings, thereby expanding the richness of their thinking.

The creative child – what do children learn?

Children are never not ready to learn. They are always learning and do so from birth, but learning is a lifelong process and involves the entire individual – thinking, feel-ing, perceiving, and behaving (Gauntlett et al., 2011). However, for the adult, a child's learning normally fits into expectations and standards for their age, which is often against the early years curriculum. The curriculum framework sets out *what* children are expected to learn in the seven areas of learning. Further, there are early learning goals which summarise the knowledge, skills, and understanding that all young children should have gained by the end of the Reception year, which then demonstrates that they have 'learnt' what is expected. These are pre-determined, assessable outcomes that adults must help children work towards (Mohammed, 2014) to ensure school readiness for the formal phase of education. What is not apparent or stipulated, however, is the *process of learning – how do children get there? What is it that the creative child is learning which is not stipulated in the framework as such?*

To be confident, resilient, and capable lifelong learners, children need to learn ways of learning. Learning can be understood as a process where knowledge is created through the active searching for meaning in, and transformation of, experience (Gauntlett et al., 2011). During the learning process, children are meaning-making, and for this they learn and develop skills and strategies, understandings of how things work and why, and where they can connect it later. They also learn and unlearn misunderstandings and internalise their concrete learning to create concepts for learning. Each one is discussed as follows:

Dispositions to, and for, learning – this refers to the ways in which children engage in, relate to, and approach the learning process. These are also described as 'relatively enduring habits of mind and action' that encourage children to respond to experiences in particular ways (Katz and Chard, 2000, p. 30). Carr (2001, p. 21) defines dispositions as 'participation repertoires from which a learner recognises, selects, edits, responds to, resists, searches for and constructs learning opportunities'. In order to do this, children need to develop a bank of dispositions that will actively engage their participation in their learning. The dispositions, often classed as 'positive', that children exhibit are taking interest, getting involved, confidence, concentration, perseverance, curiosity, commitment, flexibility, being playful, and motivation – all needed for the creative learning process. Children learn and apply these through the exciting discoveries and experiences that the early years environment and practitioner provides.

Skills – there is no doubt that children are building and developing a repertoire of skills during the process of learning – skills in mastering and controlling their bodies, skills in communication and interaction, skills in collaboration, skills in social interaction, and further in terms of technical skills, such as learning and mastering the use of equipment and resources, tackling an activity in multiple ways, fixing, joining, and using skills learnt in one place in another. Children will repeat movement and actions time after time in order to become experts and succeed at the goals they have set themselves (Fisher, 2013). The activities and the environment provided by the practitioner allow children's skills to develop, with responses and interaction to motivate and sustain them further.

Understandings and misunderstandings – children are meaning-making and developing an understanding of all that they come into contact with: understanding that a heavy object on the boat will make it sink into a water tray, for instance, or understanding that they can transport that very same water from the tray to the art easel to mix with paint. Children are learning to understand; however, during this process they can also learn misunderstandings. Fisher (2013) describes this as children making the wrong connections. In the quest to construct their own meaning for, and understanding of, the experiences they have had, this is where children can develop views about a variety of topics that are different from views of 'experts' (p. 12). The child sees something that makes sense and which connects for them, and this becomes their understanding. Yet again, if it does not fit with the adult's expectations or the learning process, it is deemed not correct – but it is the adult's role to assist children in developing their 'correct' understandings, and use the misunderstandings as a learning opportunity.

 CONNECT

What other dispositions and skills are there? What misunderstandings can children learn?

Strategies – although children may not be aware of this, they are picking up a number of learning strategies when engaging with what they do. A strategy is what children do to fulfil the aims of a task/activity or goal they set themselves. Trying things out, connecting, rehearsing, or repeating what they do are all forms of strategies, which they then develop and utilise across their learning. Other examples include:

● Persistency on activities by extending them or returning to them later

● Experimenting with resources, using additional resources in their play and activities or to solve a problem

● Using the adult as a source by asking for help when needed, responding to adult's questions and prompts, asking questions

● Use of other children as a resource by asking for assistance, cooperation, collaboration, and working together

● Directing themselves in what they do (language which indicates direction of self)

 OBSERVE

A child twice in two different contexts of learning. What strategies are they using and developing? Do they differ according to what the child is doing at that moment in the activity?

When developing strategies, there will be children who prefer to look and think before they act. Some try and try again until something comes right. Some prefer to imitate, some to instigate. Some ask questions and others wait for answers. These are tailor-made for and by each child (Fisher, 2013). They serve what the child is doing in that moment and are found to work by them. These then become part of the 'characteristics' of the child as a learner and are the basis of all strategies that they adopt.

Concepts – once children understand what they are learning, they take it from concrete form into abstract form. These are mental representations that organise their experience(s) (Gelman, 2009). Concepts can be:

- Things in the world (such as dogs, chairs, trees)

- Properties (green, happy)

- Events or states (jumping, wet)

- Individuals (mummy, Charlie the dog)

- Abstract ideas (goodness, liberty)

Concepts are generally understood to be the building blocks of ideas (e.g., the thought 'Charlie is a happy dog' requires possession of the constituent concepts), and are also embedded in larger knowledge structures, and therefore are not isolated components. Children, then, are active constructors of concepts through a range of first-hand experiences, leading them to see and understand the conceptual links between one experience and another.

Children are, as Malaguzzi states, 'authors of their own learning' (Mercilliott Hewett, 2001). The process of learning does not proceed in a linear way, determined by predictable stages and outcomes, because really, we don't know what children will learn and how until we actually observe in the environments in which they are the authors. It must be remembered, however, that how children develop and learn is complex. Some children learn effortlessly – asking questions, answering them, understanding new ideas, developing new skills. However, there are some children who do not seem to learn as easily, as they face barriers that make learning more difficult (Hallet, 2016, p. 5). These barriers need to be identified by the creative adult to allow children to access opportunities and strategies in the creative process of learning.

 FACT NOTE

William Glasser was an American psychiatrist. He developed reality therapy and choice theory. Regarding learning, he said:

We learn ...

10% of what we read

20% of what we hear

30% of what we see

50% of what we both hear and see

70% of what is discussed

80% of what we experience personally

95% of what we teach to someone else

Experiences are the key for children in the early years.

Characteristics of effective teaching and learning – how do children learn?

Engagement is central to learning in all areas of the curriculum and for all children when learning (Munns et al., 2006). When children are really engaged in their learning, they show concentration, persistence, enthusiasm, and eagerness in their inquiry – dispositions for learning. So, where we have explored *what* children are learning, we now focus on *how* the creative child goes about this learning. During the process of learning, children are without a doubt developing, mastering, and utilising certain characteristics, some of which were apparent in the previous section.

Creativity is made up of a number of characteristics, which we have identified in Chapter 2. The EYFS also emphasises characteristics in children's learning known as the Characteristics of Effective Teaching and Learning (CoETL). The EYFS curriculum areas of learning are about *what* children learn, whereas the CoETL is *how* children learn – the process. The CoETL advocate that in planning and guiding children's activities, adults must reflect on the different ways that children learn, and then reflect these in their practice. A child's individual learning characteristics will determine the way they respond to both the teaching and learning taking place in the environment, and in turn the creative characteristics they exhibit.

 ACTIVITY

Take three large sheets of paper and a few different coloured pens to stimulate your visual senses.

■ Write each CoEL on each sheet.

■ Now jot your thoughts on what each one involves when it comes to children.

■ Circle the key words.

■ Share with your tribe to gain more creative seeds!

■ Also, see if you can create a symbol or drawing to represent each CoEL.

A characteristic is a trait or quality, and these are regarded as key because they engage children through a trait that comes naturally to them. Underpinning the CoETL is the understanding that during their earliest years, children form attitudes about learning that will last a lifetime. Children who receive the right sort of support and encouragement during these years will be creative and adventurous learners throughout their lives. Children who do not receive this sort of support and interaction are likely to have a much different attitude about learning later in life – the road to becoming uncreative. The adult, the environment the adult provides, and the approaches they develop need to embed and nurture the CoETL, but without forgetting that children are individuals who bring their own needs, talents, and histories to the learning environment. The EYFS identifies three CoETL:

- **Playing and exploring** – children investigate and experience things, and 'have a go'. Playing and exploring is the way children engage with their learning environment and in turn learning; it is a natural and inherent characteristic. Children are able to choose activities (or create experiences) where they can engage with other children or adults or sometimes play alone, and during these activities and experiences they learn by first-hand experience – by actively 'doing' (DfCSF, 2007a). For this characteristic to come alive in the environment, children need sufficient space, time, and choice, with a range of activities and experiences, some of which have been planned and prepared by the practitioners on the basis of their observations of individual children's current interests, talents, learning styles, and stages of development.

- **Active learning** – children concentrate and keep on trying if they encounter difficulties, and enjoy achievements. The Tickell Review describes active learning as arising from the 'intrinsic motivation to achieve mastery – to experience competence, understanding and autonomy' (Tickell, 2011, p. 90). Active learning is not about 'being physically active', which is equally as important for young children, but rather refers to being 'mentally active and alert' (Hutchin, 2013, p. 13). Active learning describes a child's *motivation*, and is associated with the need for children to develop concentration and perseverance in order to successfully and actively learn. Learning in this way involves other people, objects, ideas, and events that can engage and involve children for sustained periods.

- **Creating and thinking critically** – children have and develop their own ideas, make links between ideas, and develop strategies for doing things (DfE, 2017). This is discussed in depth in the following section.

The observation record in the practice story below, clearly makes evident how all the CoETL are at play; they are characteristics that are continually present and in action through the interaction the child has with their environment and the people within it. The finding of the toy car prompted Gassy to initiate and explore the digging to find what else might be hidden. The adult challenged her further by encouraging her and making her think about how she was going to do so. She used trial and error with the different digging tools; in the end, her hands were the best! What is also clear is the vital role of the adult who challenged the child to take her ideas forward and try them out. This is clearly embedding a love of creative exploration.

❗ STORY FROM PRACTICE
● OBSERVATION RECORD

In the outdoor area, 3½-year-old Gassy was kneeling down near the soil on the grass when she found something poking out at her. She plucked it out with her fingers and looked at it. It was a toy car full of dirt. She brought it over to the practitioner and explained how she found it. Gassy then said, 'What else could be buried there?' The practitioner said, 'I wonder, too; are you going to find out?' Gassy jumped and said yes, so the practitioner asked her how she intended to do so. Gassy responded by saying she didn't know but would see. She then went over to the sand tray, took a small plastic spade, and went back to the area where she had found the car. Here she dug at the soil, which was quite hard; after a few tries, she could not do it, so she paused and looked around her. She went over to the shed area, found a bigger garden spade, and took it back to the soil. She then dug slightly; she tried again, but this time used her foot to push the spade in. As a hole appeared, Gassy then used her hands to dig up more dirt. Another child approached and they squealed with laughter and continued digging up the dirt until Gassy found a large stone. She went over, found a container, brought it back, and placed the toy car and stone in it. 'This is our treasure,' she said. The children continued to dig.

Creating and thinking critically

 DISCUSS

With peers/colleagues what they think 'creating and thinking critically' means.

The EYFS describes creating and thinking critically as when 'children have and develop their own ideas, make links between ideas, and develop strategies for doing things' (DfE, 2017, p. 10). It can be said that this CoETL is about 'creative thinking' (discussed in Chapter 2) and is associated with the need for children to make sense of experiences and develop thought over time. Many adults relate it to creating something; however, it is much more than this. The interactions that children have with other children, adults, the environment, and the experiences they engage in allow children to actively think about the meaning of what they are doing through perceiving patterns, inventing ideas, making connections, and developing creativity's characteristics. This then allows children to develop knowledge about when and how to use particular strategies in learning or problem-solving; vitally, they can transform ideas and rethink what they know (DfSCF, 2007b). Becoming more aware of their own thinking in this way is known as 'metacognition': an awareness of oneself as a thinker and learner, which is a key aspect of successful learning (Whitebread and Pasternak, 2010). Creativity emerges as children become absorbed in exploring what things are like and what they can be made to do (DfSCF, 2007b). Creating and thinking critically can therefore be summed up as being about 'ideas', 'making connections', 'making choices', and 'developing strategies', all of which are inherent in what children learn and which stimulate creativity's characteristics.

 RESEARCH TO EXPLORE

THINKING LIKE A GENIUS

In 1998 Michalko published an article listing the thinking patterns of geniuses. The following is his list, where I have omitted the word 'genius' and replaced it with 'children'. This is because children have the ability to do this when creating and thinking critically.

- Children look at problems in many different ways.

- Children make their thoughts visible.

- Children produce many ideas.

- Children make novel combinations.

- Children force relationships.

- Children think in opposites.

- Children think metaphorically.

- Children prepare themselves for chance.

Having their own ideas *(ideas)*

This is when children use their imagination and creativity to take on challenges and explore how problems could be solved and how their ideas can be implemented. It is about children generating their own ideas creatively through the use of their imagination; as the Tickell review states, 'being inventive allows children to find new problems as they seek challenges, and to explore ways of solving these' (2011, p. 90). Having their own ideas includes:

- Thinking of ideas

- Finding ways to solve problems

- Finding new ways to do things

Planning prompts

- Provide opportunities for children to express their ideas in a variety of ways.

- Appreciate children's ideas and individual ways of capturing and representing them.

- Give children time to explore and develop their ideas.

- Build on children's ideas as you help them to see new possibilities in their play.

- Listen to and discuss children's ideas; offer suggestions and pose questions that extend their thinking (DfCSF, 2007b).

- Allow children to revisit their ideas.

Using what they already know to learn new things (making connections)

This is when children link different activities and develop concepts – making connections. It is also how children develop an understanding of sequences, cause and effect, and how to build on thoughts through description and scientific thoughts. Here, thinking becomes more conscious as concepts are developed and connected. Making connections include:

- Making links and noticing patterns in their experiences

- Making predictions

- Testing their ideas

- Developing ideas of grouping, sequences, cause and effect

Planning prompts

- Help children to make connections in their learning by linking play to adult-led activities.

- Encourage opportunities for all children to link their ideas to new situations.

- Tell stories that present different possibilities within familiar situations to stimulate children to make new connections.

- Make it easier for children to make connections by giving them easy access to resources and allowing them to move materials from one place to another.

(DfCSF, 2007b)

- Encourage children to ask questions.

Choosing ways to do things and finding new ways *(choices and strategies)*

This is when children make choices and decisions in an organised way when undertaking new goal-directed activities or tasks. It involves children working out what to do, and how to change what they do in order to achieve where they are going with the process – developing strategies:

■ Planning, making decisions about how to approach a task, solve a problem and reach a goal

■ Checking how well their activities are going

■ Changing strategy as needed

■ Reviewing how well the approach worked

Adult approaches

■ Create conditions within which children are inspired to set themselves goals.

■ Provide resources from a variety of cultures to stimulate new ideas and ways of thinking and doing (DfCSF, 2007b).

■ Involve children in the planning of activities and environments, giving voice to their thinking.

 RESEARCH TO EXPLORE

NINE BARRIERS TO THINKING CREATIVELY

Thomas (1999) stated that creativity can be hindered due to barriers. She listed nine which should be considered by practitioners when supporting creating and thinking critically.

1) Failure to ask questions.

2) Failure to record ideas.

3) Failure to revisit ideas.

4) Failure to express ideas.

5) Failure to think in new ways.

6) Failure to wish for more.

7) Failure to try being creative.

8) Failure to keep trying.

9) Failure to tolerate creative behaviour.

For creativity to thrive, it is essential for the creative child to be actively engaged in the learning process. The CoETL support this to happen, and learning in this way allows children to master knowledge, skills, and behaviours that can lead to creativity and novel thinking. The creative adult needs to embed them in what they teach and how children learn. Duffy (2006) defines creativity as a process of learning and provides a framework for it, which clearly demonstrates the CoETL in play. The framework closely relates to the possibility thinking concept discussed in Chapter 4:

Curiosity

What is it?

Exploration

What can or does it do?

Play

What can I do with it?

Creativity

What can I create or invent?

 ACTION RESEARCH

Using Duffy's framework for the creativity process, observe three children and make notes on how visible the framework is in what they do and say:

■ What are they saying or doing under each of the headings?

■ How do they move in and out of each one, or even go back to them?

■ What does this inform you about the process of learning and the creative child?

The creative child's approaches to learning

Children's approaches to learning in the early years tend to be spontaneous, with materials and resources accepted into whatever they may be doing. This gradually changes as children become more aware of new elements that can be integrated into their learning. This is a form of 'knowingness' that increasingly replaces spontaneity and leads children to think about what they may need to do in their learning, and what may be needed for it. However, do note that previous knowledge, and a background of rich sensory experiences, nourishes and contributes to this aspect of children's learning. Where the CoETL are about how children learn, this book goes a step further in terms of how children can be observed to approach their learning – an almost personal approach.

The way children approach learning contributes to their success and influences their development and learning in other domains and in their lives. Their ability to stay focused, interested, and engaged supports a range of positive outcomes, including physical, cognitive, language, social, and emotional development. It allows children to acquire new knowledge and learn new skills, practice them, and set and achieve goals for themselves. Many early years adults view the way children approach learning as one of the most important aspects of early childhood development. Recognition of this, along with the skills and abilities that children possess, can lead to a great deal of creative learning and development of the creative child.

Over my career to date, I have observed many approaches that children take to their learning, and I share them with you below. They demonstrate that there is no uniformity in how children approach their learning – hence the unique child – and that children need to discover this with the benefit of time, pace, materials, and experiences provided in the learning context. The key is knowing children as people – *who are they? What do they like? How do they like to learn?* The adult must allow time for this and create environments to facilitate such approaches.

Table 3.1 The creative child's approaches to learning

Approach	Characteristics
The neat approach	Assembles what they need first and ensures neatness and organisation in all they do.
The scattered approach	Adds to their learning as they go along. Can be seen to be darting around the environment collecting and bringing things as they change and adapt what they are doing as they go along.
The quiet approach	Prefers quiet, but not isolation. Requires a certain level of noise but still wants others around whilst learning.
The lone approach	Wants to work entirely on their own. However, this depends on what they are doing and the context they are in.
The sensory approach	Uses the senses to explore activities/materials. Seen to touch, explore, and examine their environment and has a tactile approach to what they are doing. They are often the first to reach out when presented with resources/materials.
The reassured approach	Requires routine and the constant reassurance, support, and direction from the adult. This approach is short of ideas and confidence and uses the adult as a secure base for their learning.
The observing approach	Takes in all aspects of the environment through visual means. Often appears slow on task, but is actually processing what he/she sees visually and needs time. When you speak to them, you are astonished by how much they know and have picked up around them.

✖ **CONNECT**

In what other ways have you observed children *approach* their learning?

You must remember not to use the approaches as a way to label children, as they can be seen to move in and out of the differing approaches, depending, as always, on the context they find themselves in and the task or experience at hand. There will also be children who like to work at a table or desk, others on the floor, and many who learn by moving around the room! When looking to organise group working, think about children's preferences, too. For example, some children like to work by themselves, others in a group, and some with a partner.

❚ **STORY FROM PRACTICE**
● BUT I AM PLAYING!

In a busy foundation stage setting, 3-year-old Lara is at the mark-making area where the activity is to trace your names — very creative. Lara sits on her chair, shifting back and forth; you can see the concentration on her face as her frown forms and the tip of her tongue pokes out as she traces her name. She then looks around at her friends on the carpet area, who are engrossed in a book and giggling. Lara turns back to her name tracing; she then looks back at them again.

A practitioner deployed at the area is encouraging her to write and notices her distraction. She says to Lara, 'When you finish what you are doing, then you can go and play'. Lara continues being distracted from the completion of her task by the group. The practitioner then intervenes and says, 'Lara, what do you want to do? You either finish this or go and play'. Naturally, Lara opts to play and runs off to the group on the carpet. After a few minutes, Lara returns to the mark-making table and sits back down to trace her name. The practitioner turns to her and says, 'I thought you went to play?' Lara's response is, **'But I am playing!'**

The creative child at play

No book for the early years should fail to dedicate time to play, no matter the year group, or even age! There is much literature and research demonstrating the undeniable power of play on one's ability to think and work creatively. It is a vital characteristic of our being and, in some cases, an essential aspect of our cultural development (Huizinga, 1970). 'Play [is] a means by which children's development and learning are initiated and through which development is achieved and learning is mastered' (Bergen, 1998, p. 7). First and foremost, though, play is about joy and interest for the young child; these are the predominant emotions associated with it (Gray, 2013). Joy, for example, is associated with increased dopamine levels in the brain, linked to enhanced memory, attention, mental shifting, creativity, and motivation (Cook, Goodman and Schulz, 2011). By taking an interest in and experiencing joy, children's play evolves into helping them learn and understand themselves and their world; affect their environment and shape their world; and master important skills and concepts (physically, socially, and intellectually). Children who engage in quality play experiences are more likely to have well-developed memory skills and language development and are able to regulate their behaviour, leading to enhanced school adjustment and academic learning (Bodrova and Leong, 2005). Play, and exploration, is the first CoETL, and is therefore a basic, but fundamental, characteristic of creative activity.

Play is often viewed as what one does after work: a reward. In most cases, first you work and then you play. Many adults work so that they can afford to play (i.e. holidays, club memberships, electronic games, and many more). As adults we play; take an engineer, for example. When investigating a problem at work, for example, with a machine, they often do so by 'playing' with it. They start with a concrete problem, then think in abstract terms about how to solve it, perhaps by building a model, writing notes, taking images, and then applying the abstract solution to the concrete problem. Learning based on knowing facts or doing things by what is expected is no preparation for this type of creativity, but play is. Play must not be viewed as a break from learning, but as a pathway toward creative learning.

📖 RESEARCH TO EXPLORE
PLAY FIRST

Brian Sutton-Smith was a play theorist who spent his lifetime attempting to discover the cultural significance of play in human life. Brian spent over 65 years observing, researching, and teaching play theory, which should be explored by you.

In a 1967 study, Brian demonstrated that participants who were given a task to imagine various purposes for an object were likely to come up with more ideas than their peers if they could play and tinker with the object first.

Are children getting the play they need to thrive in the twenty-first century?

As time passes, children become less skilled at transforming everyday objects into playthings; play therefore diminishes as children go through life. Ready-made play items erode this further. Many of today's toys are linked to what children see on television. These experiences cause children to imitate what they see instead of creating their own play. Electronic devices fuel this further, as these can make child-centred play seem boring to children. For this very reason, creative play should be fuelled throughout the education system, as it is a natural method through which they develop a variety of skills and attitudes that will help to achieve success in education, life, and future work. Further, play has a cognitive function that supports and fosters creative thinking and tends to indicate a disposition towards creativity in later life (Russ, Robins and Christiano, 1999; Cook, 2000).

Children's play is rich, varied, organic, and constantly evolving. It is a deep level of engagement by the creative child; they can be seen in a 'state of flow' (Csikszentmihayli, 1997) when involved in the experiences around them. When walking into an early years setting, it is visual in every sense: the creative child at play. They are the inventors of play – as Lara demonstrated, work and play are entwined – and children do not separate it from anything that they do. Children are drawn to creative exploration and imagination through play. You just need to give them some cardboard boxes, or a set of blocks, and a whole new world comes to life in the form of forts, castles, robots, building sites, and much more. When they fall, they get back up. If their creations don't work out the first time, they try and try again. They challenge themselves to jump higher, build taller, and concentrate longer. They try out new words and make them their own.

Children incorporate into their play whatever tools, materials, and resources are available. Through this, they open up their minds to what is possible, take chances, solve problems, collaborate, make meaning, and become better creative thinkers and doers. Play is where children use what they already know to help them figure out new things, see how they work, and master skills – all vital in developing creativity. For many young children, verbal thinking is frustrating, as language can be limited. Through play, they are able to express creative energy in concrete forms, and through visual and tactile experiences – the notion of 'learning by doing'. Playful activities can also assist children with disabilities to become more engaged. It is through play that the creative child develops an appetite for discovery and a passion for what they are doing. The spontaneous and natural ways in which children play can offer insights into how eventual public displays of creativity develop and mature (Root-Bernstein in Keenan and Mishra, 2016).

Therefore, this is a reminder of play's relevance and the continuing need for it in the creativity process. It goes without saying that play should not be limited to the early years, but needs to echo in the whole of the education system. It is about making learning practical so that children at all levels can create things, work with their hands, have the freedom to tinker, and experiment with ideas. An engaging and stimulating play environment provides opportunities for learning to be experienced and crafted (Haughton and Ellis, 2016, p. 82), which are fundamental to the creative process and the engaging of creativity's characteristics. Without a play-like attitude, creative insights hide from us behind fear and uncertainty. When we don't embark on activities that involve play, being creative becomes a challenge. As the creative adult, ensuring a playful attitude in the setting is important for both children and adults to be able to approach self-expression with a greater sense of balance and, in some cases, with renewed enthusiasm, making it easier for creativity to flourish. When creative adults observe play carefully, it tells them what children know and what they are thinking about; what they are wondering, testing, and predicting; and, most importantly, which skills they are ready to master. In order to do so, creative adults should be aware of the types of play that children engage in.

Types of play

There are hundreds of different ways of playing, and the things that children do when they play are likely to be wide-ranging and varied. Bob Hughes, a playworker since 1970, is a lifelong advocate for free play, and for play as a fundamental and essential part of human development. He devised a taxonomy of play types (2002, 2006, 2011) in which he identifies 16 types of play that children display in normal play development. These categories were for playworkers to work with, so they could understand how children can explore different types at the same time, flow from one to another, and back again. They are useful in helping us to be more specific when we are talking about play and planning provision for play, but also for what we observe to help children engage further. However, this will only ever capture a narrow aspect of the wealth of children's play. Hughes' taxonomy of play types are as follows:

Communication play – using words, nuances or gestures, for example name calling and mime, backslang and street slang, whispering and song, jokes, 'mickey taking', secret languages, codes, rhymes, debate or poetry. The emphasis is on the 'message' and 'interaction'.

Creative play – allows the transformation of information, awareness of new connections, an element of surprise at how things turn out, and a new response. It involves the enjoyment of creation with a range of materials and tools, texture, and form for its own sake, with freedom to mix and make whatever you wish without the necessity of an end result. It's all about the process!

Deep play – in which the child participates in risky or even potentially life-threatening experiences to develop survival skills and conquer fear. For example, playing up high and balancing, using toys and equipment in ways that they should not or ought not to be used, rolling, running, and swinging very fast. The risk will be from the child's perspective, not the adult's.

Dramatic play – which dramatises events in which the child is not a direct participant, such as recreating scenes from the lives of others, perhaps from television or the theatre. It deals with events and experiences that do not have a direct impact upon the child and which may or may not be played out in front of onlookers.

Exploratory play – engaging with an object or area and, either by manipulation or movement, such as handling, throwing, banging, or mouthing, assessing its properties, possibilities, and content in search of factual information. The fascination is with 'what I can do with this and/or what I can make it do', such as stacking boxes, dismantling an iron or radio, or swinging objects, just to see what happens.

Fantasy play – which rearranges the world the way the child would like it, but which is unlikely to occur. It is pretending to be a monster, being on a pirate ship, being a dragon, dressing up as a superhero and flying, or doing magic and casting spells.

Imaginative play – playing at being and doing real things in unreal situations. Conventional rules which govern the physical world do not apply but the play is still based in reality. For example, imagining oneself to be a tree, a ship, or an animal, or eating food which isn't there.

Locomotor play – movement in any and every direction for its own sake to chase, tag, hide and seek, climb, swing, gallop, balance, go up, and move along.

Mastery play – which changes the physical and affective elements of the natural environment, enabling a sense of control over it, competence, and the urge to master or be the cause of something, for example, construction and deconstruction, digging, changing the course of water.

Object play – which uses infinite and interesting sequences of hand-eye manipulations and movements and the examination of and novel use of objects, such as a cloth, paintbrush, cup, or knife, using them in ways other than the purpose they were perhaps designed for. The fascination is with the object itself and what it can do, for example, using a shoe as a phone, or tins as shoes.

Recapitulative play – play that allows the child to explore ancestry, history, rituals, stories, rhymes, fire, and darkness. It is often stimulated by aspects of the outdoor environment such as forests, pools, rivers, or the weather and involves, for example, playing with puddles and streams, sticks and stones, digging for treasure, making mud pies, engaging in rituals and song, dressing up, role-play, playing wars and making weapons, growing and cooking things, building shelters, creating ancient and obscure communities, languages and religions.

Role-play – exploring ways of being, although not normally of an intense personal, social, domestic, or interpersonal nature. It is an effective way of exploring and trying out identity, status, personality, and activity that have probably not been experienced, for example, being a driver, playing teacher, playing at being asleep, blind, old, or a baby, just to see what it may feel like.

 ACTIVITY

In groups of four, describe a favourite toy or game you played when you were a child. Explore with each other:

- What did you enjoy about these games/toys?

- Where did you play? With what and how did you play? With whom did you play? What you would have been learning while playing?

- What are the commonalities and differences?

- Could you see these 'play types' in there?

- Where would you class creativity within them?

Rough and tumble play – close encounter play which is less to do with fighting and more to do with touching, tickling, measuring relative strength, physical flexibility, and the exhilaration of display. It must involve body contact. Children are seen squinting and gritting their teeth, being a kung-fu fighter, wrestling and chasing. They are unhurt and display signs that they are enjoying themselves.

Social play – during which the rules and criteria for social engagement and interaction can be revealed, explored, and amended. For example, games, conversations, making something together or playing in a group with made-up rules and agreed boundaries. There is an expectation that everyone will abide by the negotiated rules.

Socio-dramatic play – the enactment of real or potential experiences of an intense personal, social, domestic, or interpersonal nature such as recreating scenes from home, setting, doctors, or an argument.

Symbolic play – allows control, gradual exploration, and increased understanding, without the risk of being out of one's depth, by using symbols, i.e. objects, designs, or signs to represent people, abstract ideas, or qualities. It could be playing with a piece of wood and using it as a sword, using string as a fishing line, making signs and marks as a code, or making signs or noises as a language.

Every child is a creative child. Creativity is an innate ability in children and is a part of helping them discover and make sense of their world. Children who engage in quality play experiences are more likely to have well-developed memory skills and language development and are able to regulate their behaviour, leading to enhanced school adjustment and academic learning (Bodrova and Leong, 2005). The CoETL reinforce creating and thinking critically as trait that comes naturally to children, nurtured and stimulated through play. The early years practitioner's focus, then, must be on the children having positive learning experiences in environments where they can develop characteristics and abilities for creativity through their own unique approaches and play.

Next steps

 REFLECT

Observe children in their early years environment. Annotate your observations with where the CoETL are evident. Use Work Tools 1, 2, 3, and 4 to support your analysis.

Think about how the adults support the CoETL in action.

Reflect on what you have learnt about what and how children learn.

How can you take this forward?

Can you analyse Hughes' play taxonomies?

 **EXPLORE**

Articles on the Characteristics of Effective Learning: http://eyfs.info/articles/_/teaching-and-learning/characteristics-of-effective-learning-play-and-r160

■ A series of articles on the CoETL.

Discovery Early Learning Centre: Hijacking Play (2016): http://discoveryelc.blogspot.co.uk/2016/09/hijacking-play.html

■ A blog post on not hijacking children's play!

Haydon, K. P. (2014) Open letter to adults from a highly creative child: www.creativitypost.com/education/open_letter_to_adults_from_a_highly_creative_child

■ A highly creative child who is often misunderstood responds to adult comments and provides ideas on how adults can help.

Nurturing Creativity: An Essential Mindset for Young Children's Learning (2016): www.youtube.com/watch?v=OCG_2G5FYJM

■ A webinar on inspiring creative thinking across all areas of learning, as well as insightful details on the book!

Play Education by Bob Hughes: www.playeducation.com/

■ Website on the study and practice of play work.

Play England: Free Play in Early Childhood (2007): www.playengland.org.uk/media/120426/free-play-in-early-childhood.pdf

■ Literature on the value of free play.

Tedx Brum: Children as Ideas Makers: www.youtube.com/watch?v=JVsGJluJz5I

■ Debi Keyte-Hartland shares her vision for education built around children's enquiries and curiosities.

The Spoke Blog: Supporting Children's Creativity (2016): http://thespoke.earlychildhoodaustralia.org.au/supporting-childrens-creativity/

■ A blog post on supporting children's creative thinking.

Wilson, L. O. Killing or Fostering Creativity in Children: http://thesecondprinciple.com/creativity/children-creativity/killingcreativityinchildren/

■ A blog post on how adults discourage creativity in children.

Alcock, S. (2010) Young children's playfully complex communication: distributed imagination, *European Early Childhood Education Research Journal*, Vol 18, No.2, pp. 215–228: https://doi.org/10.1080/13502931003784404

■ A study on children's playfulness.

 # Creativity and imagination

 THINK

What is imagination?

How does it relate to creativity?

Is **'using your imagination'** a part of your practice?

 CHAPTER FOCUS

■ The role of imagination in creativity

■ Being imaginative in the EYFS

■ Possibility thinking

■ Strategies to develop children's imaginations through stories, rhyme and rhythm, imaginative play, building worlds, awe and wonder, humour, and creative art

Following on from the second chapter, if you have explored definitions of creativity, you may have found that 'imagination' is a reoccurring term associated with it. Often titles such as 'creativity and imagination' or 'imagination and creativity' appear together when researching for information. When asked to define creativity, 'imagining' or 'imagination' is always almost the first word used to describe it. This is because 'using your imagination' is an important characteristic of creativity. It's embedded in thinking and is what can start the process of the cognitive dance to stimulate creativity. This chapter intends to support your understanding of the key role of imagination within the early years and provide you with approaches to use in your practice.

Humans are born with a natural tendency to be inquisitive and curious about their world. Our ability to imagine a different world, and to create new possibilities, sets us apart from other creatures. Imagination is a natural way that the human mind develops and understands. When imagination is at play, thinking is deeply and energetically engaged. We just need to read a story and we transport our minds into it as if we are present; we are all capable of it. The development of the imagination during childhood is why adults are able to do many of the tasks that daily life demands. Adults constantly use their imagination to help them invent new things, visualise, solve problems, enjoy a book or movie, understand others' perspectives, make plans, come up with ideas, and, of course, think creatively. No wonder Albert Einstein felt that 'imagination is more important than knowledge'! Therefore, using one's imagination is critical to the creative process that is used throughout life, and requires development. Early years settings which encourage imagination across the curriculum have been shown to lead to even greater amounts of imaginativeness and enhanced curiosity, and to learning skills in pre-schoolers or early school-agers (Ashiabi, 2007)

 FACT NOTE

Lev Semyonovich Vygotsky was a Soviet development psychologist. He considered imagination and thinking processes as forming a special unity that helps children make sense of the world (2004). His theories explain that imagination develops as thought develops, and that language plays a central role in the development of imagination.

At this point it is important to understand that imagination is a characteristic of creativity and does not mean the same thing. Imagination is the ability to see the impossible, the possible, the unreal, and the real, and it has no limits. Imagination is where all the cognitive processes are stimulated and connecting, whereas creativity uses this ability to devise ideas and strategies, make connections, and unleash what is possible into the real world. Creativity thrives under constraints, whereas imagination has no constraints. Imagination is the root of creativity. It is the ability to bring to mind and senses things that aren't present. Creativity is putting your imagination to work (Robinson, 2015).

Being imaginative

The word 'imagination' conjures up images of children pretending with dolls, pushing trucks, or dressing up as princesses or pirates. Many adults equate imagination with the early years only. Whilst young children do spend much of their time in the land of make-believe, the imagination is not reserved just for the early years. It plays a key role in creativity in all learning, across all education stages and levels. However, it is true that imagination is encouraged to a greater degree in the early years compared to other year groups, but it is also true that early imaginative play is associated with increased creative performance years later (Russ and Fiorelli, 2010).

 ACTIVITY

In your place of work or training, find out from the adults when the last time they used their imagination was.

How difficult or easy was it for them to answer you?

Can you make links between what they have told you and the creative process?

How do they perceive the role of imagination in children's learning?

Imagining is the creative ability to form images, ideas, and sensations in the mind without any immediate input of senses such as seeing or hearing. It makes knowledge more applicable in solving problems and is fundamental to integrating experiences and the creative learning process. The EYFS specific area of learning and development, titled Expressive Arts and Design, is made up of two parts; being imaginative is one of them. This requires children to use what they have learnt about media and materials in original ways, thinking about their uses and purposes. Children are to represent their own ideas, thoughts, and feelings through design and technology, art, music, dance, role-play, and stories (DfE, 2017, p. 12). Clearly, the EYFS has recognised the role of imagination in children's learning, where art, music, dance, drama, and role-play are all forms of communication and expressions of it; these then build further on children's developing curiosity, imagination, and creativity (Isbell and Raines, 2013).

 ACTION RESEARCH

Conduct a search over a day in your setting, detailing what imaginative opportunities arise for children:

- What do the adults do?

- What do the children do?

- How does the environment allow for imaginative thinking/play?

- What conclusions and next steps can you draw from your data?

In early years settings, you will observe children being imaginative – perhaps zooming a shopping trolley from the role-play area around the room as if it were a racing car; or walking around with a clipboard and pencil, mimicking one of the adults; or being a doctor whilst holding a funnel from the water area to another child's chest, listening to a heartbeat. Children will use objects to represent something else, or assign themselves and others roles and then act them out. Children will be seen to communicate their ideas through drawing, mark-making, construction, and much more. All this can be classed as the symbolising and representation (Griffith, 2014; Ulger, 2015) of children's imaginations, which can be seen in practice in children's art, play, creations, self-talk, and so on.

It is through 'being imaginative' that children identify with the world, practice, interpret, and understand. When assigning roles, they are developing social skills in negotiation, turn taking, and sharing. They are also working out problems and experimenting with solutions by deciding what games to play, what roles to take on, who will be involved and how, what materials are needed for the game or task and what rules apply to the game, and how to overcome scenarios where something 'goes wrong', all of which are essential to the creativity process. When being imaginative, children can be anyone and do anything. By absorbing themselves in this way, in whatever it may be, children are given the opportunity to practice using their imagination, to exercise their brain and train it to think creatively, and to learn how to think for themselves. This yet again reinforcing the essential link of thinking with creativity.

> ! **STORY FROM PRACTICE**
> ● PRACTITIONER OBSERVATION
>
> Jia and David find two laundry baskets outdoors and bring them in onto the carpet. David places them against each other and crouches down, wiping the sides.
>
> David: 'I'm cleaning it, Jia, then we sail.' Jia nods in approval and busily wraps a scarf around her.
>
> Jia: 'It will get cold out there.'
>
> David: 'We're sailing now.' They each get into a basket. Jia stands up and twirls around.
>
> Jia: 'This is me dancing.' She gets out and continues to twirl.
>
> David: 'We need to sail away, get back on board matey.' Jia rushes to get back into the basket.
>
> David: 'Waves are here; quick, row.'

They both pretend to use oars to row their boat. At this point I quickly grab two small pipes from the water area and bring them over. David smiles. I ask them what they think they can use them for. David grabs one and starts to row. I stand back.

Jia: 'Waves, waves, waves! My scarf will fly away.'

I go and get the CD player and play some music in the background. Jia starts waving her scarf to the music, and stands up and dances.

David: 'Jia! You are rocking the boat. We will sink.'

Jia giggles and sits back down and pretends to row the boat again.

David: 'We're sailing back. We'll get stuck in the water.'

Both children continue in these roles for a whole class session, taking turns at different roles and involving other children.

 **CONNECT**

Can you apply creativity's characteristics to David and Jia's story?

David and Jia's practice story demonstrates both children being imaginative. They utilised equipment around them to represent what they were thinking, and the adult further supported their imaginations by providing props to fuel their continuing scenario of sailing a boat. The adult also recognised Jia's keen interest in movement and desire to use her whole body, and therefore provided a stimulus by introducing an atmospheric feature of music in the background.

Possibility thinking

 STORY FROM PRACTICE

Four-year-old Ayyan is getting ready to go to school. He chooses to wear his Batman beanie hat today. The hat can fold over his eyes as a mask which he can see through. Ayyan is Batman this morning, and he is excited to see what Batman will learn in school today. He happily skips to school holding onto his mum's hand. Batman can run to school! Batman says hi to the caretaker at the gate. Batman sees his friend and giggles. He can't wait to tell his teacher that Batman is ready to learn!

As he approaches his classroom door, both teacher and teaching assistant ask him sternly to fold the mask back onto his head, and then to take it off and put it in his tray. Ayyan reluctantly removes it, kisses his mum goodbye, and does as he is told.

The capacity to imagine is dependent on the knowledge one holds, as it is fuelled by it. Our minds always come back around to what we already know; this is evident when we compare new experiences with ones we have already had. For example, try imagining a letter that doesn't exist. The harder you try to do so, the more likely you are to keep thinking of letters that already come to mind. So, where knowledge fails our imagination, our perspectives can encourage it. One can turn knowledge on its head in order to come up with more imaginative answers to the question at hand. What if we were to imagine sounds as letters? Who's to say the door bell, or the sound of a car engine, cannot be types of letters? Suddenly unimaginable letters are imaginable, but again, only in the context of what we already know. Therefore, to develop imagination, children must continuously fuel their knowledge. One could say that there is a cognitive conflict going on between imagination and creativity, which is then drawn out through creative thinking processes. It is this that allows one to explore possibilities in learning; if one cannot imagine new possibilities, the ability to think creatively is limited.

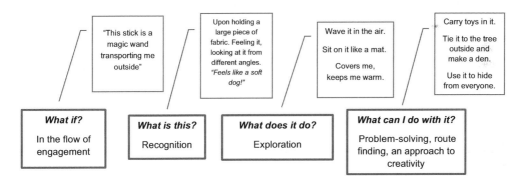

Figure 4.1 Possibility thinking at play

The term 'possibility thinking' was first coined by the renowned Anna Craft, who dedicated much of her life into researching and advocating for creativity in the early years and primary education. Craft (Cremin, Burnard and Craft, 2006; Craft, 2011) argued that 'possibility thinking' occurs through the posing, in multiple ways, of the question 'what if?' and that it involves the shift from 'what is this and what does it do?' to 'what can I do with this?' Being imaginative is vital to the 'what if' process. In young children, 'what if' can be observed on a day to day basis where shoes are used as phones, or hats as shopping baskets; a simple box turns into a powerful rocket, a laundry basket into a pirate ship, and a water tray into the deep blue sea. As children get older, the capacity for 'what if' starts forming mental images in the mind which feed off the knowledge the child already holds, as per the creative story about Indigo.

 CONNECT

What have you observed children and adults doing/saying that can be 'possibility' thinking?

❗ STORY FROM PRACTICE

Five-year-old Indigo is learning about healthy eating in her reception class. On this particular day, the children are looking at fresh vegetables. Indigo picks up a tomato and runs her hand over the smooth, rosy red surface. Suddenly it hits her: what if I were a farmer? Indigo wants to be a farmer! She imagines the smell of the soil as she plucks tomatoes and places them in crates. She pictures herself on top of a tractor, ploughing the soil ready to plant her seeds. She is off to the market now to sell her tomatoes for a good rate. She has to wake early to water her crops. Indigo smiles to herself.

When Indigo's dad comes to collect her, she tells him about being a farmer. 'What?! A farmer!' he says. 'No way, all that work and not much to survive on, work on your maths and English and get a job in a bank.'

It is not that parents mean to be abrupt towards their children, after all; they want the very best for their children, including financial security and stability – which Indigo's father doesn't see happening on a farm. His response to Indigo's budding imagination, however, squashes her ability to think of possibilities and ideas, make connections, and play with what she already knows – all of which are important to the creative process. It is almost a 'death of possibility thinking'. These tiny deaths can occur each and every day at home or in the setting, which can lead to the stifling of children's imaginations, and in turn the stifling of creativity. *Think about your own life. Find a moment from the previous 24 hours or from a couple of years ago when something or someone caused the death of your imagination.*

Further, the evolution of technology, which presents children with television, games, video games, tablets, and other media products, presents ready-made possibilities for children, leaving no room for imagining anymore. Instead of using their imagination, children are passive recipients of visual and auditory stimulation, which is a very artificial way of learning. However, it is how technology is used by the adult to provide a context for imagination to thrive in. If imagination leads to creativity, and creativity to economic success and success in life, then holding on to imagination as children grow and learn is of vital importance to the creative process. Settings need to nurture and develop possibility thinking in all aspects of their provision.

 RESEARCH TO EXPLORE
IMAGINATIVE EDUCATION

Keiran Egan (2008), a big thinker in education and a forerunner in research on imagination, has carried out extensive work on the role of imagination in children's learning. He situates imagination at the heart of all learning, as it allows the ability to envision the 'possibility' in all things. It is something adults can educate and enrich as children learn all aspects of the curriculum. Egan advocates for imaginative education as a good thing which ought to be stimulated and developed.

Stimulating imagination

As discussed in Chapter 2, being able to generate innovative ideas, novel thinking, and originality requires children to master other knowledge, skills, and behaviours to get there – creativity's characteristics. This also involves an imagination that helps children see beyond the norm, beyond reality. Children who have a limited imagination will struggle with these areas and with many aspects of learning. Children are by nature imaginative, but the imagination requires nurturing and encouragement (Hendy and Toon, 2001, p. 5). Adults therefore need to employ approaches to make what they are teaching meaningful, memorable, and inspiring, in turn allowing children to develop their imaginative possibility thinking, which will lead to creative thinking in learning. According to Vygotsky (1967/2004, p. 71), play is the initial expression of imagination and 'the root of all creativity in children', followed by drawing and storytelling. It will be no surprise that already in the early years environment, the nurturing of imagination happens in many ways.

Stories – storytelling is central to human existence. It is common to every known culture and has been one of our most fundamental communication methods. We use stories to make sense of our world and to share understanding with others. Stories can be said to be the cornerstone of imaginative development, providing unlimited possibilities; doing it well, in a variety of ways, can have a huge impact on children's cognitive processes.

Children will range from imagining characters to creating stories to liven up their learning. Hence, children should be encouraged to develop an appetite for books. Picture books are great for the youngest of children, helping language, vocabulary, and reading skills as well as fuelling the imagination. But don't just limit stories to books; it is good practice to make up your own stories and involve children in doing so. For example, they could come up with characters for you to form stories around, choose a theme for the story, or suggest ideas of what might happen next. How you use your voice to tell a story also matters! To further enhance imagination, and ensure inclusion, props and other visual aids are vital for allowing children to see imaginative thoughts in concrete form.

Stories allow children to imaginatively engage with content and help them to remember things by making knowledge more absorbing. As they listen to stories, they are constantly creating mental images of characters, settings, and descriptive language. When children eventually come to write their own stories, these imaginative visualisation skills will aid their thinking process by allowing them to create a bank of ideas that could be translated into their learning.

Planning prompts – *what's the story on what you are trying to teach? Is there any aspect of the curriculum teaching that you can present in story form, rather than just keep to carpet or circle times? What materials and resources are at the disposal of the children to spark story ideas?*

IDEA

Finish the story – tell children a story and ask them to make up the ending. What possibilities have they come up with?

Rhyme and rhythm – there is no denying that children's experiences with rhymes and rhythm promote early phonological and print-related skill development. When engaging with rhymes, music, and songs, children create mental pictures which expand the imagination. Rhymes and rhythm can be offered through story form, but also through songs, poems, music, dance, and so on. With these, children can engage all their senses and their whole body, which can actively lead to imaginative possibilities. This can give meaningful, memorable shape to any content. For example, rhymes are used for children to remember the sound of each letter of the alphabet. Making your own rhymes in conversation (for example, 'let's pat the cat' or 'see the bee in the tree') or making a funny poem can spark children's imagination and can be a fun way to learn. Encouraging children to think of their own rhyming words, create their own rhythms, form movements to music, or make up their own songs lets them get imaginative and creative.

CONNECT

How can you use 'dance' as an approach to stimulate children's imagination?

Planning prompts – *are there any rhymes or rhythms of the learning content that you could deliver through? What activities might draw attention to rhyme and rhythm? How can you support children in being expressive through their bodies and senses to communicate their imaginative thoughts and ideas?*

 AROUND THE WORLD
NEW JERSEY, AMERICA

Tools of the Mind is a research-based early childhood model in America. It merges Vygotskian theory with cutting-edge neuroscience research. Tools of the Mind gives adults in the early years the 'tools' to ensure every child becomes a successful learner by developing the underlying cognitive, social, and emotional skills needed to reach his or her highest potential.

Make-believe play is the heart of a Tools of the Mind early years setting. The year begins with adaptable play themes close to children's lives, and over the course of the year, as children's levels of make-believe play, self-regulation, and executive functions develop, the play themes develop as well.

Imaginative play – this needs no introduction, as it is very common in the early years, and is what this chapter is all about! It is also known as pretend play, make-believe play, or drama. It is naturally and inherently present in young children and utilised by them daily in their play. For example, pebbles become the vegetable soup to feed a doll, and stacked blocks represent horses on the race course. The element of 'pretend' is central to creativity as children weave easily between real and pretend worlds, real and pretend situations, and real and pretend actions with real and pretend items that have real and pretend consequences (Wood and Attfield, 2005).

Normally, early years environments contain well-resourced areas for imaginative play, and often children can be seen playing out different roles. The provision of props adds an extra element with which to engage them. Empty boxes are always a hit as children pretend they are dens or a whole other world! Pretending to be someone or something else can free children's imaginations. Fill a box with old clothes, hats, and accessories (a feather boa, a chunky necklace). They dress up and 'act' as a character – giving them a name, a voice, and a way of moving – and you can then perform a play, or have funny conversations with them 'in character'. The question is, *how well is it used to teach and learn from?*

Planning prompts – *how can children engage in pretence, drama, or imaginative play while learning about what you want to teach? How can it be employed to engage children in learning? And not just be an area set up in a corner? What resources/provision can extend and expand children's imaginative play? How can* *you use pretence to teach maths or reading? How can you guide children in jointly planning play scenarios before enacting them?*

 IDEA

Swap bodies – ask children to pretend they have swapped bodies with an animal and imitate them.

 RESEARCH TO EXPLORE
THE BATMAN EFFECT

White et al. (2017) conducted a study with 180 4- to 6-year olds. They reported that when children pretended to be Batman whilst they were doing a task, it helped them to resist distraction, stay more focused, and spend the most time working on the task. This was in contrast to those children that were not impersonating Batman and worked on the task as themselves.

An approach to assist in scaffolding children's imaginative play can be seen in what Leong and Bodrova (2012) describe as *PRoPELS*. This acronym stands for the most critical elements of children's imaginative play that can be assessed and scaffolded by adults.

 IDEA

Play with limits – give children five random items; these can be anything. Ask them to use the items to invent something.

Plan – this is about children's ability to think about play in advance of playing. Younger children may be seen observing their environment to seek out resources they might want before proceeding. Older children may come directly to adults and ask for specific things. Adults and children can also plan scenarios together.

Roles children play – including the actions, language, and emotional expressions that are associated with a specific role. Roles can be things like animals, a fly on the wall, a ghost, or a boat others stand on.

Props – the objects (real, symbolic, and imaginary) children use in play.

Extended time frame – play that lasts for long stretches of time: within one session for an hour or longer or extending over several sessions and over several days.

Language – what children say to develop a scenario or coordinate the actions of different players as well as speech associated with a particular role. For example, saying 'Aye Aye Matey' when in the role of a pirate.

Scenario – what children act out, including the sequence of scripts and interactions between roles.

Using PRoPELS to assess imaginative play gives adults an idea of how children play out their thinking. It also allows adults to plan forward to ensure that children's experiences are extended and their imaginations expanded through the provision of rich resources and environments. *How can you use PRoPELS in observing and extending children's imaginative play?*

 IDEA

Refer to a keyhole in a door and ask children to imagine what's behind the door. They can draw it, tell it in story form, or convey it any other way to represent their thoughts.

Building worlds – also known as small world play or make-believe worlds. Yet again, another very common provision in the early years. This requires creating a life scene for children to engage with, or children creating it themselves through the evolving of their imagination. The Root-Bernsteins' (1999) research with creative individuals, such as Nobel Prize winners and MacArthur Foundation 'genius' grant awardees, made clear that early childhood games about make-believe worlds were more frequent in such individuals than in control participants in their fields (Root-Bernstein, 2012). The use of such worlds in the early years thus further fuels the imaginative creative capacities of young children.

Miniature items such as furniture, a barn, small animals, and much more are used in building these worlds. The goal is for children to act out ideas from real life or to re-enact stories they know on a smaller scale, but also to create make-believe worlds. Children use their own experiences of the world to build on their imaginative skills, supporting and allowing them to express thoughts and experiences into their play whilst exploring the world in which they live. However, it also allows them to experiment with fantasy play and incorporate their own ideas. Just give children a washing up bowl and get them making a miniature garden, using grass for moss and gravel for paths, or create a house for mice or fairies in a shoe box, with cotton-reel seats and tissue bed clothes! Oh, the possibilities! Yet again, the question is *how well is small world play used to teach and learn from? Or is it just another provision set up on a daily basis?*

IDEA

What is it? – show child an object; it can be anything, i.e. paint brush, paper clip, or jug. Ask children to dream up an entirely different use and create a scene around it.

Planning prompts – *how can small world building be used to deliver teaching and learning? What are the imaginative possibilities within it? How can children be supported and encouraged to represent their imagination in small world form?*

Awe and wonder – do you remember that feeling of seeing something so amazing that you said, 'Wow, that's awesome!'? This is awe and wonder, an almost magical moment which many children experience in the early years and beyond. It has a place in nurturing children's imaginations through exploring, discovering, and recognising the wonderful in everything and how things work. 'If you don't have a sense of wonder, you really can't learn anything, you can only memorize' (Querido, 1987, p. 11). The idea is to leave room for possibilities. 'Aha' moments for children are more likely to occur in an atmosphere of exuberant discovery than one without. Adults should respond to children's questions with imaginative pictures or stories. Early years children are in a dreamy state, and their minds are more pictorial than ours and less verbal. They respond best to explanations that speak to their imaginative picture-thinking. For example, if a child asks 'why does it rain?', they are not asking for a factual scientific explanation or about how the water cycle works. They are asking for a description that makes sense to them. It could be as simple as 'when the clouds become heavy with water they burst and down comes the rain' – *how else could you explain this?*

DISCUSS

'Wonder' with peers/colleagues and the many ways it can be encouraged.

Planning prompts – *how can you encourage 'I wonder why . . .' through teaching? What activities might evoke children's sense of wonder? How can you use that sense of awe and wonder to draw out children's thinking about further dimensions of learning?*

Humour – something we don't often associate with teaching and learning, but can be vital in allowing children to play with what they already know. Humour draws from the same well as other forms of creativity and creative problem-solving (Kuchner, 1991). Children are often seen giggling and sharing private jokes that only they know the meaning of. They will most often express humour relating to experiences they have had or are still experiencing. For example, a 3-year-old who is still mastering toilet training is often enthralled by 'bathroom' humour, finds the words 'pooed' or 'pee pee' fascinating, and uses them often in sentences. Or a child who is independently learning to dress will find no humour in placing a sock on their foot, but on the ear it's hilarious! Children will giggle uncontrollably when they hear a combination of words and nonsense syllables. They understand that the nonsense syllables are different from words. The sounds are out of place – the whole thing is out of place. It is therefore hilarious! Humour, then, is a blend of imagination, creativity, and play (Loizou, 2005).

The use of humour in teaching and learning can allow children to play with knowledge that they hold or need to learn, for example by creating a maths joke! A developing imagination is important for a child to eventually be able to produce their own jokes. This starts to happen by around 2 years of age, with jokes often being object-based, such as placing underwear on the head, or conceptual, such as claiming the 'pig says moo' (Davis, 2017). Then children will move to a more logical and abstract form where riddles and jokes often contain ludicrous juxtapositions, plays on words, or logical flaws, e.g. 'Why did the elephant paint her toenails red?' When making up their own jokes, children often draw inspiration from whatever they are learning about, the knowledge they hold, and the experiences they have had. This can be at the setting or at home, and needs to be encouraged.

Planning prompts – *could children learn or create their own jokes about what you want to teach? How might they expand their understanding through playing with what is humorous about the learning? How can you develop children's humour through language – playing with words? How can resources be used to allow children to represent their humour in concrete form?*

 FACT NOTE

J. K. Rowling first imagined a world of wizards and magic when all around her were only the harsh realities of welfare benefits and single motherhood. Using her imagination, she was able to put her vision on paper, fully realising that world and conjuring from mere wisps of inspiration the stories we know today as *Harry Potter*. *What an imagination!*

Changing the learning environment – one very common feature of early years environments is that they are multi-purpose. So it is very likely that the children will spend their whole day there. An enabling environment is one that allows children to grasp the richer meaning of anything they learn. By changing the context in which learning takes place, children's imaginations can be brought to life and engage content much more richly. Just imagine that children arrive to the setting one morning to find the tables all together with cushions under them. They are going to learn phonics laying down, with images stuck under the table! Or the setting has turned into a museum for the day where certain areas and equipment are not allowed to be touched! So how will the children cope? It is about simple changes with the idea of children exploring possibilities in learning and imagining another world. There will be more about the environment in Chapter 8, on creative spaces.

Planning prompts – *what kinds of activities could change the context of the environment where children can engage with the learning? How imaginative can you get with your environment? How can you use technology and digital tools to bring an imaginary learning context to life?*

▌ STORY FROM PRACTICE
● FORTUNE READING

Name: Atabak　**Role**: Plasterer　**Location**: Essex

From the days of the Ottoman Empire through the present, coffee has played an important role in Turkish lifestyle and culture. Brought to Istanbul in 1555 by two Syrian traders, coffee became known as the 'milk of chess players and thinkers'. Derived from the Arabica bean, Turkish coffee is a very fine, powder-like grind. An aromatic spice called cardamom is sometimes added to the coffee while it is being ground. As the coffee begins to heat, it begins to foam. A rule of the Turkish coffee ceremony dictates that if the foam is absent from the face of the coffee, the host loses face. Turkish coffee is served hot from a special coffee pot called 'cezve'. Tradition states that after the guest has consumed the coffee and the cup is turned upside down on the saucer and allowed to cool, the hostess then performs a fortune reading from the coffee grounds remaining in the cup. Atabak's grandmother did the same.

Now as an adult, he recalls this favourite tradition and orders a cup of Turkish coffee. Once consumed, he turns the cup over on the saucer. After a while, he picks up the cup and asks me to tell him what I see. At first I'm hesitant, but then I see all sorts of things (I think my early years instinct kicked in!). I see a large elephant with ears; on top of this elephant is a person, looks like a man, and in his hand, he seems to have a spear, almost as if he is going to war. I realise that I am building a narrative around what I am seeing. We then look together and see birds overhead. On the other side seems to be a mountain; he asks if I can see it. I tell him yes, wide-eyed that we both can see it. We giggle at our responses, unaware of anyone else in the coffee shop at the time. It was obvious that through the use of our imaginations, we had painted a story of the shapes that we could see in the coffee grounds. We transported ourselves into the story and its many possibilities. The influence of Atabak's culture is evident in how he views his world, and the constant time spent with his grandmother in the magical world of fortune reading, which nurtured his imagination such that he could still recall and use it as an adult. As a plasterer, working with shapes has become the norm for him, and he brings to life many forms through what he observes within them and the use of his imagination.

Creative art – no surprise again, because art is regarded as the offspring of creativity. It must be remembered, though, that it is not the only place where creativity happens. In children's imaginative experiences, the role of art is a means to represent their feelings, thoughts, and ideas. Young children need concrete forms to express these and opportunities to engage in art activities that are essential for fostering cognition and imagination (Koster, 2012). It may not be in the form of creating something, as it should be open-ended and about the process, but can be as simple as children engaging with paintings or pictures, with adults building a narrative around them. For example, discussing who the bearded man in the portrait is, or where the big ship is going and what it's carrying, allows children to see the pictures as an illustrated story; their imagination will fill in the gaps. They may then want to use media or materials to keep the narrative going. This freedom to manipulate different materials in an organic and unstructured way allows for exploration and experimentation. Yet again, it is much more than resourcing an 'art area' or 'junk modelling table'. It is about giving children the means or, rather, the tools to allow their imaginations to play out.

Planning prompts – *what types of creative art forms can you introduce to children in their learning? How can you seek out experiences at museums, galleries, theatres, libraries, or dance, arts, or music venues that will offer you and others the ideas, confidence, and resources to bring to children's imaginative explorations? How can you provide opportunities for collaboration, discovery, and exploration in art experiences? Where is the 'imagination' in what you are trying to teach and wanting the children to learn?*

 **CONNECT**

How is 'art' currently being used in your setting or classroom?

 ACTIVITY

Considering all the approaches discussed, choose three and plan an activity to encourage children in 'being imaginative'.

Remember, you can prompt any one of the approaches through an object, image etc.

Remember, your activities should be open-ended to allow children's imaginations to take them where they want to.

Remember the possibilities!

These strategies, and many more, will allow children's imaginations to grow and develop all the time, leading to creative thinking and, ultimately, creativity. Imagination is an essential part of the learning/creativity process. Children learn best when they are engaged in their learning and when they are engaging their imaginations. Capitalising on innate imagination and fostering it is vital. Children with good imaginations can advance their all-round cognitive development and progress in all areas of learning. As Albert Einstein once said, 'imagination is more important than knowledge. Knowledge is limited. Imagination encircles the world' (TES, 2002). Need I say more?

Next step

 REFLECT

1) In order for children to be imaginative, adults must first have the imagination themselves to see the potential for developing children's creativity across all areas of learning. How imaginative are you?

   For the next five days, record moments when you use your imagination. What have you learnt about yourself?

2) How can you use digital tools/technology to nurture children's imaginations?

 EXPLORE

Child-initiated play and professional creativity: enabling four-year-old's possibility thinking: http://oro.open.ac.uk/31395/2/Child_initiated_play.pdf

■ A study on possibility thinking.

Early Arts: https://earlyarts.co.uk/

■ Creative training company for arts and creative learning in the early years. A valuable resource to stimulate imagination through the arts.

Marta Giménez-Dasí, M., Pons, F. and Bender, P. K. (2016) Imaginary companions, theory of mind and emotion understanding in young children, *European Early Childhood Education Research Journal*, Vol 24, No.2, pp186–197: https://doi.org/10.1080/13502 93X.2014.919778

■ A study on the effects of imaginary companions.

The cognitive tools of children's imagination. Kieran Egan www.mantleoftheexpert. com/studying/articles/KE%20-%20Cognitive%20Tools%20of%20Children's%20 Education.pdf

■ Various 'tools' as approaches for encouraging and developing the imagination.

Imaginative Inquiry: www.imaginative-inquiry.co.uk/planning-units/

■ Ideas for developing imaginary contexts for learning.

ImaginED: www.educationthatinspires.ca/imaginative-education/

■ A blog designed to support and enable imagination-focused teaching in all contexts.

The Imagination Education Research Group: http://ierg.ca/about-us/what-is-imaginative-education/

■ This website introduces new theories, principles, and practical techniques for making education more effective.

Tools of the Mind: https://toolsofthemind.org/

■ A research-based model to develop the imagination.

10 Easy Ways to Fire Your Child's Imagination: www.parenting.com/article/10-easy-ways-to-fire-your-childs-imagination-21354373

■ An easy-read article for parents, by parents, regarding imagination.

Rhythm, rhyme, repetition, reasoning and response in oral storytelling: www. teachingenglish.org.uk/article/rhythm-rhyme-repetition-reasoning-response-oral-storytelling

■ David Heathfield is a storyteller and English teacher who explains how storytelling works for language.

Tech tool

The benefits of fantasy play (2017): http://bold.expert/the-benefits-of-fantasy-play/

■ A blog on learning and development hosts this video of Sonja Perren, Professor at the University of Konstanz, Germany, and Thurgau University of Teacher Education, Switzerland.

5 The creative adult

 THINK

What are the key features of a 'creative adult'?

What is meant by 'teaching creatively'?

What is meant by 'creative learning'?

CHAPTER FOCUS

- Exploring and understanding your own creativity

- Overcoming misunderstandings and creative blocks

- Teaching creatively and creative learning

- The role of the 'creative adult'

- Developing creative practices in 'being creative'

If you were asked about your own creativity, what would you say right now? 'I'm not creative!' 'I didn't do well in the arts.' 'Is creativity not for the young?' When adults are asked if they believe they are creative, they tend to respond negatively and, of course, associate it with the arts. Quite often adults do not reflect on their own creativity; many times this can stem from their own experiences of education, which can then limit what they can do in the context of early years education. This chapter is intended to assist you in exploring and understanding your own creativity, and to help you to use various strategies within the chapter to develop your confidence. This will hopefully then help you to embed these into your creative approaches for children, ultimately leading to becoming and being a 'creative adult'.

In the last two decades, there has been an increased emphasis on how a well-qualified and appropriately skilled early years workforce makes a real difference to the quality of provision and outcomes for young children. As a result, overhauls of qualification structures have taken place and investment has been made to ensure that children have access to high quality practitioners who will support their progression and play a vital role in ensuring that they get the best start. However, creativity is seldom mentioned as a key feature of this. Early years practitioners have a crucial role to play in finding ways of engaging and collaborating with children for creativity, for creating interesting and purposeful opportunities, experiences, and approaches to stimulate creativity's characteristics, both indoors and outdoors, and planning adult-child interaction that supports children's creative thinking. It is about being a skilled and effective creative practitioner.

 DISCUSS

With peers/colleagues how creative they think they are. When was the last time you all did something creative?

Is there such a thing as a 'creative adult'? If we can clear our misconceptions and see beyond them, then yes, there is. The idea that creativity cannot be fostered or applied within teaching and learning is based on our misunderstandings as adults. Firstly, a misunderstanding of what creativity actually is, as discussed in Chapter 2: many believe it is an inherent ability, or just art-related. Secondly, a misunderstanding of what the role of teaching actually is: very often this stems from our own experiences of education – learning something in school without understanding it through approaches that hardly facilitated creativity. The dominant model in my life has been direct instruction, in which creative teaching hardly existed and, for many, the thing they were good at, talented in, brilliant at, was not valued. This then shapes our view of creativity's place in teaching and learning, and the emerging trap of adulthood.

The trap of adulthood

There is a popular perception that creativity is for the young, and that it does not mix with adults. It is agreed that we do become less creative as adults; however, our decline in creativity does not happen because of age. It actually starts, believe it or not, at the time one starts formal education. It is amazing that in the earliest years, at around the age of 5, children are using around 90% of their creative potential – that's right, 90%! You will often find children in the early years playing with possibilities, inventing and innovating without fear. This is their creativity at play. The unfortunate truth is that around the age of 10, this creative potential declines to 30%, and keeps on doing so; it then generally stays there for the rest of their or, rather, our lives. Research studies mostly agree that children are more creative before they enter education, and once there, it is possible to either encourage creative further, or inhibit it altogether (Meador, 1992). There are also trends in creativity of continuities and discontinuities throughout an individual's lifespan (Runco, 1996). Bruce (2004, p. 12) further supports that emergent possibilities for creativity, which are in every child, quite often do not develop, or can be quickly extinguished. Adults play a large role within this.

 RESEARCH TO EXPLORE
DECLINE OF CREATIVITY

Originally to test for divergent thinking, Land and Jarman (1998) conducted a study that followed the creative capacity of children. They used a test at different stages of 1,600 children's lives, and the results are as follows:

- At 5 years of age: 98%

- At 10 years of age: 30%

- At 15 years of age: 12%

When 200,000 adults were given the same test, only 2% tested at the genius level.

What this demonstrates is a downtrend: the older we are, the less creative we become – but why?

 ACTIVITY

Think about all the adults that have taught you, or you have observed teaching.

Rank them in order of creative teaching.

Why have you ranked them in this order?

What is it that they do which is 'creative'? Use post-its!

As adults, we are caught in the trap of adulthood through conformity, which slowly creeps into every aspect of what we do. To live in a society, we have to follow laws, rules, and standards; we conform. We are often straightjacketed into what is expected of us and what we should do. It can be said that education drills this into children through the one way of thinking when learning. One right answer to a problem, many times in direct relation to what the adult is thinking and expecting. We are told to read questions and answer them in tests or exams, regardless of whether we understood them or not. Marking consists of accurate answers, rather than creative ones. We pick up the practice of looking for the 'right answer', which very often remains with us throughout our lives.

FACT NOTE

Ursula K. Le Guin was an author of novels, children's books, and short stories, mainly in the genres of fantasy and science fiction. She is famous for the quote 'The creative adult is the child who survived'. However, many do not know that this is just a sentence from within a larger quotation. The whole quote is as follows (Le Guin, 2017, p. 120):

> The creative adult is the child who survived, after the world tried killing them, making them 'grown up'. The creative adult is the child who survived the blandness of schooling, the unhelpful words of bad teachers, and the nay-saying ways of the world.

As discussed in the first chapter, education was not designed to produce creativity. Children were taught to obey, not to challenge or think creatively. The adult walks in or goes to the front; children stand up or go silent. Further conformity can be seen in the expectation of uniforms, and children being grouped by ages and abilities. This whole pattern of conformity leads to the process for university entrance (if we get there, that is) or work, where we further conform. So, when we step out as adults, we are functional members of society, ready to contribute to the economy, but during this process our creativity has been stifled. What we have achieved, though, is the ability to 'know' and, in return, repeat this knowledge with little or no creativity required.

Unfortunately, this doesn't stop once we reach adulthood; it continues, as creativity fades because it is not used. For most of what we do in our day-to-day lives, creativity is not really required, and therefore is not thought of. Adults tend to stay with what is familiar to them; it becomes our comfort zone. Children, on the other hand, have the benefit of not knowing what is not possible. For them, everything is feasible. What's more, young children get praise and encouragement from their parents and other adults for almost any work they do – particularly for imaginative stories or weird ideas and creations. They have heard tales of magic and they see around them technology doing all sorts of amazing things. As far as they are concerned, every problem can be solved. Adults, though, are only too well versed in what they cannot achieve and what cannot be done. They are surrounded by rules, regulations, laws, and compliance. They have experienced rejections, failures, and even humiliations. At some stage, they have worked for a difficult manager who was not interested in their ideas – just in getting the job done on time.

Adults concentrate on what they cannot achieve and what cannot be done, blaming time and pressure. This is understandable when constant policy changes dictate our work with children and provide unpredictable landscapes in which to function. With busy lives, adults tend not to expand their reading, research further, or even take up a hobby. On the other hand, the more we know as adults, the harder it is to see things differently because we hold on to old ways of thinking, 'because it works' or 'it's always worked!' There's no blame here, because it is our educational systems that have emphasised the learning of knowledge and built a culture of conformity. As parents, we become the source of knowledge for our children by being authoritative and certain that all we know is right. We teach children that this is what is expected as adults, with little or no emphasis on creativity, thus triggering the cycle for the trap of adulthood once again. As adults, we don't lose our creativity; we just haven't been taught to develop it. We learn habits which stop it emerging and thus learn to become uncreative – something we don't want for the children we are working with.

It is vital at this point to state that the trap of adulthood does not class every adult within it – only a majority. There are many creative adults in differing disciplines who have contributed fascinating creative insights; who's to say what their education was like or what they experienced leading into their adulthood? Take creative practitioners, for example, in the fields of art, music, dance, photography, architecture, and much more – and don't forget the outstanding early years practitioners that thrive on creativity. *Where does their creativity come from?* These adults teach us that there are practices that can be undertaken to avoid losing creativity in our work and in our lives; it is this that adults in the early years need to develop in order to emerge from any trap that hinders creativity – something we explore a little later in this chapter.

 **CONNECT**

Find someone you deem to be creative in your setting. What makes them 'creative'?

Creative blocks

When one finally pops their head out of the trap of adulthood to understand creativity and its inherent role in their teaching, they come face to face with mental blocks or, as Constantinides (2015) describes them, 'creative blocks'. Several things cause these blocks, and many are created by the individuals themselves. To start with, most of what we do outside our work with children, we don't need creativity, i.e. driving. So then there is no need to think about it – our minds often remain cluttered with things we need to do, how we are going to do them, and if they will ever get done. Here we concentrate on the outcome, rather than the process of getting there. In addition to the creative mental locks within, there are also external blocks that play a role.

ACTION RESEARCH

Carry out some research on what the biggest road block to creativity in settings is.

- Adults?

- Preparation and teaching time?

- Senior leadership?

- Other?

What can you learn from this?

How can the blocks be overcome?

- **Training blocks** – creativity can be a foreign concept to many adults at the beginning, and it is not really high on the list when choosing teaching as a profession. Programmes designed for adults working or intending to work with children often lack any exploration of creativity in their content. Often, the content of training does not contain learning objectives, such as demonstrate 'creative teaching' or 'the ability to facilitate children's creative thinking skills', that adults are expected to apply in their roles. Adults are not trained in creativity, but are asked to integrate it into their teaching.

AROUND THE WORLD
PORTUGAL

A study asked 576 teachers in Portugal schools what they thought about the concepts of a creative pupil and a creative teacher. It was concluded that the teachers' responses helped to identify a **need for teacher training about creativity**. It was also noted that this kind of training should be developed in a very practical way, taking account of real experiences in schools and not only theoretical concepts. It should be done through case studies, class observations, planning and assessment, and structurally creative tasks, applicable to what really goes on (Morais and Azevedo, 2011).

- **Environment blocks** – being in a fast-paced technological era, where the emphasis is on 'get in there and teach', can reinforce the education system as a block in developing creativity in both adult and child. Education leadership may be more concerned with setting and achieving targets, rather than valuing the role of creativity in the learning process; this can ultimately lead adults to not think about it – 'if it's not accounted for, why bother!' Ofsted standards and regulations add further pressures to the role of the adult by expecting conformity, which then leads into the **'poverty block'**. I'm not talking about money here, but being too time-poor, knowledge-poor, network poor, and short of resources and equipment-poor to get the job done. The challenge is then to achieve as much as possible within the constraints within which one has to function.

- **Perception blocks** – adults adopt perceptions through their interpretation and understanding of creativity. One such perception is that some adults are gifted with natural creative abilities, and the rest of us beg and borrow from elsewhere because we lack this ability. This is far from the truth, because actually, creative adults are masters at gathering ideas from all kinds of sources. Further, perception is also based on how an adult views a teaching and learning situation – for example, a lack of creativity because it is time consuming to create extra resources for the activity and spend extra time planning for it. Knowing your perceptions about creativity can help you to understand the needs, misconceptions, or even prejudice ideas held, and to discern positive beliefs that should be reinforced, leading to better practices for fostering creativity in the setting.

- **Values block** – as always, we all have beliefs about how early years education should or ought to be, and because certain practices have always worked, we hold on to them strongly. This is a challenge in itself. As stated earlier, our own experiences shape our values and how we perceive creativity. Values are the core beliefs, concepts, and philosophies we hold about life, in this case about teaching, learning, and, of course, creativity. They keep us grounded and clear on who we are, guide us to connect with others, and direct us towards meaningful work. Values also shape how we deal with challenges and triumphs, and are deeply connected to our creative core. Therefore, they can also sometimes unknowingly undermine our creative aptitudes. Although having values is a good thing, sometimes this can be negative as it makes individuals unable to accept new sets of values and ideas, even if they are proven to work. What we value and believe to be important in early years education and in our work with children and families will largely determine our practices (Arthur et al., 2008, p. 176). The same can be said for creativity. It can be extremely eye-opening to clearly define our values and discover how they can sometimes quietly block our creativity under the radar.

 **CONNECT**

What values do you hold about children and creative learning? How can you identify them?

- **Self-image blocks** – this normally stems from confidence: confidence in our own ability to be creative. The trap of adulthood can beat it out of us, but often, adults do not try new and innovative ways because they are not confident in doing so. An adult can easily burn out because they stay with the same ideas and techniques without trying something new, not realising that this rubs off on children, too. As adults, we might have creative ideas rolling around in our heads, but we stop ourselves. We don't want to look silly. We don't want to say something that might have us look different in the eyes of our peers or leaders. This self-image block prevents us from being creative as per the practice story about the toothpicks and jelly beans.

! STORY FROM PRACTICE
● THE JELLY BEAN STRUCTURE

A group of adults from various educational backgrounds attended a training session. To start with they were given a task using jelly beans and toothpicks: to build the tallest free-standing structure possible in 20 minutes using these materials. It first required some work on the facilitator's part to get them started, and then he stood back and observed. It was clear that this creative task seemed like an unwanted chore to them. They were stiff, unfunny, and thinking too much about what was required. When they finally finished, the facilitator informed them that this task was performed with a group of 5-year-olds in a setting. They set themselves a competition over who could build the tallest tower, and there was noise, giggles, planning, trial and error, etc., going on. Children were creating and thinking critically about all aspects.

The group discussed at length how they perceived the activity. Many said that they had a few ideas but didn't want to look silly sharing or trying it in case it didn't work. There seem to be a consensus that there is always a strong social pressure to conform and be ordinary when coming to 'train', and that they didn't really think about creativity within it. The facilitator shared the following on the screen:

Asif: 'I like to put cold water in my coffee so it cools quicker to drink.'

Saranna: 'You're weird, you know?'

Nadhia: 'What are you doing?'

Bobby: 'I'm painting my letterbox.'

Nadhia: 'You're crazy.'

Gurmit: 'Why don't we add a little garlic?'

Julie: 'Because the recipe doesn't say garlic.'

Zena: 'Why are we going this way? It's longer.'

Tony: 'Because I like the drive.'

Zena: 'Did anyone tell you you're strange?'

Finally! There were giggles and humour amongst the group. The group discussed which conversations indicated creativity, and which did not, and how perception and self-image could get in the way.

■ The practice story about the jelly bean structure suggests that children are more creative and are natural inventors. Their worldview is incomplete and demands discovery. They prosper because they embrace their ignorance instead of ignoring it. And they are willing to explore, investigate, and put their ideas to the test because they are willing to fail. Unlike adults, they don't care how other people perceive or evaluate their ideas, and they're unconcerned with the impossible or what doesn't work.

The creative blocks discussed are just some examples of the many challenges that adults are faced with when trying to nurture creativity. To promote creativity amongst children, adults need to unravel their pre-conceptions and blocks about what it means to be creative not only as part of their professional learning process, but also as part of their creative teaching process. Adults need to be aware of and identify the blocks, and then establish how to overcome them in order to develop their role as a creative adult. Work Tool 5 is a creative profile designed to help you gain insight into your own thoughts around creativity. Take some time to complete it and really think about what is being asked – it may well be an eye opener!

Teaching creatively and creative learning

You may have come across these terms interchangeably when one speaks of creativity in education, or through your research on it. On the path to becoming a creative adult, understanding the distinction between 'teaching creatively' and 'creative learning' is vital, because one is about the learner – the child – and the other is about the teaching – you.

Teaching creatively is about the adult making learning more interesting and effective. It focuses on the children and includes giving them many choices of what to explore and how it is to be explored. It is about how adults use imaginative creative approaches in the setting to engage children with content, some of which were discussed in Chapter 4, and more will be in the chapters to follow. The creative adult is an expert in teaching creatively through facilitating, mentoring, encouraging, and inspiring children, as well as in developing materials and approaches that fire children's interests, motivate their learning, and nurture and stimulate creativity's characteristics. The creative adult has confidence in children, with the belief that they can learn what it is that they are being taught. This is a necessary part of all good or, rather, creative teaching. Studies have suggested that adults feel creative most when they are in control and take ownership of their practice (Craft and Hall, 2015); practice includes their approaches to teaching creatively.

Teaching creatively can also be considered a craft, with the creative adult as the craftsperson. When crafting, you are indeed connecting various materials, or elements, together to produce something. Creative teaching is exactly this: where one crafts together to produce a learning experience for all involved. Crafting plans can include elements such as use of time, differentiation, resources, room arrangement, participation strategies, monitoring understanding techniques, and children's engagement through creativity's characteristics, all unfolding in the early years context. Whether one sees it or not, adults engage in everyday creativity when they plan and improvise activities or provision to meet the needs, interests, and abilities of children, whilst still conforming to the formal curriculum and available resources.

 **DISCUSS**

With peers/colleagues both 'teaching creatively' and 'creative learning'.

There is no denying that teaching creatively is a challenge, because it is about inspiring creativity in children whilst remaining creative ourselves. Adults can easily stifle children's creativity by being prescriptive in their teaching. They can discourage fantasy or imagination, or have low expectations of how and what children can do and achieve. Early years practice is a high-pressure role, with the weight of children's progression largely resting on the teachers' shoulders. There is a pressure on adults to focus on math and literacy, a lack of early years training of creative practice, and a tension between meeting the needs of a whole group and, at the same time, encouraging the interests of each individual child. Adults have various responsibilities, ranging from planning and assessing to behaviour management and beyond. Teaching creatively means considering how creativity can be applied to these everyday responsibilities, too; if children are interested and engaged enough to ask probing questions, then creative learning is taking place.

OBSERVE

A peer/colleague/teaching. What is it that they do/say which is 'teaching creatively', and what do children do/say which is 'creative learning'?

Creative learning, then, is about the child, and how adults identify and foster creativity within the learning content for children to engage with. Creative learning involves innovation, control, relevance, and ownership, which are also characteristics of teaching creatively (Jeffrey and Woods, 2003). Creative learning is about investigating, discovering, inventing, and cooperating. At least one of these will be present in creative learning experiences for children; ideally, it will be all four (Rosen, 2010, p. 11). For creative adults, creative learning occurs through the forms of teaching approaches that are intended to develop children's own creative thinking, creative behaviour, and creative strengths and potential: 'creativity's characteristics'. It is where children use their imagination and experiences to develop their creative capacities. Woolf and Belloli (2005) define approaches for creative learning by adults as:

■ The provision of a range of materials to help children represent their unique and individual perception of the world, unrestricted by adult ideas

■ Valuing each child's individual creativity and demonstrating respect for their ideas

 RESEARCH TO EXPLORE
CREATIVE TEACHERS (2011)

Research was conducted in 13 qualitative case studies and two quantitative studies of teachers, who demonstrated every day creativity in their work. It proposed an emergent creative teaching framework, highlighting three interrelated dimensions of creative practice, namely the teacher's:

■ Personal characteristics

■ Pedagogy

■ School/class ethos

■ Providing young children with time, space, and high-quality resources

■ Offering scaffolding for young children's learning, giving them a secure structure to work within by demonstrating techniques and skills or initiating ideas

■ Letting the young child take the lead

It goes without saying that creative learning involves teaching creatively, an almost middle ground. Children's creative abilities are more likely to be developed in an atmosphere in which the adult's creative abilities are properly engaged, too. To put it another way, adults cannot develop the creative learning of their children if their own creative abilities are suppressed. Creative learning is a demanding process which cannot be made routine, and requires encouragement, identification, and fostering, with the opportunity to practice creativity's characteristics frequently. 'Teaching creatively' and 'creative learning' are intertwined and should be considered as an equal creative partnership, where one cannot exist without the other.

 AROUND THE WORLD
REGGIO EMILIA, ITALY

The Reggio adult is known as a teacher-researcher, a resource and guide as she/he lends expertise to children (Edwards, 1993). Teachers are:

- **Co-constructors:** partners, guides, nurtures, solves problems, learns, hypothesises

- **Researchers:** learns, observes, revisits

- **Documenters:** listens, records, displays, revisits

- **Advocates for children:** involved in the community, politics relating to children, speaks for children, and presents work to other educators and community members

It is a fact that creativity is demonstrated in different ways by different people, and at different times, provided the context is right. It should come as no surprise by now that the ability to be creative and solve problems in novel ways is manifested in early childhood. Clearly, the more children know and the more eclectic their knowledge, the greater the potential variety of creative learning. However, for children to get here, an essential first step to fostering and supporting creativity is for the adult to question their own way of viewing it, and then to go on to understand and be confident with it. Yes, we believe there is more creativity in the early years, but how it is understood, used, and facilitated by the adult is the key question.

What is a creative adult?

Creative adults, together with teaching creatively, are key for fostering creativity in young children and their learning. Overcoming creative blocks and understanding the difference between teaching creatively and creative learning is a start. Next, it's about asking *what is being a creative adult all about? What makes a creative adult? Is it about how they deliver the curriculum for children's learning? Is it the ability to seamlessly incorporate real-world experiences into the setting? Is it about blending outside creative interests with the curriculum? Or is the creative adult someone who just isn't afraid to take a few risks?* The answer: yes, yes, yes, and more yes! There is no such thing as a perfectly creative or a non-creative adult in the early years; simply put, it's what an outstanding early years practitioner is, or ought to be – someone who is always striving to develop themselves and their creative confidence.

❗ STORY FROM PRACTICE
● THE HUNT FOR PENCIL POTS!

I'm in Wilko, exploring the notebook section. I glance to the side and see two men standing looking. I go back to looking at the notebooks. I glance again and realise they are still looking at me, and then one of them waves! It suddenly dawns on me that they are teacher trainees who have just completed the course and are ready for their first year in teaching. I go over and we say hi. They seem happy to see me and ask about what has been happening on the programme since they left.

After some exciting discussion about the two teaching in Reception in September, I ask what they are shopping for. They tell me pencil pots. They go onto to tell me how they have been to several stores and can't seem to find pencil pots for their classes for September. I give them 'that look', the one they know so well, and they smirk. I say, 'Have I taught you nothing about being creative?!' They reluctantly shake their heads and look like two schoolboys being told off. I ask them if pencil pots need to look a certain way. They reply no, so I ask them what the purpose of the pencil pot is – of course, to hold pencil! I then tell them, 'What can you find in this store that you can turn into pencil pots?' They straighten up, almost as if accepting a challenge, and set off to hunt down their pencil pots.

Adults in the early years have what it takes to think about education differently. They have studied and worked with creative colleagues, and have used their imagination to create engaging activities for children. *How do adults come up with creative ideas for activities and lessons? What do they do when they are planning?* Being a creative adult may not be something we think of when analysing our roles in early years practice, but it is inherent within it because the act of teaching itself demands creativity – *how am I going to engage children in learning?* This question weighs heavily on every adult as they create and develop learning plans and environments to engage children. It is something every adult working in early years education is expected to, and can, do.

A creative adult is the one who encourages reasonable risks and unpredictable situations, while reinforcing creative teaching and learning. Creative adults, although aware of the requirements of the curriculum, often give precedence to children's social and personal learning intentions over content outcomes. They strongly defend their right to shape the curriculum in response to children. This is a value they hold close to them. Creative adults know a great deal about children's interests and passions and see this as vital and essential knowledge in order to make connections and widen children's perspectives within and beyond the areas of learning. Creative adults are able to present materials in many diverse ways, where children have a better chance of understanding it and using it in their own creativity. Being a creative adult encourages children to be creative learners and thinkers too.

Creative adults bring more to teaching than just knowledge. They are educated in other areas and have rich work and life histories; they can draw on their experiences and outside interests to inform the creative partnership. Personal interests, passion, and knowledge of the wider world are all contributing factors to teaching creatively and creative learning which should not be underestimated. In fact, what creative adults do with all this is to build, develop, and maintain a repertoire of strategies and tools which they utilise within their approaches with the children – these are their 'creative practices'.

CONNECT

What personal interests or wider knowledge do you hold that can inform your work with children?

Creative practices of the creative adult

When observing good or outstanding adults in settings, it is evident that they understand their specialism of early years education. They have read widely into children's literature in order to bring the art of storytelling into their setting. They have undertaken science experiments and watched videos of them and have brought this into the activities they create. They have practiced writing on various surfaces so that when they model writing for children it is clear. They have hunted down resources to use in their teaching through scrap yards and even building site skips! They have read recent research to inform their approaches with children. It is their *practicing* of this that leads to the quality of what they offer in the early years context. Similarly, only by having experienced 'practicing creativity' will adults be able to fully develop it in their approaches and, through this, the children.

It is vital to note that creativity is inherent in the roles we have in the early years, but is not simply an inherent ability. It needs to be practiced and honed (Keenan and Mishra, 2016). It is about the development of creativity and the use of different strategies that can be used to exercise the characteristics of the creative process – just like the children! Simply put, it is about adopting creative practices and *practicing* them, which starts with the adult inviting creativity, embracing it, and allowing it to be nurtured and encouraged.

RESEARCH TO EXPLORE
THE *PLURAL* PRACTITIONER

The role of the adult in early years settings is complex and demands many different responsibilities and fulfilment of different tasks. The plural practitioner reflects the different 'selves' that make up the adult role and their work with young children. It discusses seven distinctive dimensions and how these manifest in daily interactions between adults and children. The seven selves that constitute the plural practitioner have particular characteristics and encompass particular forms of behaviour, but, like rainbow colours, each characteristic or self blends into and helps to create the next (Rose and Rogers, 2012).

■ The critical reflector

■ The carer

■ The communicator

■ The facilitator

■ The observer

■ The assessor

■ The creator

Creative practices when planning for teaching creatively are about *playing* with the knowledge, experiences, and tools the adult holds. Being creative lies in what can be done with the knowledge of children, the learning, teaching, creativity, approaches, and early years practice as a whole, while at the same time drawing on other experiences and strategies that inform it practically. This then leads into planning to engage children in learning, creating environments to facilitate it and responding to what children say and do to ensure progression – creatively, of course. Many of these creative practices are shared with you here.

 IDEA
100-DAY CHALLENGE

Depending on how you perceive creativity so far, do something creative for 100 days and log your progress.

What has this process taught you?

Being creative – a beginning strategy, for those practitioners who feel this creativity thing is all new and daunting, is to prime yourself to make a creative contribution in your work. This is simply by always practicing 'being creative', even in a hobby (Root-Bernstein in Keenan and Mishra, 2016), through undertaking a creative project of some sort, a personal interest, or trying the idea of the 100-day challenge suggested here. It is not about attending a class to learn about creativity, but rather about having experiential learning in other places. *What about baking or glass making? Or even a class on flamenco!* Even if this practice of 'being creative' results in creativity that is more personal than observable to others, using those cognitive skills will develop your ability in your professional role in early years education. For example, by using a critical eye on activities and the environment – *how can you make them more interesting and motivating for children through your 'being creative' experience?* Yet again, the emphasis here is on the creative process and developing creativity's characteristics as you undertake 'being creative'. By being creative outside of your role, you will remain inspired and motivated within it.

 ACTIVITY

Plan and create a web page for your early years setting which is about the children 'being creative'.

If this was an EYFS learning intention (being creative), what would the explanation for it read?

How would it be visible in practice? What would children be doing?

Imitating – Root-Bernstein (in Keenan and Mishra, 2016) identified a useful strategy for practicing creativity as 'copying'. This term can have various criticisms attached to it in the form of being unethical, hence why I am using 'imitation' alongside it. Root-Bernstein explains that if you do not know how to do something, how to think and put something together, then you can't be original. You have to go through the process of learning how to do so. The best way to do this is by seeing how something else was put together. An example of this can be as simple as a teaching session from another colleague. Imitate some of their techniques and strategies, such as behaviour management or questioning of children, and increasingly make it different by trying differing ways yourself. With a variety of experiences and knowledge will come the ability to adapt your imitation, which moves it away from copying or, rather, imitating and towards producing your own ways.

IDEA

Writer Ernest Hemingway famously laid down a challenge to write a story in six words. Try it!

Why not update this to a Facebook or Twitter challenge and write an entire story in just 240 characters?

Become a noticer – Guy Claxton once said that 'creative people are expert noticers' (Ingledew, 2016). They have highly developed abilities in visual searching – spotting, gathering, and utilising things that most others overlook. A good example of this was on one of my many train journeys. I was trying to pass time, as you do, and spotted a poster advertising a television channel. It was the title that grabbed my attention: 'late excuse generator'. The excuse then was that the train track had been taken over by eight giant slugs, so whoever it was couldn't get to where they wanted to go on time – how original! A day later, I noticed my students coming in late from lunch, and realised it was a regular occurrence. So, I put up a slide titled 'Late Excuse Generator'. I then asked students to come up with the best creative excuse ever of why they are late from lunch on a daily basis. Having an active rather than a sluggish curiosity about your surroundings can reveal ideas, as did this poster. So, be a noticer, be nosey, and be eye-sy! Work Tool 6 has been designed to get you going!

Thinking tools – in 1999, husband and wife duo Robert and Michele Root-Bernstein developed and published 13 creative thinking tools in their much-acclaimed book, *Sparks of Genius*. The tools were created by examining the writings of a range of highly creative thinkers, in multiple disciplines, to find out how they experienced their processes (Starko, 2014). It is where they 'learned to mix, blend and savour an entire range of mental ingredients' (Root-Bernstein and Root-Bernstein, 1999, p. 1). Creative adults in the early years need to adopt and practice many differing approaches of 'thinking' to inform what they intend to do when teaching creatively, and these tools provide multiple ways of doing so. Work Tool 7 explains each tool for you to explore in developing and practicing your creative thinking. A few more are shared below.

- **Play with possibilities** – as explained in Chapter 3, children do this all the time, so why not take a page out of their book! Playing is a strategy for developing creativity and is not just the privilege of the young (Root-Bernstein, 2014). We see most things – objects, buildings, spaces, materials, technology, and much more – through the lenses of habit and familiarity, often overlooking any possibilities. By playing with things, concepts, or processes, you ask yourself 'what else can I do with this?', which can open doors to new ways of thinking, ideas, and even new discoveries for teaching creatively and approaches to creative learning. Playing with possibilities allows work and thought processes to shake traditional constraints and become both fun and creative in an open-ended exploration of possibility (Keenan and Mishra, 2016).

- **Use alteration** – altering how something is viewed can also reveal new possibilities and ideas. You do this by seeking every possible viewpoint and shifting the context it is in. Take something from its usual place and put it somewhere completely different – what do you get? For example, take the kettle from the staff room and place it outdoors – you could grow flowers in it. *How can you use alteration when designing learning approaches? How can you apply alteration to what you intend to teach?* The idea is to look at something in a different context altogether, maybe also by being in a different role.

- **Translation** – creative ideas are greatly stimulated through the behaviour of translating. Converting things from one form or medium into another can guide thoughts in totally new and exciting directions. One idea leads to another – and then you're off on the ideas trail. Russian artist Wassily Kandinsky translated classical music into abstract paintings, selecting different colours to signify the varying sounds and emotions the music provoked. He also invented a machine that translated musical sounds into instructions for paintings – *what and how can you translate content to teach? For example, can you translate some form of knowledge you want the children to learn through music or miming instead? Like a mathematical concept, for instance?*

Practice varying roles – sometimes if we take on a different name for our roles, but with the same purpose of viewing creativity for children, it can make it easier to adopt practices to develop. Roger von Oech (1998) is a pioneer behind the creative revolution in the world of business. He distinguished four main roles in creative thinking in adults and calls them the 'Explorer', the 'Artist', the 'Judge', and the 'Warrior'. He claims that these roles are present in all of us, but some may be more developed and pronounced than the others. We may find that we love to perform one of the roles, but do not like another one. However, a creative adult draws on all four roles.

- The **Explorer** is our role for searching for new information and resources. The Explorer reads books and magazines, talks to people, goes out, looks around and collects things, goes to the library, and goes online. In short, the Explorer collects materials and information.

- The **Artist** is our role for turning these resources and information into new ideas. People often limit creativity to this thinking function, though without the other three, it cannot create anything but beautiful bubbles of fancy ideas.

- The **Judge** is our role for evaluating the merits of an idea and deciding what to do. Our Judge will tell us which of our ideas best meets the objective and which is feasible within the constraints of resources, time, content, and practicalities.

■ The **Warrior** is our role for carrying our idea into action. The Warrior will carry out the plan the Judge selected from the ideas the Artist came up with, using the materials and information collected by the Explorer.

 CONNECT

Which roles can you identify with? How can you use these roles to develop your role as a creative adult?

Strengthen your technology skills and tools – there is always room for growth with technology, and with the speed that it is evolving, there is no getting away from it. Technology has become a much-embedded tool in education, and to practice and develop this will fuel your creativity both personally and professionally. There will be more discussion on the use of technology in Chapter 9. Take deliberate action to improve and practice your skills by assessing where you are with them and where you want to go. A good place to start is by becoming a Google Educator. It's a certification that marks you as having a solid foundation in Google's online tools. You work through a series of free online courses that prepare you for online exams. These include your knowledge of Google Apps for Education (Google Docs and Drive, Sites, Calendar, and Gmail), and you can choose one elective exam (options include Chromebook and Google Chrome browser).

Becoming a Google Educator is the first step toward becoming a Google Certified Teacher, which is a much bigger deal and involves on-site training for just a small group of adults every year. See this chapter's Explore section to learn more about Google for Education exams and certifications. Once you have developed your confidence with simple Google tools, then there are varying apps and online tools designed to assist in creative teaching and learning; find out what these are and how they can be used. Of course, if you are a tech expert, then develop yourself further by trying some challenging apps such as Prezi or animations to form an activity for children.

 ACTION RESEARCH

Carry out some research on what technology/software/apps are used in the setting or classroom.

■ How are they used in teaching creatively?

■ What training did staff undertake to be confident with it?

Become a researcher and collector of teaching ideas – the creative adult wants to be a 'know it all'; they want to know about all kinds of things, because they never know when they may need it, or it comes together when planning creative approaches. Research can be as simple as observing other adults and their teaching styles – *how did the children engage with it?* It is also about using this role to take on creative reflection of teaching and learning, which moves beyond the traditional cognitive processes, something which is discussed in depth in Chapter 10. By researching and collecting, it will nudge you on the way to creativity where you can adapt and experiment with them. Try ideas, adapt old ones, stop for a minute, think, and evaluate. Kirby Ferguson, a writer, film director, and producer, is famous for saying that 'we're all copying and transforming and combining . . . you can't get something from nothing, you can't just summon it out of the air' (Ferguson, 2012). Creative adults use what is around them to create innovative ideas and teaching approaches. They are willing to try new strategies and are not afraid of failure.

IDEA

TEN ACTIVITIES!

Choose an image, text, song, or video. Now brainstorm ten activities that can use it as a base in a different form altogether!

A good place to start collecting ideas is an online tool called *Evernote*. There is the Microsoft version of *OneNote*, and Google's *Google Keep*, but Evernote has been tested and found the better note tool. It is like a ring-binder, but one you keep online. Of course, if you are more of a hard copy person, then a ring binder is for you. On Evernote, you can store directly typed notes, snap a picture and file handwritten notes, and upload various files, including Word documents, PDFs, image files, screenshots of webpages, and much more. You can also store voice notes if you don't have the time to type. Once you save notes, you can organise them into notebooks and stack groups of notebooks so that they become digital, *searchable* files.

The tools are cloud-based, so you can access it through your desktop computer, tablet, smartphone, or anything that has internet access. You get an idea when you're sleeping? You can plop it in right then and there. Have your meetings for the year been scheduled by the setting that you want to remember? Snap a photo and file it. As a creative adult, you can use these online tools to keep ideas for future lessons, along with links to materials, images and research articles, webpages etc.

Store notes from planning meetings, professional development sessions and discussions. Keep a reflective log on your teaching which includes images, pictures, and quick notes. This is just some of the potential of tools; there is so much more! Table 5.1 has been designed to give you some ideas to start collating your research and ideas around, whatever method you choose.

Table 5.1 Build a creative toolbox

Use the following headings to start forming a toolbox of creative resources to support your creative practice. The idea is for you to begin to research and collect, and in time you will find a method to collating in a way that works for you – i.e. e-portfolio, blog folio, ring binder, etc.

	✓ *Progress*
Websites – resources, information, teaching ideas. etc.	
Teaching and learning apps and software	
Resources in the local community	
Events taking place during the year	
Teaching and learning videos	
Images	
Music	
Resources, websites for the learning environment	
Good practice from other colleagues	
Colleagues from other disciplines	
Things children have said – their conversations and ideas that can be embedded into teaching and learning	
Research and latest discussion in the field	
Forums, blogs, vlogs, etc. by the early years community i.e. EYFS Forum, Kathy Brodie	
Notes from meetings, discussions, etc.	
Parents – what they do and how to utilise them in children's learning	
What else can you add to your creative toolbox?	

Find your tribe – ideas need 'tribes'. The early years profession is such that we do need each other. The more connections we have, the more powerful creativity becomes. Huberman (1995) defines the term 'open networks' as such that practitioners should remain open to insights from other practitioners, children, and parents in order to develop their approaches and practices. Connect with other adults, writers, online bloggers, early years forums, national organisations, and many more for inspiration. Creativity is difficult in isolation; your tribe can inspire you, ask you questions, provoke you, and plant further creative seeds. It is also about extending beyond the setting to reach out to experts. Get them in if you can't get out! Bounce ideas off colleagues and students, and try things out. It is in this way that creative adults share their thinking and practice, explore creative ways to build more meaningful early learning environments, and learn about opportunities to nurture children's creativity. Common challenges can also come into the light where alternate approaches and ideas can be explored as a result.

Think about experts outside your discipline, too. Creative practitioners come in the form of artists, dancers, photographers, and storytellers, but also come from other disciplines, such as architecture. An early years practitioner once got in touch with a local architect who provided him with A2 sketches of a building. The practitioner mounted these on a wall in the construction area for children to engage with and create their own sketches on graph paper, to later use to build outdoors. This type of networking not only provides a wider experience and learning opportunity for the creative adult, but provides creative confidence in using a multi-disciplinary approach to ensure that the role of creativity in learning is manifested in every aspect of what children do and learn. Lave and Wenger's (1991) situated learning theory on developing 'communities of practice' requires practitioners with a common aim or passion to interact with each; the passion is the place of creativity in children's learning.

FACT NOTE
THE MARIGOLD EFFECT (GONZALEZ, 2013)

Many experienced gardeners follow a concept called 'companion planting': placing certain vegetables and plants near each other to improve growth for one or both plants. For example, rose growers plant garlic near their roses because it repels bugs and prevents fungal diseases. Among companion plants, the marigold is one of the best: it protects a wide variety of plants from pests and harmful weeds. If you plant a marigold beside almost any garden vegetable, that vegetable will grow big and strong and healthy, protected and encouraged by its marigold.

Marigolds exist in our settings and schools as well – encouraging, supporting, and nurturing growing practitioners and adults on their way to maturity. If you can find at least one marigold in your setting and stay close to them, you will grow. Find more than one, and you will positively thrive. *Where's your marigold? And whose marigold are you?*

Another vital aspect of developing a tribe is for you to be accessible. Don't forget you are a creative adult and an expert in early years. For this reason, you should develop an online professional profile where you can not only share your expertise, but can also connect with people from other specialisms, and they can find you too. These profiles normally state your current role and location, your experiences to date, what you are passionate about when it comes to early years education, and what you would like to network on – creativity! There are many ways to achieve this, but start locally first and build your way up:

> Research with your local authority and early years networks and provide details of your setting and role which they can publish. Very often these places organise training and events, which you can tap into.

> Join recognised online forums and organisations where you can share expertise, but also tap into others. Early years forums are a good start, but don't just limit yourself to this; think about creative practice sites, too, where you can then invite other professionals from other areas into your setting.

> Create professional profiles online, such as on the networking site LinkedIn. It provides a way to connect with other professionals and helps you stay in contact with millions of users, where you can exchange knowledge, ideas, and even employment opportunities, as well as expand your networks in your field. There are more out there – find them, join them.

The creative adult needs to understand their own creativity, and their own willingness to take risks, which will hopefully lead to the promotion of creativity in children. By developing a sense of themselves as creative educators, it is only then the creative adult will understand that good teaching is actually creative teaching. 'You're human, and you have an imagination. You are wired to be creative' (Gerard Puccio in Barras, 2014). Once adults master this understanding, then the creative adult's role deepens in the designing of learning, creating environments conducive to creativity, and using the many creative approaches in children's learning to facilitate, nurture, and stimulate creativity. All of these are discussed in the coming chapters. Trust in your creative instincts and exciting ideas!

Next step

 REFLECT

Do you know people who feel they are not creative? Why? Explore this further.

What practical approaches can adults take to inspire creativity within themselves and the learning environment?

What steps need to be taken to achieve a more creative approach to teaching and learning?

EXPLORE

Bramwell et al. (2011) Creative Teachers: http://spectrum.library.concordia.ca/974917/1/Creative_Teachersfinal.pdf

■ A research study on creative teachers which provides a framework.

Cremin, T. (2014) Creative Teachers and Creative Teaching: www.steveslearning.com/Teacher%20Training%20resources/cremin.pdf

■ A chapter focusing on the key features of creative teachers and how it is visible in their characteristics and practice.

Learning to become creative practitioners: www.teachearlyyears.com/learning-and-development/view/learning-to-become-creative-practitioners

■ An article on two projects to facilitate practitioners' developing their creative confidence.

Grete Skjeggestad Meyer & Margareth Eilifsen (2017) The challenges of creativity in Norwegian Early Childhood Teacher Education, *European Early Childhood Education Research Journal*, 25:3, 425–435: https://doi.org/10.1080/1350293X.2017.1308166

■ A research study on the challenges of creativity in adult learning.

Tech tools

The Creativity Quiz: http://thecreativityquiz.com/

■ An online quiz to test your creativity!

Evernote: https://evernote.com/

■ An online tool to collect and collate all your research and ideas.

Google for Education Training: https://edutrainingcenter.withgoogle.com/

■ Information on how to become a Google Educator.

Lynda.com: www.lynda.com/

■ Delivers top-quality training videos to help anyone learn technology, creative, and business skills. Log in to watch expert-taught courses in photography, graphic design, business training, web and interactive design, 3D animation, audio, and much more.

6 The creative curriculum

 THINK

What do we need to teach children?

What is your definition of a creative curriculum?

CHAPTER FOCUS

- Defining 'curriculum'

- The EYFS and the issues with interpretation

- Exploring the notion of a creative curriculum

- Elements in constructing a creative curriculum – includes embodying children's voices, creating holistic experiences, and pedagogical approaches underpinning it

This chapter explores the building of the creative curriculum, which should remain statutory but engage and motivate children to keep on learning. The aim is not to provide you with a 'ready-made curriculum', but to give you food for thought in how you go about shaping and delivering your own. It is about taking what you already know and have, along with the contents of this chapter (or, rather, book) – not only to really think about what it is that children need in relation to a creative curriculum, but also about what they bring to the creative process of learning.

What is a curriculum?

The very notion of the term 'curriculum' is elusive, as its meaning is often open to multiple interpretations (Ang, 2014, p. 3). A curriculum can refer to the knowledge, understanding, and skills children are expected to learn or achieve by a certain stage, in various areas of learning or subjects. It can include the learning aims and objectives children need to meet; the units, themes, topics, or lessons that the adult teaches; the tasks and resources given to children and used in teaching approaches; and methods and assessments used to evaluate children's learning. Ornstein and Hunkins (2009) broaden the definition of curriculum by referring to it as a 'design', to include the imparting of essential concepts, attitudes, and skills to learners. It is clear here that 'curriculum', as with creativity, gives rise to many differing definitions, but also, more essentially, to perspectives from both those who use it in their teaching (you) and those who are learning from it (the children).

 ACTION RESEARCH

Access a setting or school's curriculum for the early years. Annotate where the curriculum speaks of:

- Knowledge

- Understanding

- Skills

What is it that education is trying to teach children?

How does it link to Chapter 5 about what the 'creative child' learns?

In many settings and schools, the curriculum moves between topics, themes, and areas of learning as a means to cover the content stipulated by the government. This has contributed to a stressful situation of planning and workload issues that the adult has to deal with. However, many individual settings and schools have made changes to their curricula in terms of delivery in individual contexts to make it look different, but the key question is *are the outcomes for children any better?*

FACT NOTE
ETYMOLOGY

The word 'curriculum' began as a Latin word meaning 'a race' or 'the course of a race' (which in turn derives from the verb *currere*, meaning 'to run/to proceed') (Oxford Dictionary). The first known use in an educational context is in the *Professio Regia*, a work by University of Paris professor Petrus Ramus, published posthumously in 1576. The term subsequently appears in University of Leiden records in 1582. The word's origins appear closely linked to the Calvinist desire to bring greater order to education (Hamilton, 2014).

By the seventeenth century, the University of Glasgow also referred to its 'course' of study as a 'curriculum', producing the first known use of the term in English in 1633. By the nineteenth century, European universities routinely referred to their curricula to describe both the complete course of study (as for a degree in surgery) and particular courses and their content.

The Early Years Foundation Stage (EYFS) is a mandatory framework for all early years settings in the UK responsible for the teaching and learning of children aged zero to five years. All schools and Ofsted-registered early years providers must follow the EYFS, including childminders, pre-schools, nurseries, and school reception classes. My career has predominately been in the early years, and the widely held belief is that there is more scope for creativity here than in the upper age/year groups. Of course, this is debatable, but it is fact that the current EYFS supports a play-based pedagogic approach and advocates the centrality of the CoETL, which are fundamental to the development of every child as a lifelong learner (Pascal and Bertram, 2017a).

The EYFS supports an integrated approach to early learning and care. It gives all adults a set of common principles and commitments to deliver quality early education and childcare experiences to all children. The framework is about providing quality and consistency in all early years settings, so that every child makes good progress and no child gets left behind. It is expected that a secure foundation will be provided through learning and development opportunities planned around the needs and interests of each individual child, and are reviewed and assessed regularly against the framework. There is partnership between practitioners and parents and/or carers, and equality of opportunity and anti-discriminatory practice to ensure that every child is included and supported.

The EYFS specifies requirements for learning and development and for safeguarding children and promoting their welfare. The learning and development requirements cover:

- **Seven areas of learning and development** which must shape activities and experiences (educational programmes) for children in all early years settings.

- **The early learning goals (ELGs)** that adults must help children work towards. The goals summarise the knowledge, skills, and understanding that all young children should have gained by the end of the Reception year, i.e. the year that they turn 5 years old.

- **Assessment arrangements for measuring progress** in terms of when and how adults must assess children's achievements, and when and how they should discuss children's progress with parents and/or carers.

- **Safeguarding and welfare requirements** which cover the steps that providers must take to keep children safe and promote their welfare (DfE, 2017).

DISCUSS

With peers/colleagues what they consider a 'curriculum' for young children.

ACTIVITY

Using Wordle (at www.wordle.net/), create a 'word cloud' of what you expect children should be able to *know, understand, do,* and *be* by the end of the EYFS phase. What stands out to you?

Figure 6.1 has been devised to give you the teaching and learning requirements of the EYFS in a nutshell. This book deliberately only provides this because, first, the EYFS should be considered as only one part of a broad and balanced curriculum, and secondly, this book is after all about creativity, and therefore this provides a prompt for you to create your own creative curriculum. It's about bringing creativity to life! What is apparent from Figure 6.1 is that the CoETL and the prime and specific areas of development are interconnected (Pascal and Bertram, 2017a).

Educational Programmes

Communication and Language:
- opportunities to experience a rich language environment; to develop their confidence and skills in expressing themselves; and to speak and listen in a range of situations.

Physical Development:
- to be active and interactive; to develop their co-ordination, control, and movement; to understand the importance of physical activity; to make healthy choices in relation to food.

Personal, Social and Emotional:
- to develop a positive sense of themselves, and others; to form positive relationships and develop respect for others; to develop social skills and learn how to manage their feelings; to understand appropriate behaviour in groups; to have confidence in their own abilities.

Literacy:
- to link sounds and letters and to begin to read and write; access to a wide range of reading materials (books, poems, and other written materials) to ignite their interest.

Mathematics:
- to develop and improve their skills in counting, understanding and using numbers; calculating simple addition and subtraction problems; to describe shapes, spaces, and measures.

Understanding of the World:
- to make sense of their physical world and their community through opportunities to explore, observe and find out about people, places, technology and the environment.

Expressive Arts and Design:
- to explore and play with a wide range of media and materials; opportunities and encouragement for sharing their thoughts, ideas and feelings through a variety of activities in art, music, movement, dance, role-play, and design and technology.

The EYFS is based on Four Principles

To shape practice in the early years
Activities and experiences for children must involve:

A Unique Child
The belief that every child is unique.

Positive Relationships
Children learn to be strong and confident.

Enabling Environments
Where they learn and develop.

Children learn and develop in different ways and rates.

The EYFS Areas of Learning and Development

There are seven areas of learning in the early years.

The areas are inter-connected.

Prime Areas

- Personal, Social and Emotional
- Communication and Language
- Physical

Specific Areas

- Expressive Arts and Design
- Understanding the World
- Mathematics
- Literacy

EYFS Characteristics of Effective Teaching and Learning

These are used to guide teaching and learning – How children learn

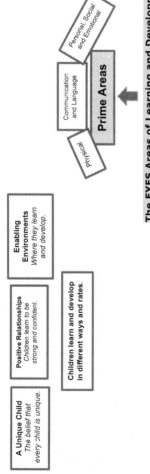

Active learning
children concentrate and keep on trying if they encounter difficulties, and enjoy achievements.

Creating and thinking critically
children have and develop their own ideas, make links between ideas, and develop strategies for doing things.

Playing and exploring
children investigate and experience things; 'have a go'.

Figure 6.1 The EYFS in a nutshell

EYFS Early Learning Goals (ELGs)

Goals children work towards meeting by the end of the EYFS – What children learn

C&L	**Listening and attention:** children listen attentively in a range of situations. They listen to stories, accurately anticipating key events and respond to what they hear with relevant comments, questions or actions. They answer 'how' and 'why' questions about their experiences and in response to stories or events.	**Speaking:** children express themselves effectively, showing awareness of listeners' needs. They use past, present and future forms accurately when talking about events that have happened or are to happen in the future. They develop their own narratives and explanations by connecting ideas or events.
Physical	**Moving and handling:** children show good control and co-ordination in large and small movements. They move confidently in a range of ways, safely negotiating space. They handle equipment and tools effectively, including pencils for writing.	**Health and self-care:** children know the importance for good health of physical exercise, and a healthy diet, and talk about ways to keep healthy and safe. They manage their own basic hygiene and personal needs successfully, including dressing and going to the toilet independently.
P,S&E	**Self-confidence and self-awareness:** children are confident to try new activities, and say why they like some activities more than others. They are confident to speak in a familiar group, will talk about their ideas, and will choose the resources they need for their chosen activities. They say when they do or don't need help.	**Managing feelings and behaviour:** children talk about how they and others show feelings, talk about their own and others' behaviour, and its consequences, and know that some behaviour is unacceptable. They work as part of a group or class, and understand and follow the rules. They adjust their behaviour to different situations, and take changes of routine in their stride. **Making relationships:** children play co-operatively, taking turns with others. They take account of one another's ideas about how to organise their activity. They show sensitivity to others' needs and feelings, and form positive relationships with adults and other children.
Literacy	**Reading:** children read and understand simple sentences. They use phonic knowledge to decode regular words and read them aloud accurately. They also read some common irregular words. They demonstrate understanding when talking with others about what they have read.	**Writing:** children use their phonic knowledge to write words in ways which match their spoken sounds. They also write some irregular common words. They write simple sentences which can be read by themselves and others. Some words are spelt correctly and others are phonetically plausible.
Maths	**Numbers:** children count reliably with numbers from 1 to 20, place them in order and say which number is one more or one less than a given number. Using quantities and objects, they add and subtract two single-digit numbers and count on or back to find the answer. They solve problems, including doubling, halving and sharing.	**Shape, space and measures:** children use everyday language to talk about size, weight, capacity, position, distance, time and money to compare quantities and objects and to solve problems. They recognise, create and describe patterns. They explore characteristics of everyday objects and shapes and use mathematical language to describe them.
U of the W	**People and communities:** children talk about past and present events in their own lives and in the lives of family members. They know that other children don't always enjoy the same things, and are sensitive to this. They know about similarities and differences between themselves and others, and among families, communities and traditions.	**Technology:** children recognise that a range of technology is used in places such as homes and schools. They select and use technology for particular purposes.
E Arts & D	**Exploring and using media and materials:** children sing songs, make music and dance, and experiment with ways of changing them. They safely use and explore a variety of materials, tools and techniques, experimenting with colour, design, texture, form and function.	**Being imaginative:** children use what they have learnt about media and materials in original ways, thinking about uses and purposes. They represent their own ideas, thoughts and feelings through design and technology, art, music, dance, role-play and stories.

Figure 6.1 Continued

The issue with 'curriculum' is all the interpretation

> **▌ STORY FROM PRACTICE**
> ● TEACHING MATHEMATICS IN THE LIBRARY
>
> Whilst working at the library, I could overhear a group opposite me trying to teach a child math. I'm not sure what the concept was, but it quickly became apparent that they were expecting her to solve a sum on paper. After 20 minutes, the child was still unable to solve it, and I could hear the dissatisfaction being expressed from the adult. She was then told that if she didn't learn she would fail. After some time, the child was told to go for a walk and come back ready to attempt it again. I then saw the girl walking around the library shelves, looking 'phased out'. As she came closer, I said to her, 'Why not go for a walk outside instead? It will refresh you'. The girl was shy and went back to her table, where I could hear the adult whispering and asking her what I had said to her.
>
> The thought that occurred to me at the time was, 'Is there any creativity in this learning?' No! 'Could the adult not form a game to engage the child to think and problem solve? Creative maths?' It was obvious that there was a set curriculum that this was expected to work towards, and the child was preparing for a test to move on to the next stage. How was this being interpreted by the adult through their teaching method?

Building a curriculum which embeds creativity as central to it means taking ownership of the EYFS and designing creative learning opportunities around it. It's exactly the sort of thing creative adults should be doing. However, there have been so many changes to the curriculum over the last decade that many of us have not had the time or the thinking space to do this. There has been no period of consolidation during which adults have been able to implement, develop, and take ownership of the EYFS before it changes again (Mohammed, 2014, p. 34). There are adults who are desperate to open their environments to more innovative kinds of ideas, but this is quite difficult when there is a political agenda around standards that they must pay attention to – bold beginnings is one of them – to say nothing of dreaded funding cuts across the sector.

A curriculum that emphasises teaching to pre-determined, assessable goals does not do enough to help creativity flourish in either child or adult – hence it is deemed a restrictive and prescriptive curriculum. But the main issue here is one of *interpretation*. It is crucial to explore the notion of 'curriculum', as its *interpretation* drives the everyday practice decisions and approaches adults choose and make (Ang, 2014). A curriculum only becomes restrictive and prescriptive from how the adult views it, understands it, interprets it, and in turn implements it. Early childhood practitioners play a significant role in the interpretation, delivery, and maintenance of the curriculum (Mohammed, 2014). One such example of interpretation follows.

OBSERVE

An early years setting (any age group). How is the EYFS being interpreted and implemented by the adults for children?

Although the content of the EYFS was reduced following the Tickell Review, a supporting document titled Development Matters (Early Education, 2012) was published. It is a non-statutory guidance which supports all those working in early years settings to implement the requirements of the statutory framework for the EYFS. Development Matters demonstrates how the four themes of the EYFS framework, and the principles that inform them, work together to support the development of babies, toddlers, and young children within the context of the framework. The document also illustrates how the CoETL may be supported and extended by adults, as well as how they underpin the 'prime' and 'specific' areas of learning and development.

All those working to support the early learning of young children use Development Matters as part of daily observation, assessment, and planning. It is also used at points during the EYFS as a guide to making best-fit summative judgements, with parents and colleagues across agencies, in relation to whether a child is showing typical development, may be at risk of delay, or is ahead for their age (Early Education, 2012). The document contains age/stage bands, which overlap because these are not fixed age boundaries but suggest a typical range of development. The creators of the document, the British Association of Early Education, stress that when using Development Matters it is important to remember that babies, toddlers, and young children develop at their own rates and in their own ways. The development statements and their order are not necessary steps for every child and should not be used as checklists.

 CONNECT

How is your setting currently using Development Matters?

Yet today, many settings have adapted the document as some form of tick list or checklist to measure children's learning and development against, for children to fit into, rather than it being about one aspect of a child's education. A checklist is a list of items required, things to be done, which then gives the impression that each box needs to be ticked in order for it to be complete. The interpretation and use of the document in this way implies that it is generic, one size fits all, and that children go through a sequential process. The individuality and uniqueness of each child, and what he or she brings to the process, are not considered. This is the danger of how a curriculum is open to interpretation by those using it. The focus needs to be on the curriculum fitting the child, not the child fitting the curriculum. As stated earlier, the EYFS framework is just one part of a broad and balanced curriculum for children. It is a framework, a support structure of information, designed to guide early years practice, but it is not set in stone in terms of *how* it is to be achieved. Its content is to be used and implemented, but flexibly, creatively, and with what the children bring to the process.

 RESEARCH TO EXPLORE
BORN CREATIVE (2010)

Ahead of the revised 2012 EYFS, a series of essays were released by leading thinkers in the field of early education, which reinforced that children with access to creativity in the early years are more likely to succeed in adult life by developing the skills they need to perform in the workplace and wider society, as entrepreneurs and citizens, than those children without. This ultimately identified creativity as an important dimension of the early years curriculum. It also reinforced the essential role of the creative adult in fostering creativity from the early years onwards.

Ornstein and Hunkins (2009) go on to suggest that although curriculum development models are technically useful, they often overlook human aspects such as personal attitudes, feelings, and values, which should all be involved in curriculum making. There should be a consideration of children's learning styles, social interactions, and personalities. There is also individuality in cultural and language backgrounds, life experiences, temperament, interests, skills, and talents, which a curriculum cannot capture. A curriculum is not a recipe and should not be used as a substitute for the adult's professional and personal judgement on what a good creative approach to enhancing learning ought to be. Practitioners need to gain professional autonomy, creativity, and flexibility in the use and implementation of the curriculum.

What is the creative curriculum?

There is no doubt a tension between the EYFS as a curriculum and the concept of a 'creative' curriculum. Early years practitioners are faced with the dilemmas of practice in terms of how the curriculum can be organised to stimulate creativity, and how they are meant to balance professional creativity and judgement against the requirements of the curriculum to teach in certain ways (Craft, 2003). Root-Bernstein and Root-Bernstein (2016) note that

> part of education is to pass on what we already know, but if we don't also make sure there's some part of our education that trains children to make new knowledge – how to take all that and go one step further, that's where we have a problem.
>
> (p. 202)

Many different interpretations exist for the concept of 'the creative curriculum'. In some settings, it means topics or themes; in others it means observing children and

CREATIVE CASE
A CURRICULUM IS ALL ME

Name: Christopher   **Role**: Head of Learning   **Location**: Children's Centre

In my first year of teaching about a decade ago, I was given very straightforward instructions for what I was to do. I was told to follow the curriculum, ensure that my children didn't disrupt the classroom, meet the standards for each subject, and make sure that the children passed the expected stages. To meet these goals, I was provided with a curriculum, policies and procedures, and prep materials, and was wished good luck.

For anyone on the outside looking in, all the materials I was given meant that I was well-prepared. Technically, I was given all that I needed to succeed. Unfortunately, none of the tools I was given considered the complexities of teaching that I faced once I entered the classroom. The curriculum was so scripted that it allowed little to no time or space for me to be **creative in teaching**. For children who asked a lot of questions, think deeply, and wanted to create a true connection to what was being taught, my teaching did not work. The script I was given was so structured that it forced me to ignore children who were asking brilliant questions.

The children quickly grew frustrated, and before long, became increasingly disengaged. As they grew more disengaged, they began to feel disconnected from the learning. Before long, their frustration turned into either behaviour problems or complete disinterest or behaviour problems. I still remember that day when 4-year-old Janet said to me, 'Why do I need to sit at the table to learn phonics?' It was an innocent question, but caused me to ask several in return to myself – *was a curriculum really all that children needed to learn? Could I not deviate and offer it in another way if I covered the basics? What is it that children need to know and do?* From this point, I started using my observations of the children to inform my teaching. Yes, I used the curriculum to ensure statutory content was covered, but how I presented learning and delivered teaching was down to what I knew about how children learned and approached their learning. **A curriculum is all me and what I bring to the learning.**

involving their voices in what they want to learn. In some, it is about investing heavily in the arts and music, whereas in others it is just about adding the word 'creative' in front of the title 'curriculum'. Critics of the creative curriculum dismiss it as lacking rigor and structure, thinking that it is about allowing children to roam around free to do as they please and day dream all day. Those in support of it reinforce that it is the best way to engage and motivate children in the learning process. There are also many settings and schools that have embraced the concept of a creative curriculum and shown innovation in their teaching by working with what they have.

   A curriculum is no longer something that can be created based on the previous traditions of education. As time and the needs of generations change, so does the concept of the curriculum. Thus, the curriculum is the knowledge, skills, strategies, dispositions, and concepts that children are to learn. Creativity is in the use and provision of the various approaches of teaching and learning. Together these form a 'creative curriculum' in which creative learning occurs. The creative curriculum gets beyond rote learning and focuses on big ideas, interesting projects/themes, and individual children's passions, needs, identities, and talents; these are all terms that are missing from a curriculum. One should not be thinking about eliminating the current curriculum, but rather about restructuring it to embed creativity – *how can this be achieved?* Ornstein and Hunkins (2009, p. 15) contend that curriculum development encompasses how a 'curriculum is planned, implemented and evaluated, as well as what people, processes and procedures are involved'.

Creating curriculum models should help adults to systematically and transparently map out the rationale for the use of particular creative teaching, creative learning, and creative assessment approaches. For creativity to flourish, and for children to realise their talents and potential, a well-planned curriculum is required, one with good effective creative approaches. However, a curriculum only truly emerges from the play of children and the play of adults. It is co-constructed by children and adults within the environment itself. It is not about having pre-planned goals and a checklist of what children must learn, because really, we don't know what the children will learn – but we can create the conditions for it. To develop a creative curriculum, adults must notice children's questions and invent ways to extend them, document what happens, and invent more questions (Jones, 2012, p. 67). This indicates that a creative curriculum is an ongoing process (not product) and a live document that needs to be constantly updated and reviewed as interactions in the setting unfold. *So, where do we start?*

 AROUND THE WORLD
FINLAND

In 2015, Finland embarked on one of the most radical education reform programmes ever undertaken by a nation state. Its Finnish Curriculum scrapped traditional 'teaching by subject' in favour of 'teaching by phenomena', a combination of different skills to teach a topic. The idea for the change was so it prepares children for the future with the skills that are needed for today and tomorrow. Finland stated that there is still teaching in the old-fashioned way in their schools that was of benefit at the beginning of the 1900s – but the needs are not the same and there is now a need for something fit for the twenty-first century (Khoo, 2015).

Not a single person I have met finds it easy to nurture and unleash their own creativity, let alone direct it into a curriculum. As adults, we have to deal with all sorts of fears that may keep us from being creative, including fear of change, fear of accepting failure, fear of rocking the boat, fear of standing out, fear of disappointing children, and fear of uncertainty. Working in an environment that does not value creativity is another huge mountain to climb. Having worked with hundreds of adults, I know from experience that discovering that we can actually begin to create is the real trigger. There are no magic wands and no easy tricks; there is no such thing as right or wrong, only having the ability to trust in the process. Having to form a creative curriculum from scratch can be a daunting process; a certain amount of bravery is required to take this step – and don't forget the support needed from your colleagues and other early years professionals. It is even more difficult if your current curriculum is based solely on the EYFS document, and this is all that one has to work with.

As a practitioner, you may have little control over course content, but that does not mean that you can't think outside the box with how you deliver it – the curriculum is the box to think outside of. If you expect change, then you will have to take the first step in what educationalist John Lear (2015) refers to as 'going guerrilla'! This means you have to take the fight underground and continue to do the best for children despite the constraints you are faced with. Here, I am not asking you to become all rebellious and get the children to stand on tables and strike, nor am I asking that you paint your face and wrap ties around your foreheads in an aim to ambush senior leaders! No, I'm asking you to work with what you can, which is very often possible within your own domains. Before attempting anything, though, a little reflection is required to interrogate your thinking around your current curriculum and around your present practice and understanding. Figure 6.2 is designed to help you start thinking about the basics that underpin a creative curriculum.

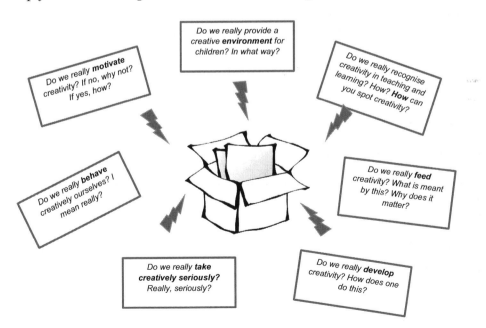

Figure 6.2 Questions to encourage self-reflection for designing a creative curriculum (Adapted from Ben Sandbrook, 2012)

Key question: *where are we currently allowing room for creativity in our curriculum?*

Constructing a creative curriculum

The most important aspect for any curriculum design is to remember that it involves seeing the big picture. The idea is that just about every element of a curriculum should be approached creatively, which becomes a hallmark of effective creative learning. A creative curriculum is one that incorporates big ideas and is varied, exciting, and engaging; all allow the nurturing of creativity's characteristics. There should also be a sense of continuity throughout it to stimulate children, practitioners, and families. It starts with how much we know our children and where we see the place of creativity in the curriculum and, ultimately, in their learning and lives.

 CONNECT

Are some areas of learning more creative than others? Is it possible to develop creativity in all areas?

While some areas of the curriculum are more inclined to consist of creativity's characteristics than others – for example, expressive arts and design – a creative curriculum acknowledges that it is not limited just to this area and must be developed in all areas: a holistic approach to creative learning. Developing a creative curriculum cannot be viewed as a project that has a start and an end. A creative curriculum should be viewed as a living, organic instrument to help adults and settings find optimal ways to educate children (Sahlberg, 2006, p. 8). It should not take much; it's not that you need to learn a whole course on creativity, but rather that you need to know what creative tendencies you want and need to keep alive in children (Epstein, 1996) – *what are these? Where does one start?* The EYFS stipulates what children must be able to do by the end of the foundation stage. Taking this content, it then provides rationales in terms of how children will be provided with provision and opportunities to reach these goals. These are discussed as follows.

The creative curriculum recognises children's creative lives – outside the setting, our creativity emerges in the situations we encounter or create in our daily lives. It is in our responses to challenges and opportunities that our creativity is required, applied, and revealed. By adopting a life-wide concept of education, which embraces all the spaces and places for learning and personal development of children's lives, the creative curriculum can do much more to recognise and value the creative development of the children it serves, rather than having an 'off the shelf' approach that offers the same content year on year. *How does the curriculum accommodate children's life-wide experiences and recognise their creativity in those experiences? Is there scope for developing this aspect in the curriculum experiences that follow?* These are questions to consider when focusing on the big picture.

RESEARCH TO EXPLORE
ANTICIPATING CURRICULUM CONNECTIONS

Katz and Helm (2011, p. 12) describe a series of phases adults may use to guide children's projects or investigations. One suggestion, once a possible topic emerges, is to have adults complete 'anticipatory webs' of possible questions, curriculum opportunities, resources, and field sites that may arise and support children's learning as part of the project.

Creating webs in this way can allow adults to make connections to the EYFS, as well as to any learning outcomes/benchmarks. It is a live, emergent curriculum approach.

The creative curriculum embodies children's voices – a creative curriculum has children's ownership and filters their voices into their own learning. This is a participatory approach. Involving children in the design of the learning, projects, and experiences that both fulfil curricular requirements and address children's interests and concerns is vital. Talking to, and observing, children to find out what their interests are and what they want to learn is a must in constructing a curriculum. However, with young children, the creative adult needs to develop an approach to listening, which means listening to children's thoughts, observing their thoughts in action, and analysing what theories, ideas, interests, questions, and answers they have. By doing this, practitioners are treating children's thoughts and their voices seriously and with respect.

The creative adult takes what is learnt from children's ideas and builds a curriculum around their interests. This should still cover all the essential skills they need: reading, writing, mathematics, scientific investigation, and much more. This approach to curriculum design creates children who are excited about learning and promotes a love for it. It creates dispositions towards listening and understanding children's curiosity as platforms to authentic teaching and learning . . . rather than seeing the curriculum narrowly (MacDonald, 2007).

The creative curriculum creates 'holistic experiences' – the creative curriculum is more than just areas of learning or subjects; it is about an entire experience for children. The result of experiences – good or bad – stay with children forever (Fisher, 2013, p. 4). We don't know where children's learning journeys will end, so we cannot predict what children will learn in advance, but we can offer experiences through the curriculum for them to experience, regardless of the outcomes. When devising a curriculum, you need to think of what experiences you want children to engage with throughout their time in the setting. It is this that will assist you in devising creative approaches and environments for the curriculum to be visible in the holistic experiences:

■ Create meaningful opportunities and spaces that foster curiosity, wonder, experimentation, and creativity

■ Facilitate children to creatively communicate thoughts, experiences, and points of view using many different forms of expression

■ Support children in listening to, attending to, recognising, and thinking with multiple others – other children, setting adults, parents, and beyond

■ Encourage exploration and thinking to identify and try possible solutions to problems in meaningful contexts, and experiment with creativity, spontaneity, and flexibility

■ Acknowledge and respond to the multiple ways in which children's creativity and explorations can be experienced and expressed and the diverse ways that children represent what they know in ways that are respectful of self, others, materials, and the environment

■ Provide access to, and engagement with, materials, places, community members, and other resources to support creative activities that are reflective of children's common worlds

■ With children, families, other educators, community members, and other resources, co-construct opportunities for children to build, design, create, and experiment with a broad range of multimodal materials through mediums such as music, song, stories, poetry, visual arts, dance, mathematical concepts, natural environments, and the dramatic arts.

■ Co-construct opportunities to experience and explore language learning through culturally appropriate and meaningful techniques and resources, including the stories and symbols of their own and other cultures.

■ Support children in acquiring and differentiating multiple meanings in concepts, seeing interconnections, and discovering new ways of understanding their surrounding world.

(adapted from The Early Childhood
Pedagogies Collaboratory, 2017)

 CONNECT

Where can you connect these experiences to the requirements of the EYFS in Figure 6.1?

The creative curriculum is underpinned by early years pedagogic approaches – derived from the Greek (paidagogos, παιδαγωγός = to lead and guide the child), pedagogy is known as the art or science of educating children. This means the process of teaching and learning, how children are guided, and how learning and development are facilitated and supported by the adult. Pertrie et al. (2009) define it as education in the broadest sense of the word, where care and education meet and which concerns upbringing, child-rearing, nurturing, socialisation, and the support of learning and development. It is a holistic approach in working with children, with practitioner roles embedded in it as the 'pedagogue'.

Underpinning the creative curriculum are the pedagogical approaches that will nurture and support children's experiences, lives, and voices, the knowledge, skills and understandings they will develop, and how they will progress. A creative curriculum makes transparent what approaches to children's experiences of learning it will adopt and use. This becomes the ethos, philosophy, and shared understanding amongst the setting practitioners, and is visible in all that they do and say. Pascal and Bertram (2017b) mention four pedagogical approaches for the early years: 'play-based', 'child-initiated', 'relational', and 'participatory'. I will endeavour to provide an explanation for each one.

- **Play-based pedagogies** – we know that children 'learn through play'; they use it as a medium for exploring and manipulating their physical environment. Play allows children to explore, identify, negotiate, take risks, and create meaning. It is through this context for learning that children organise and make sense of their social worlds, as they actively use their senses to engage with people, objects, experiences, and representations. It is also fact that research on playful pedagogy points continually to better learning outcomes for young children (Hirsh-Pasek et al., 2009). Within a play-based pedagogy, the play is co-constructed between practitioners and children, where the practitioner interacts in playful ways with the children (Goouch, 2008). The intention is to shape curriculum outcomes without 'formal' approaches, instead shaping through creative and innovative ways both teaching and learning.

- **Child-initiated pedagogies** – the EYFS guides state that each area of learning and development must be implemented through planned, purposeful *play*, and through a mix of adult-led and 'child-initiated' activity. Child-initiated pedagogy, then, is about recognising and respecting children's individual and collective views, interests, and motivations in their learning. This occurs by shaping curriculum experiences and approaches to allow children to choose their own pursuits and learning explorations, take ownership of planned activities and adapt them to their own purposes, and incorporate their own experiences into the many learning opportunities provided (Kinos et al., 2016). Practitioners take forward and facilitate what the children initiate in their learning.

- **Relational pedagogies** – treat relationships as the foundation of teaching and learning by placing strong emphasis on, nurturing, and developing them. Relational pedagogies focus on the connections between people, ideas, and places, and place communication, interactions, and dialogue at the core of educational practice that underpins social, cognitive, and therefore creative development of children (Papatheodorou and Moyles, 2009). These connections/relationships are reciprocal between the practitioners, children, parents, families, and communities; it is where 'relationships and learning coincide' (Malaguzzi, 1998, p. 66).

- **Participatory pedagogies** – building on the child as a competent and active agent in their learning, this pedagogy is about children participating in their learning where they are acknowledged, listened to, and involved. Children are enabled, by the adult, to participate in decision-making processes, respected, given a voice, and supported on the ideas they initiate (Sinclair, 2004). Participation can be seen as a common activity to interpret the world with early years practitioners who respect and listen to children and are interested in their affairs. This means that children are listened to and have an opportunity for independent initiatives, choice-making experiences, and chances to take responsibility (Kangas, 2016).

 OBSERVE

Your setting. How are these four pedagogical approaches visible?

'Creative pedagogies', then, become an amalgamation of all four, where creativity's characteristics interplay in how children learn. Lin (2011) describes creative pedagogy as about creative teaching, teaching for creativity, and creative learning. 'Creative learning' is an essential part of creative pedagogy since its focus is on children's action, and it embraces children's intrinsic curiosity. 'Creative teaching' focuses on teaching and practitioner actions. Lin (2011) refers to creative teaching as a creative, innovative, and imaginative approach to teaching in the moment and acting spontaneously. The practitioner may have planned the activity one way, but a creative practitioner has the courage to take the ideas that have arisen from the children and change the activity to finish it in another way (Sawyer, 2006). 'Teaching for creativity' considers the significance of a creativity-supporting environment (Lin, 2011). The environment denotes both the external and social contexts that support and inspire learning. It is where the environment nurtures and stimulates characteristics and abilities for creativity. Teaching for creativity encourages children to ask questions, argue, discuss their thoughts, and actively engage in their own learning; it aims for creative learning and the development of a creative person (Craft, 2005).

There is no doubt that all five pedagogical approaches must underpin the devising, implementing, and maintaining of the creative curriculum. In 2010, the Effective Provision of Pre-School Education (EPPE) longitudinal study concluded that there is not 'one' effective pedagogy; instead, the effective pedagogue 'orchestrates' pedagogy by making interventions (scaffolding, discussions, monitoring) which are sensitive to the curriculum concept or skill being taught, taking into account the child's 'zone of proximal development'. I argue that the early years practitioners must know, identify, and recognise quality pedagogic approaches that exist, and be able to 'orchestrate' by drawing from them when interacting with children.

IDEA
SKILLS PROGRESSION GRIDS

If changes can't be made to the curriculum, why not take on John Lear's suggestion of creating 'skills progression grids' for each area of learning? Going through this process means that, alongside the EYFS, adults (and leaders) have a clear understanding of which skills to include where, and how these skills are developed throughout the experiences provided to children. These can then be filtered into the planning formats.

The creative curriculum makes transparent, alongside the EYFS content, what skills and characteristics it intends to develop; including creativity's characteristics in the curriculum is a helpful starting point for them to be taken seriously in settings. Early years practitioners are familiar with various creative skills and characteristics; however, they rarely think of them as creativity, or combine them for a creative purpose. When designing learning, you need to think in terms of what you want children to be able to know and do after it is over. *Why are these pieces of knowledge or skills important?* If you can't answer this question, then you need to start again. Day-to-day planning falls into place much more easily once you have sketched out the big picture; it's almost a backward design to curriculum, where you start at the end and work backwards to think about what particular activities and experiences will start moving children. If you don't have a big picture or end goal in mind, you may lose track of your own purpose. If you don't know where you're going, it's really difficult to help the children get there! Figure 6.1 gives you what the educational programmes for children must involve. Start by mapping creativity's characteristics to it – *how can you use creativity's characteristics?* – this will help you visualise what skills, behaviours, and attitudes you want children to develop overall, which can then filter into individual planning – *what's the big picture?*

The creative curriculum is visible in practice – once there is a clear idea of the experiences, skills, knowledge and understandings, and pedagogical approaches that the creative curriculum intends to embed, it then becomes about how these are visible in practice through the environment, through the learning opportunities children will receive, through the interactions and dialogues, and so on. For example, the creative curriculum may intend for children to *imagine and create, master skills, have meaningful experiences, express their thoughts and ideas, solve problems, engage in thinking,* and *explore diverse ways of knowing, thinking and learning.* This is the overall big picture. *How is this then visible?*

In practice, this may be:

- Through the environment by providing open-ended materials

- Active learning opportunities through play, imagination, and creativity

- Flexible seating

- Allowing children to feel a sense of ownership and responsibility for their environment

- Letting them choose how they approach their learning

 ACTIVITY

Using Figure 6.1, mark where you see the connections of these examples discussed in how the creative curriculum looks in practice.

What else can you come up with?

Through learning opportunities, this may be:

- Teaching children techniques

- Ensuring sensory experiences

- Providing opportunities to explore and experiment

- Use a range of books, sources, and other media texts

- Allowing time

- Integrating music

- Adopting a creative approach to routines, for example lunch times as a restaurant

- Opportunities for children to collaborate with each other

Through interactions, it may be visible through:

- Encouraging children to pursue their ideas

■ Interpretations and expressions

■ Involving children in reflection and solving problems

■ Collaborating

■ Allowing children to make mistakes and see it as new learning

■ Modelling

■ Asking open-ended questions

■ Encouraging children to ask questions

■ Encouraging initiative

■ Encouraging children to have a go

■ Commenting to help children progress

These examples become basics of a creative curriculum as it unfolds and develops on a day-to-day basis through the child and adult interactions. It is about how the curriculum will look in practice. Documentation becomes the key to adding to and changing it as experiences and learning take place.

The creative curriculum embeds live documentation – this means scribbling notes, making mental notes, and taking photos, images, and videos of the children as they convey their theories, misconceptions, ideas, interests, and talents through discussion and play. It adds to the curriculum as a live process. By observing and documenting, further ideas of how the creative curriculum is visible in practice and interplays – together with what pedagogical approaches facilitate it – can bring further ideas into light which can then be added to the environment, learning opportunities, interactions, and what you intend the creative curriculum to do as an experience. It also keeps the focus on the now for children, rather than the previous.

Next steps

 REFLECT

1) Does the purpose of education change from the EYFS to the Primary phase? If so, why? And in what ways? How does this then impact the notion of a creative curriculum?

2) What other pedagogical approaches do you know of and can you use in your approaches?

EXPLORE

Lifting the Lid on the Creative Curriculum (2007): http://dera.ioe.ac.uk/7340/1/down load%3Fid%3D17281%26filename%3Dlifting-the-lid-on-the-creative-curriculum-full-report.pdf

■ Innovative cases of leaders embedding creativity through curriculum ownership.

Born Creative: www.creativitycultureeducation.org/born-creative

■ A series of essays placing creativity in the curriculum.

The Creative Curriculum for Preschool: A Touring Guide: https://teachingstrategies. com/wp-content/uploads/2016/07/The-Creative-Curriculum-for-Preschool-Touring-Guide.pdf

■ A 60-page colourful document with more ideas for a creative curriculum.

Ornstein, A., & Hunkins, F. (2009) Curriculum Design. In Curriculum: Foundations, Principles and Issues (5th Ed.): https://talkcurriculum.files.wordpress.com/2014/09/ ornstein-a-hunkins-f-2009-curriculum-design1.pdf

Tech tools

How they do it in Sweden Pre-schools: www.teachingchannel.org/videos/examining-pre-school-curriculum

■ A wonderful video demonstrating the curriculum in practice underpinned by play.

Creative Curriculum podcasts: www.hays.co.uk/podcast/education/creative-curriculum/

■ A series of podcasts by leading thinkers around creative schools.

Teaching Strategies: https://teachingstrategies.com/

■ Digital tools, resources, and support for practice.

7 Creative planning and assessment

THINK

How does planning inform children's creative learning?

How is creativity assessed, and against what?

CHAPTER FOCUS

■ Exploring the purpose of planning: long, medium, and short-term

■ Planning approaches suited to the early years to capture and nurture creativity – cross-curricular, emergent, and 'in the moment'

■ Assessing for creativity through the formative tool of observations

Children and adults alike are ongoing learners, and we all develop and learn in different ways. The cycle of planning and assessment helps early years practitioners to purposefully support children's continual creative learning and design meaningful learning opportunities. To do this, adults need to observe children and collate evidence to then plan the environment, resources, teaching strategies, and effective ways to monitor and assess children's learning. It is where the development of creativity across the curriculum can happen. When done well, the quality of the learning experience is enhanced, and of course, it plays a vital role in sparking the creative process for the practitioner. It's where the birth pangs of creativity start when thinking about creative approaches. This chapter will both explore the role of planning and assessment and provide some creative approaches for you to consider and adopt.

Planning

Why does one plan? It's a simple question, but do we actually sit and think about it? There are various reasons, such as planning being the 'cornerstone' or 'foundation' of learning. The EYFS describes planning as adults considering the individual needs, interests, and stage of development of each child in their care, and using this information to *plan* a challenging and enjoyable experience for each child in all areas of learning and development. This, in a way, makes planning statutory, but, the question remains: *what is planning?* Planning is the process of deciding in detail how to do something before you actually start to do it. It implies that it is created before the event, or in this case, before the teaching and learning of children. In settings, planning normally takes the format of a document to be completed as a result of a planning meeting amongst practitioners, which includes the creative curriculum and what is known about children and their creative learning.

 DISCUSS

With peers/colleagues how they perceive the role of planning in their day-to-day work. What are the benefits? What are the challenges?

Planning is one of many creative tools for early years practitioners, used to ensure that creative teaching and learning are at the heart of practice. Traditionally, planning takes content from the curriculum as a means through which learning is devised and delivered, and knowledge and skills are developed progressively. In the previous chapter, we explored the creative curriculum as the big picture, but planning is what sets it into motion. Planning is where the curriculum is modified to fit the unique characteristics of the children, through the resources the setting has. It is a merging of the curriculum with children's individual needs and interests, and where they are in their learning; this cannot be taken from a curriculum in advance and therefore needs to be 'planned' for.

Planning should and must develop learning and ensure progression. It needs to have an impact on children; otherwise its purpose is futile. It is the 'key to making children's learning effective, exciting, varied and progressive' (DCSF, 2008, p. 12) and, of course, creative! However, my work with many adults over the years, and till this day, has revealed that, at times, they feel documentation is onerous and time consuming. They are caught up in what documentation of planning should look like rather than knowing or understanding the requirements. When we think about planning, we should be thinking that documentation is only one part of the process. The focus should be on gathering, analysing, and interpreting information to implement in practice. So, *what does a good plan look like? How do you know whether your plan is effective or not? And does a plan need to be in a written format?*

ACTIVITY

Think of a time you entered an activity session or lesson with a hastily written plan or no plan at all.

■ How did you feel?

■ How would it have been improved with more thorough planning?

Types of planning

There are three types of traditional planning formats in education, known as long-, medium-, and short-term plans. Figure 7.1 outlines the current role of each one.

Long	Medium	Short
Annual plan.	Termly or monthly plan.	Weekly or daily plans.
Covers all EYFS areas.	Could be a detailed plan for each learning and development area.	Draws from long-term and medium-term plans.
Includes seasonal, festive, and other planned events that occur during the year.	Outlines planned activities and resources that may be needed.	Takes account of individual children needs and is responsive to their ideas and spontaneous play.
Informs medium-term plans.	The learning outcomes that are intended.	Sets learning outcomes.

Figure 7.1 Types of planning

 ACTION RESEARCH

Get hold of a setting or schools planning cycle – long, medium, and short term.

■ How do adults use these plans in children's learning?

■ Are creativity's characteristics evident in the long- and medium-term plans?

■ If not, can you connect them by using Work Tools 1 to 4?

Long-term and medium-term planning are implemented into settings in a variety of ways. Long-term planning may look at the learning opportunities for the whole year; this may include setting up the learning environment indoors and outdoors, organising areas of provision, deciding on core equipment, making decisions about regular routines, and devising a strategy to ensure coverage of the seven areas of learning and development. This can be challenging; planning should be adaptable and not planned months in advance, as the needs of the setting and children change and evolve all the time. Bearing this in mind, some settings look closely at their areas of provision, both indoors and outdoors, and regularly monitor and evaluate these as part of their medium- and short-term planning. By doing so, adults enhance the areas based on the children's interests and adapt environments accordingly for creativity to be nurtured. The following advises on how each of these traditional plans can be approached.

Long-term planning

■ Is the creative curriculum and all its requirements discussed in the previous chapter – holistic experiences, pedagogical approaches, the skills and understandings you wish to develop alongside the EYFS.

■ Outlines all the aims and objectives that the setting or school intends to achieve and sets out their core philosophy. For example, what will the child gain at your setting or become? A well-rounded creative individual who fulfils their potential? How will this happen? What will need to happen?

■ Includes how you will organise your environment and the strategies you will use to support learning. How do you perceive creative teaching and learning? And how will this be visible in practice? What will your environment look like? How will children use them? Think Chapter 3 – what children learn in the forms of dispositions, strategies, concepts, and skills.

■ Includes holistic types of knowledge, skills, and understanding you wish the children to gain throughout their time at your setting or school, not just what the EYFS framework states. This means that they are not divided into categories, and are a reflection of what the adults in the setting want children to gain by the time they leave or move on to the next stage.

■ Collates the everyday routines like snack times, transitions, group reflections, circle times, story session, and explains how each of these items map to the standards you are following, i.e. the EYFS, the creative curriculum, and creativity's characteristics.

■ Can become a core document and be referred to if settings are asked how they fulfil criteria by regulating bodies such as Ofsted – for example, keeping children safe.

Medium-term planning

- Based on children's observations that have been collated over time, this can be an overview plan of opportunities for exploring projects and interconnecting themes. This incorporates genuine interests or explorations communicated by children in their various forms during their creative learning that warrant detailed planning.

- May include a list of resources to be collected, or a description of some of the key materials within different areas of learning that the setting will provide. These should be everchanging.

- Can highlight key skills to be developed, as well as creativity's characteristics – for example opportunities to imagine, explore, and investigate (these will likely come from observations) – and can fit with a project the setting is following.

- Daily/weekly schedules could also form a part of medium-term plans, and stories or songs that the setting plans to share.

Short-term planning

Short term planning, sometimes known as weekly planning, brings together a collection of children's individual observations, group observations, children's interests, and parent contributions. It draws on elements from the EYFS and creative curriculum, as well as the long- and medium-term plans. It is a joint record of what you observe the children doing, their fascinations, questions they are asking, and their clear patterns of play. An analysis of this data (what learning is taking place?) is then used to determine what will happen next. *How might you encourage those interests further? How could you encourage the interests to be more complex? How could you bring that interest into other areas of learning/ activities?*

FACT NOTE
LAY DOWN!

Joydeep Bhattacharya of Goldsmiths University in London has shown that people in a relaxed mood are more likely to arrive at **creative solutions** when problem-solving. Another study by Australian researchers showed people are more likely to solve puzzles lying on their back than standing up. Perhaps it's because when people are mellow, their wandering mind encourages them to review a diverse array of ideas, rather than get stuck in a more focused, narrow mode of thought. *Go on, lay down and start planning!*

- These plans could be daily or weekly records of what is provided in the environment, and the adults' role within it.

- These plans should be simple and flexible so they can be changed and adapted easily according to the learning that is unfolding.

Every setting and school develops their own planning system, and there is no one format or anything set in stone. However, there are some similarities in terms of the content which have proven to assist in planning effectively; these are shared in Work Tool 8. This can be used in those settings and schools where devising plans in advance is necessary. They are prompts to help you think about what you are planning and why. The Work Tool is vital for students, as they will be new to practice and therefore need to master skills in written planning first. It is not intended to be more paperwork or a tick box exercise. It is about using the prompts to activate your creative thinking to form ideas for teaching creatively and children's creative learning.

Skills required to plan effectively take time to develop. Those new to it, or in their early days, will evolve as they become more experienced and knowledgeable. They will find themselves moving from planning individual activities, to planning a sequence of activities and projects. More experienced practitioners will be able to plan in no time; however, the challenge is *do they plan for creativity's characteristics in their activities? And do they actually look for them during children's learning?* Even though they may not be planned for, activities, lessons, and observations of children in child- or adult-led play often contain examples of creativity's characteristics being used. They just need to be identified and nurtured.

Planning in advance

 CREATIVE CASE
PLANNING DOCUMENTS

Name: Maureen   **Role**: Tutor   **Location**: FE College

Afiz is on a two-year childcare programme at the college. This is his final year and I have been allocated as his placement tutor to observe him in practice. Afiz submitted a lesson plan for an experience that he intended to introduce to children in pre-school.

He planned to read a story about a baby bird and have the children colour a line drawing of a baby bird breaking through a shell. To complete their picture, he planned for the children to paste different coloured shell fragments to the page. He wanted to make sure that the project would be sent home with the children at the end of the day 'so the family could see what the child was learning at pre-school'. In preparation for the lesson, he planned to dye several dozen eggs the night before the lesson 'to make it easier and give the children a choice of colour to make their picture'.

When I asked Afiz to reflect on the content and teaching approaches in his plan, he responded by saying the lesson was 'hands-on', and he thought that the children would have fun pasting the egg shells. I had several reactions to Afiz's response, the first of which was, 'But, what did the children learn as a result of the experience, or how did the experience maximise opportunities for teaching creatively and children's creativity? But also, how were children going to use their imagination and creative thinking with these ready-made possibilities?'

Planning in the early years needs creative thinking. Very often early years practitioners grab wordings from the EYFS and put them up as a result of meeting the needs or settings protocol. Learning outcomes or objectives are also just a copy of terms from the EYFS, with little attention to what they actually mean to children's learning. It is often vague, and does not show any relation to the big picture. This is because planning seems to be a draining task to many, and another 'thing to do', but also as per Afiz's story, an underestimation of children's creative abilities, with too much care and attention on resources rather than the process of 'learning', and what he himself may know about the children. Creativity's characteristics are seldom incorporated into planning or even assessing children's progression against them, because as always, other objectives take priority. Adults also do not pinpoint creativity's characteristics, even though they are apparent. Thinking about planning for creativity is only about enhancing the process further – *how would you plan Afiz's intentions to ensure creative learning and teaching creatively?*

 **CONNECT**

How can you use the approaches in Chapter 5 to assist in creative ideas for planning?

Planning should excite us and not be an exhausting task that needs to be completed. When sitting down and thinking about what you are going to do, ideas strike – *how can I engage children in their learning? What is the expectations of the adult? What are the expectations of the children? What will happen? How will it happen?* By answering these questions, and utilising the approaches for creative adults in Chapter 5, you give way to experiencing the birth pangs of creativity and the unlimited possibilities within teaching and learning, just like the children. This is exactly what the planning process is about. It gets you thinking; your imagination is aroused to think of the possibilities, and to then explore those that can be turned into a reality.

A note of caution, though; when planning, excitement of creative opportunities can often get us carried away. Many can be fun and exciting, but may not necessarily promote learning. While exciting and fun is a must, learning is challenging and needs to be underpinned by a clear rationale. The term 'effective planning' makes it implicit that planning has to be effective for children's learning. Teaching does not necessarily equal learning, and planning requires careful thought to ensure that what adults do in their activities/lessons supports and promotes learning, and enables children to make progress (Sewell, 2015, p. 11) – but creatively, of course!

Successful planning involves thinking about the relationship between the environment and individual activities/lessons, the children, and longer-term outcomes from the big picture of the creative curriculum. Too frequently activities fail because they have been designed backwards, i.e. resources, activities, learning intentions, and then success criteria. There is a necessity to planning in the opposite way, i.e. children's ideas and interests, their current abilities and knowledge, their thoughts, success criteria, learning intentions, activities and experiences that will deepen thinking, and resources. Planning should generate a learning environment in which children can ask questions, make suggestions, explore differing approaches and ideas, and manage their own learning through the available resources – this is where creativity is cultivated.

❗ STORY FROM PRACTICE
● STAFF PLANNING SESSION

I had the pleasure of staying back at a Children's Centre one night to sit in on a planning session. At first, my thoughts were that it is 6pm on a Wednesday, staff will be tired, and will they really be in the mood for this? I was surprised to hear that this meeting took place weekly in the evenings; tea and coffee flowed, and snacks were provided. I walked into a room where there were conversations flowing to find some staff sprawled across the sofas, others on the floor sitting on bright cushions or laying on their front with arms raised to their faces, chin in hand. The manager was perched on a table against a massive wall covered in blank paper. All of a sudden, a cushion hit me in the face, a staff member told me to sit down, I joined them on the floor. I wasn't sure what to do with my long legs, so I chose the safer option, which was to cross them.

Discussions were taking place about individual children and what had happened so far during the week, including last week. There were giggles and laughter about what some children had said or done. Ideas were being formed and recorded in large on the blank wall. Some staff drew pictures to represent their ideas. There were debates and discussions. The manager asked the staff to think of what knowledge, skills, and attitudes they wanted children to develop through the activities. These were represented in large on different coloured post-it notes pinned to the wall. Then, using another colour, skills were mapped – thinking, creating, problem-solving, asking questions, trial and error, and much more.

I went away with the thought that adults must plan together in developing creativity's characteristics which help children learn better, no matter what is being taught. There was so much fizz around the room, and planning is also about encouraging children to generate fizz and take it forward.

Planning approaches for the early years

In the early years, planning tends to be holistic and aimed towards individuals: their skills, their interests, and their capabilities. Therefore, there is much more potential to develop creativity, though only a few plan specifically for this. There are various planning approaches that are more suited to the early years than the normal planning in advance documentation.

 RESEARCH TO EXPLORE
LEARNING DESIGNERS OF EXPERIENCES

Dr James Paul Gee (2011) states that human beings learn from experiences – our brains can store every experience we've had, and that's what informs our learning process. Following that logic, he says, the best kind of learning comes as a result of well-designed experiences.

Adults in settings and schools need to redefine themselves as 'learning designers'. Game designers create well-designed experiences and social interactions. Adults are 'designers of learning' and can create experiences tailored to suit their outcome: creative learning. If we 're-professionalise' adults as designers, they can create their own scripts of what they want children to learn.

Cross-curricular planning – when the skills, knowledge, and attitudes of a number of different areas of learning/subjects are applied to a single experience/ activity/ lesson, theme, or idea, it is called working in a cross-curricular way (Barnes, 2007). This way is regarded as a creative approach to curriculum planning. Planning in this way encourages children to make connections across areas/ subjects and to draw on a range of approaches in learning and make connections. The connection is between the prior knowledge and skills children hold to the new information being taught and learnt holistically. Cross-curricula approaches are believed to open up the curriculum, to ensure greater breadth and balance (Driscoll, 2012). It intends to cater for all learning styles of the creative child by addressing them, whilst the need for children to make connections in their learning is being met (Barnes, 2011). However, a word of caution: cross-curricular planning must ensure that the distinctiveness of each area of learning is not diminished by another, that equal weighting is given to all areas combined in an activity/lesson and experiences.

A key success to cross-curricular planning is the unlimited collaboration with your tribe, but also beyond your tribe to the tribe of other areas and departments in your setting or school. It just takes a swim across the hall to collaborate with another adult from a different area of specialism. Early years adults can collaborate with colleagues from science, maths, and literacy disciplines, where they can find common topics and themes to plan jointly rather than separately. Many settings and schools are time-poor and financially strapped. If we share what we teach, observe other's techniques, and recognise through this where there is a repetition of learning, then we may just rule out presenting children the same thing each year. Whether inside or outside the setting, every aspect of every field is connected to every other. Find these connections and you find the means of making learning real, making it creative.

 **CONNECT**

Where is cross-curricular and emergent planning visible in your setting?

Emergent planning – created in the 1960s by Loris Malaguzzi, the Italian Reggio Emilia pre-school ideal has become a world-renowned model of the documentation of children's active learning at play and work, and an emergent curriculum built on the strengths of the child (Jones, 2012). Emergent planning, sometimes referred to as emergent curriculum, is defined as a process where adults plan activities and projects based on the specific group of children they are working with at that particular time, taking into account their skills, needs, and interests in the present. It 'emerges' from the children, from their interactions, from their experiences. The adult considers all that he/she knows about each individual and the particular group of children he/she teaches and then plans accordingly. In this approach, the creative adult and child are co-constructors of learning; short-term planning is the key. It happens all the time in the early years – maybe not in writing, but physically when adults build on what the children say and do throughout the day. Although the creative curriculum is the big picture, emergent planning allows adults to really 'listen' to children and use what is learnt to build a bridge between the creative curriculum and children's interests. Emergent planning therefore focuses on the process of learning, rather than just the products of it.

A key aspect of this approach is the use of planning conversations with young children to gain ideas and understand their thinking. As this book is about creativity, 'creative conversations' are more suited! Creative conversations normally start with capturing an interest from a child or group of children:

■ An interest that has been observed by the adult is used to engage the children as a springboard for discussion. Often children will bring in objects of interest from home, such as a book, a favourite toy, or an item from the outdoors. Adults may also choose to introduce a topic using a stimulus object, e.g. a bird's nest, something from the local environment, or a letter in the mail.

■ It is then about what children already know about the interest/stimulus. Children are invited to share their knowledge of the topic and pose thought provoking questions – 'I wonder how?', 'What might happen if?', 'What could we use to?' – to stimulate interest and activate possibility thinking and imagination. Children can be encouraged to represent their thoughts visibly by drawing, telling, building, constructing, and much more. Adults here need to tap into the many forms of communication and interaction that children exhibit.

■ As the above is happening, adults are recording ideas and suggestions on a whiteboard or paper, making a list of questions, or creating an ideas web. Each of these tools enables children's ideas to be recorded simply, added to, or referred to over a few days, or even weeks. These ideas are very much part of the creative process. Representing children's thinking in written form or through drawings also helps children to see that their ideas are valued, and that writing and drawing have a purpose and can convey meaning. In addition, parents, families, and carers can see the kinds of learning experiences the children are engaging in, and add to it!

■ It is then about how adults take these creative conversations forward through short-term planning. It may require research on their part (books, other people, research) to find out more and to refine it in order to offer children all the possible experiences as a result of these emergent creative conversations.

 AROUND THE WORLD
NEW ZEALAND

In the New Zealand curriculum, Te Whāriki ('planning') is used to describe the sum total of the experiences, activities, and events, whether direct or indirect, which occur within an environment designed to foster children's learning and development. These experiences, activities, and events may be based on forward planning or may evolve in response to a particular situation.

'In the moment' planning – in 2009, National Strategies, which are professional programmes that aim for improvements in the quality of learning and teaching, published a document titled *Learning, Playing and Interacting*. Within this, the concept of 'moment-by-moment' emerged. The document made a case for how planning in the early years is very different to what may be expected in schools. It stated that babies and young children experience and learn in the here and now, not storing up their questions until tomorrow or next week. It is in that moment of curiosity, puzzlement, effort, or interest – the 'teachable moment' – that the skilful adult makes a difference. This is achieved by using a model to observe, assess, and respond on a moment-by-moment basis:

- The adult will always be alert to individual children (*observation*)

- Always thinking about what it tells us about the child's thinking (*assessment*)

- Always ready to respond by using appropriate strategies at the right moment to support children's well-being and learning (*responding/planning for the next moment*)

(pp. 22–23)

'In the moment' planning is a child-led approach. The term planning implies it is written down and created in advance; in this case, *adults do not plan ahead*, but rather remain 'in the moment' with the children as they explore and learn. 'In the moment' planning is where early years practitioners do not spend time writing down what they plan to do with the children, or detailing focus activities and their requirements. The practitioner observes carefully and enhances the learning whenever they spot a 'teachable moment'. Practitioner observations, interactions, and the outcomes are recorded afterwards. For many practitioners working in the early years, this type of planning is simple and effective as it reduces their own anxieties about 'what to plan', and allows those crucial moments to be captured and extended there and then rather than introducing these as next steps in a week or two. The following quote reinforces this:

> When children are playing and selecting what to do themselves, they become deeply engaged. While this is happening, the adults should be observing and *waiting* for a moment in which they feel they can make a difference. They should then interact to 'teach' the 'next step' as appropriate for that unique child at that precise moment. Each time they interact with a child, they are observing, assessing, *planning for*, and responding to, that individual child. Such interactions are the most important and powerful teaching moments.
>
> (Ephgrave, 2017)

This is child-led and real-time planning. Children's current interests are identified regularly and practitioners can plan and evaluate from moment by moment as opposed to week by week. Enhancing and nurturing creativity's characteristics can also be more effective in a moment by moment response than waiting a while. Early years practitioners understand what the children enjoy, are interested and engaged in, and plan an active learning environment that supports this. It is the children that give the adults the ideas and possibilities. Adults then create core provision plans for the environment, for these 'in the moment' 'teachable moments' to take place in, which offers the children core elements of creative learning. This can be achieved through consulting the curriculum and creativity's characteristics, which can shape the provision on offer. Both indoor and outdoor environments must be reviewed regularly through planning to ensure they are adapted to meet the children's level of involvement in their learning. The environment needs to be engaging, stimulating, and contain plenty of resources for this approach to work. An in-depth discussion of the environment follows in Chapter 8.

A child-led approach to creative learning is of importance. At the same time, however, it is important that adults incorporate teachable moments that they would like the children to learn; this can be adult-led, creating a balance of both adult- and child-led activities. Teachable moments are also about recognising that children often learn in an unconscious way during casual or less formal interactions. Adults have to make instant decisions like these – what does the child need from me now? – every moment of their working day. Knowing children well enables the adults to choose the right strategy at the right moment (Fisher, 2013).

 **CONNECT**

What are 'child-led' and 'adult-led' approaches in early years environments?

When it comes to 'in the moment' planning, it can be difficult to provide for, or recognise and take advantage of, individual 'teachable moments' as you are looking for opportunities to allow learning to take place through child-initiated play. However, here are some approaches to help you with this:

- Provide opportunities and environments that stimulate curiosity (each child will have different things that stimulate them).

- Provide children with the opportunity to choose of their own accord with what or where they will play instead of being told or focused by the adult on what they should do.

- When you engage with the child, go to the child to enquire about the activity, rather than calling the child to you. This shows your curiosity and enthusiasm about what the child is doing.

- Observe and listen closely so you can follow the child's lead.

- Pick up on the thing/place/person/idea that has sparked the child's interest.

- Use open-ended questions that ask for a description, rather than a yes/no or other single word answer – these usually start with what/how/why, rather than do/is/can – (*'What do you like about that?' rather than 'Do you like that?'*).

- Praise and reinforce positive learning experiences.

Clary (2017) advocates that 'in the moment' planning starts with the child. The children throw us an idea; we think about it and toss it back to them from a new angle or in a more exciting way, and this back and forth continues as we learn and develop together, nurturing creativity. She advocates starting with the child:

- What are the children learning and what do they already know?

- Why are the children learning (interests and fascinations)?

- How are the children learning?

- Which resources/materials do they find motivating?

- What is my role as the adult in extending this learning? What resources can I provide? How should I present them? How could I present this learning in a different context? What questions could I develop further?

 ACTIVITY

Can you give an example of your own planning 'in the moment'?

What did you observe?

What did it tell you about the child/children?

What strategies did you use to respond to make it a teachable moment?

Planning is just one of the many tools of the creative adult which has importance in how creative learning experiences for the children are devised and offered. It is how it is implemented in practice that is the key to creative teaching approaches. Adults who implement 'in the moment' planning will gain a stronger understanding of the child's knowledge, skills, and level of progress. For children, this will create more opportunities for making progress in one or several areas of the EYFS and developing creativity's characteristics. Crucial elements to 'in the moment' planning are quality interactions from adults, creative conversations, clear observations, and effective ways of extending children's thinking. An important point about 'in the moment' planning is to remember when planning in this way that the practitioner's role is not to let children do as they wish. The practitioner's role is to reflect on how the children learn, interact with the children, and work as part of a team that shares ideas for the benefit of the children and their creative learning.

 OBSERVE

Peers/colleagues/students. How do they identify and provide for the teachable moments?

Creative assessment

No matter how carefully we plan and implement experiences, what children learn cannot be predicted with certainty. It is through assessment that adults can discover whether the experiences and provision that the children engaged with did actually result in any kind of learning. Assessment, then, is the bridge between teaching and learning (William, 2013). It is where the impact on learning and progression is known and supported further. *What progress did children make? What knowledge and skills did they exhibit? How did each child approach their learning? Where were creativity's characteristics visible? What does this tell me about the children? What does this tell me about my planning and teaching approaches?* Let's be clear when using the word 'assessment'. Assessment does not equal marking, nor is it just about providing a judgement at the end of a particular teaching and learning experience. They are different, but build upon each other. Assessment in itself is a process where the many forms of it interweave with each other:

Marking is checking, correcting, and giving a mark or comments on 'work' children produce, whether written, pictorial, or in concrete form. Often regarded as being used in the 'end product' of learning, it is merely a snapshot of each child's content knowledge and understanding. Marking is often an offshoot of what is known as 'summative' assessment.

Diagnostic assessment happens at the planning stage to enable decisions about how to approach teaching. Children's current level of learning is considered here: what content have they already mastered, what knowledge and skills they hold, what they will need to do to be successful in the planned approaches.

Formative assessment happens during teaching and learning as it unfolds in the environment. It is used to ensure that learning outcomes are clear, children are on track, and if something new occurs, how children can be moved forward. Here, ongoing feedback is provided to the children on what they are doing, which they understand to move forward. This is known as assessment *for* learning and ties in with teachable moments.

Summative assessment takes place after teaching and learning to evaluate progress that children have made. This is known as assessment *of* learning and involves assessing children's learning at the end of a particular stage by comparing it against a set criteria or standards, i.e. the early learning goals, the CoETL, what children have achieved, and what is outstanding that they need to progress towards.

The above can be regarded as a cycle of assessment, where each can be used in various ways to gain a holistic idea of where children are in their learning and what we as practitioners offer.

 ACTIVITY

Develop a tracking system and for a day or even a week, keep track of all the ways you assess children – questions you ask, discussions, activities they participate in that allow you to observe their learning.

Assessment for creativity

Creativity and its process should be assessed, not only to observe its impact, but to prove that creativity has a vital role in children's learning. If we want children to be creative, then we must assess it. If we want creativity to be valued as much as content, then it must be assessed. If we want to teach creatively and want creativity learning to take place, then it needs to be assessed. In the early years, day-to-day assessment of children's learning is documented as a journey and is very child-oriented. Whilst there are tools to teach and assess content, creativity can be said to be another matter. Assessing creativity is as challenging as the quest to define it (Starko, 2014, p. 307). There are difficulties in the confidence of practitioners in assessing creativity, mainly because of how it is understood and, unlike everything else, has no set criteria for it to be evaluated against. There is, of course, the danger that assessing creativity will lead to the measuring of settings or schools; this then places additional accountability on early years practitioners, something we don't want.

Current assessment methods can be said to be anti-ethical to creative learning, as children have become what is known as 'data storage centres'. Here, they are tested and assessed to pass certain attainment goals, so that they are ready for the next stage of education – almost a fixation on right answers. The bottom line, however, is that assessing creativity must be intentional when planning; it must be designed to promote and stimulate creativity. This is the single most powerful tool adults have for recognising creativity when it occurs, and for making a place for creativity in children's education. *How can we have assessment for creativity? What kind of assessment is supportive of creativity? What will assessment for creativity look like?*

FACT NOTE
THINKING CREATIVELY IN ACTION AND MOVEMENT (TCAM)

Devised by Torrance in 1981, TCAM examines fluency and originality as they are expressed in movement. Designed for children as young as pre-school, the test asks them to move across the room in as many different ways as they can, to move in designated ways (e.g. like a leaf in the wind), to put a paper cup into a basket in as many ways as possible, and to generate possible uses for the paper cup. The tests are not timed and are scored for the number of ideas and originality, rather than marks and levels of intelligence.

In the early years context, better and useful assessment is defined as 'formative'. This is ongoing assessment that informs planning, teaching, and learning, and is regarded as assessment *for* learning. It happens by monitoring children's learning and providing ongoing feedback that can be used by practitioners to improve their own teaching, and by children to develop their learning. It is in the word 'formative': to 'inform' teaching and learning, to 'inform' planning, to 'inform' the environment, to 'inform' creativity, to 'inform' feedback, and so on. Do note – one cannot then complete a summative assessment on children if they have nothing to 'inform' it with. Without formative assessment, there is no clear evidence of progression for the summative assessment to be made; hence why ongoing assessment is the key to assessing creativity. Formative assessment is about the intervention that a practitioner can have on children's creative learning constantly. It provides much-needed quality insight to adjust teaching and learning approaches while it is happening, and not afterwards. A single learning session doesn't necessarily indicate how effectively children have built, say, the use of problem-solving or thinking skills during the process. Ongoing assessment, however, can do this.

Formative assessment, even if informal, is necessary for early years practitioners to set up experiences in which creativity is hoped for, and in order to determine that it has occurred. It happens every time adults speak to children; it's walking around the room watching what children are saying and doing and building; it's looking over their shoulders; it's pointing out misconceptions quickly; it's modelling and scaffolding where and when needed; it's ensuring the availability of resources and provision as learning is unfolding; it's nurturing creativity's characteristics;

it's challenging children; it's asking questions to encourage further investigation or thinking; it's having whole-group and individual conversations throughout the day; it's about knowing when to be very specific, when to be encouraging, and when to push; it's using it in planning to create learning experiences; it's in the teachable moments. It is happening all the time! *So, how do we capture it?*

 CONNECT

What else do adults do that indicates formative assessment is being used?

Observational assessment

Observation is a tool of formative assessment and the best approach for understanding if and how children are learning creatively. It can be described as an unbiased and uncritical method of 'capturing the facts' demonstrated by a child through their actions and speech (Sancisi and Edgington, 2015, p. 6). Observations require practitioners to engage in a process of look, listen, and note, where they carefully watch children engage in their learning and pick out what they are doing, what they know, and what they need help with to develop further. It is also a vital tool in finding out more about them as individuals, how they approach their learning, and how they use the many creative characteristics associated with learning. Observational assessment is the key to understanding what children really know and can do, and it is the most reliable way of building up an accurate picture of a child's creative development and learning (Brunton and Thornton, 2013).

Observation can be managed and used in ways that are conducive to creativity, and is a fundamental and crucial aspect of the creative adult's role in moving the children forward. It can be used to answer the following:

- What is interesting and motivates children as individuals or groups?

- How are children responding to a particular activity, experience, or area of provision?

- How are children using and developing their CoETL and creativity's characteristics?

- What do children know and understand in terms of the EYFS areas of learning?

- How are children interacting with adults and other children?

- How are children approaching their learning?

- Which areas of provision and activities do they choose to access regularly?

- How are creativity's characteristics being used and stimulated by what I, as the adult, offer?

AROUND THE WORLD
NEW ZEALAND

Margaret Carr's widely acclaimed approach to assessment is known as 'Learning Stories' (2012). These are longer observations, made over a much longer period of time. They are written as a story in the first person, as if the adult were talking to the child and explaining what they had observed. The relevance of each step is explained and reflected on at the end of the 'story'.

Types of observations vary in the early years, and there are several to choose from. They can be used differently depending on the observation focus and context. It is about finding an approach that best suits the situation, and the children.

Participant – observations are carried out when adults are playing and working with the children. These tend to be more structured than spontaneous observations.

Spontaneous – spontaneous things that you see a child doing or saying which you feel are significant. These are the briefest observations that you can make. They are usually captured on post-it notes or sticky labels, which can be easily put into a child's developmental folder. This is the quickest way to record an observation and usually the most convenient for practitioners, who can often be seen carrying notepads, or rather iPads, around the setting.

Narrative – is an extended written account of what children are doing. It may include a verbatim record of the language used by the child, their level of involvement, and other children that they play with, and may also include photographs and/or images. It usually takes from 20 minutes to half an hour, so as much information as possible can be recorded. As this method takes much longer, and is much more detailed, it may be planned in advance to ensure that every child in the setting is observed in this way to gain the maximum information about their learning.

Time sampling – an observation of a child is made every five minutes over a set period of time, usually an hour. The observations are only brief, but will include the activity the child is engaged in, which area of the setting they are in, and the level of involvement at that particular time. The practitioner will need to be able to make the observations regularly, which can be a challenge in a free flow environment, but each observation will take less than a minute to record. This type of observation is very useful for recording a child's level of interest in types of activities, and their dispositions for learning.

DISCUSS

With peers/colleagues what other observation tools they may use. How effective are these in capturing creativity in action?

Tracking – this requires having a floor plan of the learning environment, including the outdoors. The practitioner observes and notes on the plan the area in the setting that the child visits, and how long they were at each activity or area. The child may be tracked for a long or short time, depending on the type of information required. For example, if the observation is to help understand why a child seems to flit from activity to activity, the adult could observe for the morning session.

 ACTION RESEARCH

Select two types of observations discussed. Research and find out more about them.

Then select two children from your setting to observe using them.

■ How effective were these approaches?

■ What was challenging?

■ How could you adapt them for future use?

To make obtaining observations more effective, the use of differing recording strategies should be considered. These can be post-it notes, photographs, work samples, recordings/transcripts, short and long observations, conversations, discussions, and feedback from parents. By employing different approaches, it allows practitioners to build up a 'holistic picture' of children providing evidence of what they can do and what they need to continue doing (Smidt, 2005). This will make it easier for the adult to assess the children and support them within their creative learning, through their own creative approaches.

Assessing creativity

Observation is only the first stage in the process of understanding and addressing children's creativity. It is what is done next with this information that will impact on children further. Assessment is then the analysis of observational information that will not only inform adult's planning, provision, and teaching approaches for creativity to occur, but will inform us about children's creative learning and development – *what do the observations and any other evidence of learning tell us? How were creativity's characteristics visible, stimulated, and used? What else do we need to do?*

The early years practitioner thinks about what they have seen and heard, and pulls this information together to gain an insight about the child. This 'pulling of information' should not be a judgement; it is about promoting creativity further and improving learning. It should help specify and clarify what creativity means, especially as there are many different views surrounding it. Assessment is integral in asking *are we teaching what we think we are teaching? Are children learning what they are supposed to be learning? Is there a way to do things better? For better learning? For better nurturing of creativity?*

Identifying creativity is extremely difficult if we are not sure what it is. For creativity to be identified within observations, practitioners need to look at ways to change criteria to pay attention to it in teaching and learning. The most important aspect of the assessment process is creativity itself! Adults teaching art and design are more confident about assessing creativity, than those that teach other subjects. Tapping into this may be a start – *what criteria do they use to determine creativity?* It is then about devising a tool for assessing children's creativity within the observations – something to analyse the observations against. It is not about having a checklist approach to assessing creativity, but a tool that guides us to constantly ensure that our teaching, provision, and interactions are nurturing creativity. Such tools are an important step to raise daily awareness of creativity's characteristics and the skills in this, and to see them materialise in children's learning.

IDEA
CREATIVITY ANALYSIS TOOL

Using Work Tool 1 and the CoETL 2, 3, and 4, see if you can devise an analysis tool for your observations of the children.

You could use a rubric maker app – see Explore.

Start by developing a common criterion to monitor children's progress in, say, creative thinking, use of imagination, creative strategies used, problem-solving techniques, and idea generating. Use Work Tools 1 to 4. *Can we develop a simple formative tool? Can you use creativity's characteristics as an analysis tool? How creative can you get with this?*

Observation recordings then need to be analysed against both creativity's characteristics and the CoETL. This needs to be done regularly for evidence of children's progress over time against these – *what creative characteristics are evident? Where can we go with this?* And, vitally, *what progression have children made as a result of creativity?* Not only this, but data from across the setting should also be drawn together to reflect on progress different groups of children are making and how approaches and provision can be developed to improve creativity for children.

RESEARCH TO EXPLORE
OBSERVATION ANALYSIS

Focusing on children's creative thinking, Robson and Lowe (2012) conducted a study using observations of activities in 3- to 4-year-olds in an English Children's Centre. These were then analysed using the Analysing Children's Creative Thinking (ACCT) Framework. The observations revealed that child-initiated activities featured the highest levels of involvement and were associated with 'trying out' and 'analysing ideas', 'flexibility' and 'originality', 'imagining' and 'hypothesising', and 'persistence'. The framework provided the researchers with a tool to analyse their collected data against and to identify creativity.

Next steps

 REFLECT

What is a creative experience for children's learning that you've designed recently?

■ What did you plan for?

■ What happened that you didn't plan for?

■ Where did you use 'in the moment' planning?

■ What were the teachable moments? And the responses you provided?

■ Can you identify creativity's characteristics within what you did and what the children did as a form of assessment?

 EXPLORE

Articles from Anna Ephgrave on 'in the moment' planning:

■ Moment by Moment Planning Anna Ephgrave: http://my.optimus-education.com/sites/optimus-education.com/files/anna_ephgrave_2c.pdf

■ Planning next steps in the moment by Anna Ephgrave: http://eyfs.info/articles/_/teaching-and-learning/planning-next-steps-in-the-moment-r217#

Progression in Creativity: Developing new forms of assessment Background Paper for the OECD conference *Educating for Innovative Societies* (2012) www.oecd.org/edu/ceri/50153675.pdf

■ Findings on creating a framework for assessing creativity.

The Analysing Children's Creative Thinking framework: development of an observation led approach to identifying and analysing young children's creative thinking (Robson, S. 2014) www.deepdyve.com/lp/wiley/the-analysing-children-s-creative-thinking-framework-development-of-an-bEnROPNGRx

■ Observation-led approach to assessing children's creativity.

Tech tools

■ Rubistar – rubric maker to help you form a tool to analyse observations against the CoETL and creativity's characteristics: http@//rubistar.4teachers.org

■ Planboard – an interactive lesson planning tool: www.chalk.com/planboard/

■ Planning apps and websites: www.commonsense.org/education/top-picks/lesson-planning-apps-and-websites

Creative spaces

 THINK

What might a creative environment feel and look like?

If you were to visit a creative space, how would you recognise it as such?

How is a creative space similar or different to a 'good' or 'effective' space?

CHAPTER FOCUS

■ Flushing out the environment to create creative spaces

■ Providing a climate conducive to creativity

■ Constructivist creative spaces

■ Elements in planning creative spaces for creativity

■ Developing outdoor creative spaces inspired by the forest school approach

The environment plays a central role in nurturing, stimulating, and supporting creativity in any early years educational setting. It either fires it to move forward or drains it, often extinguishing it all together. Ineffective environments can stifle the true capabilities of young children, and can end up silencing imagination and creativity (Tarr, 2004). Curriculum, planning, and assessment also become ineffective if the environment does not allow them to interplay. Creative approaches, 'in the moment' planning, and teachable moments do not happen in isolation, but involve the development of a creative environment or, as this chapter names them, 'creative spaces'. It is within these creative spaces that creative expression and creative learning, of both the child and practitioner, can be cultivated, nurtured, and developed. In previous chapters, the environment has reoccurred as vital to all aspects of nurturing creativity; this chapter builds upon this to explore how to create spaces for bringing forth creativity.

What does one mean when they say they are interested in nurturing and supporting creative spaces? What makes up a 'creative space'? What do adults in creative spaces do? What do the children do? What can one do to develop a more creative space? These questions need interrogation when thinking about developing creative spaces in order to understand the role of creativity within them. The EYFS guides learning and development on a principle of 'enabling environments'. It reinforces the key role of the environment in supporting and extending children's development and learning through experiences that respond to their individual needs and where there is a strong relationship between the adults and children.

Enabling environments are said to offer stimulating resources relevant to children's cultures and communities, are rich in learning opportunities through play and playful teaching, and support children in exploring and taking risks. In the EYFS, the environment is described in terms of three aspects: the 'emotional' environment, the 'indoor' environment, and the 'outdoor' environment. These three aspects together make up the environment for play and learning in the EYFS. We, of course, add the 'creative' environment into the mix! The EYFS does not provide guidance on how the environment should be set up, as it is more focused on how it meets the outcomes. Many settings use the areas of learning and development of the EYFS as the starting point for creating an environment, with further guidance from the document Development Matters (Early Education, 2012). However, this can very easily steer away from the focus of these spaces being based on children's interests and the use of creativity within them.

 ACTION RESEARCH

Research what the EYFS means in terms of the environment having three aspects:

- The emotional environment

- The outdoor environment

- The indoor environment

What, then, makes a 'creative environment'?

The environment is more than simply a planned space; it is everything that is encountered from point of entry to the setting to point of departure. It includes the resources in the setting; the images that are promoted; the messages that these convey around what the setting is about (Langston and Abbott, 2005, p. 70); and the value of creativity within them. In a well-designed creative space complemented by quality approaches to teaching and learning, children will be able to learn mostly on their own. In a creative space, practitioners are respected for their expertise and appreciated for their faith in the children's abilities; they will be asked for their help, encouragement, and clarification when the child needs it. In turn, children are appreciated for their willingness to take responsibility, become involved, and do what is needed to progress. *Where does it begin?*

Flushing out the environment

> **! STORY FROM PRACTICE**
> ● STUDY OF EARLY YEARS ENVIRONMENTS
>
> From a small chair in a corner, I counted 19 different, decorated, scalloped borders segmenting portions of the bulletin boards lining the walls. The boards were filled with words: a word wall, class rules, a calendar, alphabets, numbers, shapes and colors, and a plethora of cartoon people and animals, each with a message and at least 50 of them with horseshoe-shaped smiles rather like a capital U . . . St. Patrick's Day mobiles created from brightly painted rainbows and black-line masters hung from the ceiling just above the children's heads. Rainbows, leprechauns, and pots of gold jiggled before my eyes.
>
> (Tarr, 2004, p. 88)

Tarr (2004) wondered how this 'visual busyness' influenced children's concentration. She also questioned the choice of materials and whether 'the mass of commercial stereotyped images silences the actual lived experiences of those individuals learning together' (Tarr, 2004, p. 90). I think it is safe to say that children know the difference between an open creative space and a manufactured one, and those that are cluttered for the sake of having displays, clearly illustrated by Tarr. Visual busyness can disrupt this and cause creative blocks in adults and children alike, and in turn stifle or silence imagination and creativity. The impact of displays and walls need to be considered, especially for those children who have difficulty concentrating or staying focused. *What messages do the walls and displays convey to children?*

IDEA
DE-CLUTTER YOUR SPACES!

Teaching and learning spaces can often be full of unintentional knick-knacks. Simplify your spaces and surfaces. Once it is uncovered, imagine, as children do, the possibilities that exist within the space.

Creative spaces are about conditions for creativity to take place, a stage for powerful learning, or, as Tarr states, 'lived experiences'. Therefore, a creative space has a spark of innovation, excitement, and passion that distinguishes it from other types of spaces. It is where children engage, wonder, and imagine. The physical aspect of the space is not all about overdoing it, but rather about simplicity where children can be masters of their domain. The space available in different settings will vary, but a very common complaint is, 'We don't have enough space'. Although availability of space is certainly an issue, we frequently make this even more challenging by not making the best use of what we have. Often you walk into settings or classrooms where the adults have taken great care in the layout, but despite this there is often overwhelming clutter and lack of purpose for things in the environment. One can associate it with how one's attic or shed looks! However, as humans, sometimes we stop seeing the environment in which we live, and there is a need to overcome this by looking beyond. It's about flushing out the environment of all the clutter and providing a canvas upon which both the creative adult and creative child can work.

The practice story about the tribe walk illustrates that it is important to look at spaces with fresh eyes and a questioning stance. It is in this way that a creative space can be kept in which children engage with multiple learning opportunities which adults may not even imagine. Taking a walk offers early years practitioners a platform from which to begin examining and dialoguing about their practice. Creative seeds can be planted amongst each other for looking at inventive ways to make changes (one at a time, though) and to flush out the environment in order to develop a creative space.

STORY FROM PRACTICE
THE TRIBE WALK!

A Foundation Stage Phase Leader took the EYFS team (the tribe) for a walk in their setting. This was through the entire space, room by room, while he asked the staff to talk to each other about the purpose behind the choices that had been made by them, and others, for their environments.

'*What is the purpose … (of this or that)?*' If the response was a shoulder shrug or a blank look, then the Phase Leader informed the adults that they needed to talk to each other about what these choices communicated about the view of children alive in this environment; as well as the possibilities, what these choices *eliminated* for their children. It was things like, what was the thinking behind the couches, plants, storage of paints, materials to be thrown away, mirrors, light tables – basically everything.

The Phase Leader told the group that clutter communicates something to the children and plays out in their engagement and behaviour. He asked the group to think about the following:

■ *What spaces have you created for your children?*

■ *Are they clearly identifiable?*

■ *Are they easily redefined to respond to children's activity and interests?*

■ *Are they provocative and suggestive without limiting engagement?*

■ *Where is the creativity?*

Inducing a creative climate

 ACTIVITY

Create a map of the environment in which you work or train. Annotate the map with the ways in which the environment is working or is challenging, and the ways in which it is not. Discuss with your tribe. What changes can be made?

The aim of a creative space is to encourage children to generate new ideas, stimulate and develop creativity's characteristics, and help their learning to progress and grow. It allows children to explore and implement creative ideas more effectively, and utilises all the characteristics of effective teaching and learning approaches. Therefore, practitioners are tasked with planning, creating, and shaping favourable conditions. When one thinks of a space, it is mainly around what can be observed, maybe just on the physical aspect of it. However, the space is much more than what the eye can see; it is also about how it feels from a child's perspective.

When adults look to buy a new car or home, it is often associated with feelings: 'it felt right' or 'I didn't get that feeling'. Or maybe you are working on an important project, but can't do so at work, or at home, and therefore find a small cosy coffee shop because 'it's where I concentrate'. The same can be said for creative spaces. These spaces go beyond what can be seen with the eyes; it is where bodies and minds can actively pursue knowledge, gain understanding, and develop and practice skills. Creativity can come through interactions amongst adults and children, the processes they engage in, and the space in which they work, which is often beyond the physical experience. Some spaces can drain creativity, whilst others foster it. So, it is about breeding a 'creative climate' that is observable, but at the same time nourishes creativity. It is through a creative climate that children will absorb what is valued in learning.

A creative climate embodies behaviour, attitudes, and feelings, and through these sets the life of the creative space. The climate sends children a variety of positive messages about their learning (Dodge et al., 2010) by ensuring children 'feel' safe enough to learn creatively, but also are able to perceive from it how learning is expected to happen, and its importance. It communicates to them that this is a good place to be, that they belong here, that there are places that they can be by themselves if they want to, that they can do many things here on their own – that it is a place to explore and try out their ideas. The climate also conveys expectation about which behaviours and attitudes are acceptable. For all this to happen, there are certain characteristics connected with a creative climate, which Figure 8.1 illustrates. By using this as an audit, you can determine if your spaces

Aims of a creative climate

    o Attitude, feelings, and behaviour
   o Building, developing, and practicing skills
  o Acquisition of specific knowledge and understanding

Playful atmosphere & humour

Relaxed atmosphere in the space; non-threatening. Decreases anxiety and thus makes children more open to new approaches.

Support

The right resources to give new ideas a try. Encouraging children to make links and connections.

Social

Establishing positive relationships amongst peers and adults – building of tribes!

Play and explore

Finding out and exploring the environment. Playing with what they know. Being willing to 'have a go.'

Freedom and autonomy

Choice of tasks and ways that children approach them. Choosing ways to do things. Finding interests and problems.

Active learning

Being involved and concentrating. Keeping trying. Enjoying achieving what they set out to do.

Feedback and recognition

Clearly specified objectives and expectations. Approval and support. Appropriate feedback to children.

Ideas and creative thinking time

Having their own ideas. Sufficient time to explore ideas and possibilities. Encouragement of ideas and thinking.

Allowing mistakes

Opportunities to make errors and learn from them.

Encouragement of sensible risks

How the adult provides and responds to to this.

The rewarding system

Encouraging methods and role modelling of preferable patterns of behaviour of children. Rewarding creative ideas and products.

Figure 8.1 Characteristics of a creative climate

are climatised for creativity. You must remember that the creative climate will only work when complemented by supportive, creative adults, flexible learning conditions, clear direction, and inclusiveness.

I think it is worth mentioning creative 'culture' here, as often it gets confused with the climate. A creative climate is different from a creative culture. A climate is observable habits that characterise the life of a creative space. Culture is the values and beliefs that reflect the deeper foundations of the setting or school. It can be said that climate is observable through interactions, behaviours, and feelings, whereas culture is deeper, lasting, and less observable. Where the climate allows children to perceive what is expected and valued in the space, culture is about why this is expected and supported. Culture is the values that drive spaces to function in a certain way, and is often needed at a broader level from the setting.

A constructivist space

Based on the theories of early childhood (Vygotsky, 1978), constructivism is a concept about how one learns. It advocates that children construct their own understanding and knowledge of the world through experiencing and then reflecting on those experiences. When we encounter something new, we have to reconcile it with our previous ideas and experience, maybe changing what we believe or discarding the new information as irrelevant. In any case, we are active creators of our own knowledge. To do this, we must ask questions, explore, tinker, think, and assess what we know. In a creative space, the constructivist view of learning can point towards different teaching and learning approaches, and how the space is set up for it. In the most general sense, it usually means encouraging children to use active learning (use of senses, experiments, real-world problem-solving, playing, exploring, working in pairs or groups) to create more knowledge and then to reflect on and talk about what they are doing and how their understanding is changing.

The EYFS advocates each child as unique; this goes for their learning, too. The constructivist approach supports the child to follow their instinct and create knowledge and strategies for understanding learning. A well-planned creative space embeds the constructivist approach, as here the children learn how to learn and construct their knowledge. The main means of learning through this approach is using the senses, which causes the brain to build a full understanding of the surrounding context. This leads us back to the understanding that each child is an individual creating unique responses and experiences in the space they come into contact with. The experiences and interactions children have are created by learning through doing and engaging in their spaces. Prior knowledge is key as it is used to build and grow through adult interactions and approaches for children to make connections. Children construct their understanding of what is being taught by combining what they already know with what they newly experience. This 'combinatorial' process is a creative process (Vygotsky, 2004, p. 9).

 OBSERVE

A child or group of children and analyse how they are constructing their learning through the space.

The constructivist approach does not dismiss the active role of the practitioner or the value of their knowledge. It actually modifies that role, so that they support and facilitate children in the construction of knowledge, understanding, and skills, rather than reproducing a series of facts. Constructivism transforms children from passive recipients of information to active creative participants in the learning process. Always guided by the practitioner, children construct their knowledge actively rather than just mechanically ingesting knowledge. This gives them ever-broadening tools for creative learning.

Creative spaces

So far, this chapter has advocated the de-cluttering of spaces, the inducing of a climate conducive to creativity, and the application of a constructivist approach within them. This then naturally takes one towards the modification of the spaces to support children's creativity: *how is the curriculum offered through the planning of creative spaces?* But more importantly, *how do creative spaces allow for teaching creatively, and for creative learning? Do they allow for 'in the moment' planning? And for quality 'teachable moments'? How is the space set up to stimulate creativity's characteristics?* The goal is to spark children's curiosity and creativity by turning the spaces not only into a place to learn, but also into a place to explore and make discoveries. Creative spaces are where children are the authors and the provision is open to interpretation. It is where children can use crayons to draw, but can also learn that when they are melted, they can be re-sculpted. It's where the traditional game of 'Simon Says' can further be enhanced by being able to record their own directive on a Dictaphone or iPad and play it back. It's about the many possibilities achievable through a creative space.

 DISCUSS

With peers/colleagues how the curriculum is interpreted in the spaces they provide.

Children in creative spaces interact socially, share jokes, giggle, and communicate in their own special ways. It is here that they take part in dramatic and fantasy play, tell many stories, and so much more. These become their vehicles to build their skills and further their learning and understanding. The space is critical, therefore, in offering opportunities to think, construct, and create. A place where fizzy children can be seen everywhere, using their own approaches to learning. The creative adult is there to put at the disposition of the children the space, materials, and resources, through which the children make new stories, new worlds, and new possibilities, fuelled by their imaginations. *So how does one go about this?*

In order to develop a creative space, children must be considered as active participants in the process, and must be involved in the development of spaces they then have ownership of. Children must own their space. Very young children can be involved in choosing and organising areas and resources, whilst the older children can take ownership and responsibility by being asked how they want their space to look and feel, with the creative adult valuing their voices and ensuring it is visible in the environment – *how can this be achieved?*

AROUND THE WORLD
REGGIO EMILIA, ITALY

Known as the **third teacher**, the Reggio environment is recognised for its potential to inspire children. An environment filled with *natural light, order and beauty*. Open spaces free from clutter, where every material is considered for its purpose, every corner is ever-evolving to encourage children to delve deeper and deeper into their interests. The space encourages collaboration, communication, and exploration. The space respects children as capable by providing them with authentic materials and tools. The space is cared for by both children and adults.

Planning creative spaces – inspiration for your creative space should be found by observing children during play. Identifying children's changing interests, and how they engage, will assist you in planning a space tailored to the children's individual preferences and what they may need for it. Of course, as children leave and transition in and out of the setting, this process of documenting how the space is used needs to happen again. When planning spaces, you need to fully understand the value of the different types of learning you are offering children – e.g. outdoor play: what is this offering the children? And then move on to the rationale behind the resourced areas, such as sand, water, small world. If there isn't any, then start again! Look beyond your setting into other settings and see what can inspire your own space. Research online to get an idea of the many quality practices that are happening. Look at the space as a team by taking a walk around it, capturing images, and drawing up floor plans to sit down and discuss together; this will support you greatly in sharing your thoughts and planning a constructively creative space.

The space is constructively playful and has a 'hands on' approach to teaching and learning. It has a 'workshop style' atmosphere, which consists of practical working areas with materials freely accessible, to be moved wherever the child's creativity takes them. The space is more than just 'resourcing corners' or 'areas of learning'; it is about providing resources – real resources rather than manufactured ones – that make the creative process of learning possible. Dodge et al. (2010) recommend ten common interests for the early years that you can use to start thinking about your creative space. These are construction, imaginative play, toys and games, art, books, investigation, messy play, music and movement, cooking, and technology. *How can you use these to design creative spaces?*

 **CONNECT**

What does 'workshop style atmosphere' mean? How can it be applied to your setting?

The whole setting or school should also be used as a fluid creative space, or individual spaces dependent on structure, not just confined to one room. This can be difficult to achieve as often early years spaces are limited, with multi-purpose rooms where learning, eating, and sleeping all take place. However, children do not need to be in a certain space to take part in learning. Children in creative spaces move around the setting daily to different areas, classrooms, and spaces. They also work with differing age groups. *What about a 3-year-old working with an 8-year-old? What about creating reading nooks or quiet spaces in corridors?* Movements between sessions or lessons in this way are used as adventures in creative spaces; children love adventures!

The structure of the space considers the need for creative thinking, encourages excitement, and creates opportunities. Organising the space is a must as children need to know where to find toys, resources, and materials, or be able to use the space to make decisions about what they will incorporate into their learning and how. The structure needs to consider whole group learning, small group learning, and individual learning. Children should be freely allowed to learn where they want through the provision of flexible seating. This means letting children choose where to work: the carpet, the floor, the corridor, on the cushions, outdoors, and so on. Tables and chairs are avoidable, so no excuse. It's all about children working, playing, experimenting, and collaborating, and how this is achieved through the individual approaches to learning of each child. Watch them and learn!

Creative spaces are high-energy places, and similar to adults, children sometimes need time and space to relax on their own. You can help children meet this need by offering spaces that are limited to one or two children. The reading area, a cosy corner or nook, quiet games, or other spaces of your setting can help children calm themselves, especially when behaviour issues strike! Consider how the use of sheer fabrics or the placement of furniture can help create these cosy nooks and still provide good visibility. An approach to consider is one that Thornburg (2014) advises by using time-honoured concepts to describe spaces:

- **Campfires** – places where large groups can gather to share the same experience through listening/watching, such as storytelling, circle times, whole group sessions.

- **Watering holes** – places where children can work in small group collaborations or socialise.

- **Caves** – individual spaces with barriers to audio and visual stimuli for quiet times, activities that require quiet, reflections, or even a nap.

- **Life** – real world spaces where children can apply what they are learning to real situations and problems. These are the projects and approaches that the adult provides.

Regardless of the metaphors that are used, creative spaces must provide children and adults with the flexibility to access the right kind of space at the right time in their learning. One must also remember that children are observers, so creative spaces should be ever changing and not always the same. Children will also create their own spaces in which to learn, too; this is directed by their own imaginary worlds, and practitioners need to offer spaces for this to happen in.

Routines and timetables are reviewed to connect with the space, which may mean taking time off where children can have a day to explore and investigate for some settings, or where in the timetable it can be embedded for others. However, through the constructivist approach, the whole space, with its resources and teaching, should allow the achieving of knowledge, understanding, and skills anywhere, anytime, with the mastering of creativity's characteristics. Within this, creative spaces have modifiable rules. Classroom management is important, but not more than raising a child who can do things for themselves and think freely (De Matteo).

Creative spaces give children time and opportunities to become absorbed in what they are doing, repeating things again and again, practicing skills and mastering them, and testing out their ideas. This includes time to play on their own, with friends, and when part of a larger group. Certain projects and activities may need to be extended over several days or weeks, providing the opportunity to come back to things and explore them in greater depth. Practitioners need to think about offering a flexible approach to take account of this. As stated before, settings can be multi-purpose, which cause children to have to tidy away what they are doing. By thinking about routines and timings, it will give children the opportunity to concentrate for longer, investigate resources, and explore situations that are led by their interests, but also come back to them time and time again to take forward.

RESEARCH TO EXPLORE
AESTHETICS

Aesthetics, or **aesthetic codes**, is the conscious use of design elements of light, colour, texture, sound, and smell that support children's learning. Curtis and Carter (2015) shed a spotlight on North American classrooms that have consciously used these design elements to engage children's curiosity and wonder. Their *Designs for Living and Learning: Transforming Early Childhood Environments* is an excellent reference for any adult wishing to reconsider aesthetics in their spaces.

Characteristics of effective teaching and learning – creative spaces are designed to cater for all three of the CoETL to ensure children are playing and exploring, learning actively, and creating and thinking critically, in order to nurture and stimulate creativity's characteristics. This provides a way for children to integrate all their new experiences into their rapidly developing minds, bodies, emotions, and social skills. Children are exploring, experimenting, and learning basic knowledge through direct experience of using the CoETL. *How do your current spaces allow the interplay of the CoETL and creativity's characteristics?*

 OBSERVE

How is your space set up to allow for all CoETL to be used by the children?

From the displays of children's work, they learn what is expected of them and what is approved, including mistakes. For this reason, the purpose of displays on walls and the messages that they convey need to be considered. The displays should document children's learning in its different forms through different modes – for example, photographs, videos, children's presentations, learning stories, and much more. Displays send powerful messages to children about the value of their work. They communicate to children that this is a place to test their ideas and helps adults more easily track children's developmental progress, but without causing visual busyness and wall clutter!

The creative space opens up what is being taught and shows that ideas and inventiveness gain as much respect as skills and technical knowledge. It provides an insight into the content and facilitates connections for the children. Flexible tools are used both physically and digitally to do so. Teaching and learning are also complemented using local resources, i.e. buildings and communities. This is especially useful where space is limited within the setting. The following practice story demonstrates how one adult opened up the content of what they intended to teach.

❗ PRACTICE STORY: THEFT IN THE CLASSROOM!

I had arrived one morning to observe a trainee in the Reception setting of a school. As I walked down the corridor towards her class, I noticed the children all outside. There were gasps with a lot of 'oh no'. As I approached, I saw a red tape had been sealed across the classroom door and when I peered through, the classroom had been ransacked! Chairs were upside down, tables were on their sides, and some resources were all over the floor. I joined in with the gasping.

It was only then the adult told the children that there had been a break in! and she thought something had been taken but was not sure what. The children were to become the investigators; they were given cameras to take photos of the scene, which later were played on a projector for all to see and discuss. Some children dusted for fingerprints, whilst others found unusual things that they had to wear gloves to remove and place in a bag. The space was used as an engaging space, which opened what was being taught.

Creative spaces invite engagement – practitioners in early years settings normally plan for what is known as 'continuous provision'. This is resources, materials, equipment and spaces that are available continuously and are set up differently each day with enhancement to engage the children. To add a creative dimension to provision, is through the Reggio Emilia inspired approach known as provocations. Put simply, provocations provoke! A provocation is a picture, experience, or item that provokes thought, an interest, questions, or creativity (Edwards, 2003), as well as discussions and ideas. Provocations can also *expand* on a thought, a project, an idea, and an interest. Provocations can be as simple as a photo of a rock sculpture next to some pebbles in the sand tray, or as elaborate as a table with an assortment of recycled materials next to a book on robots and resources to make upcycled robots. Ultimately, the intention of provocations is to provide an invitation for a child to explore and express themselves in the creative spaces. It should be open-ended and provide a means for expression where possible.

Creative spaces offer open-ended 'loose part' materials and resources – these can be used in numerous ways indoors and outdoors by babies, toddlers, and young children. They can be moved, carried, combined, and redesigned in any way the child decides. These materials can be natural or manufactured and can be sourced in several ways: in nature – simply by going to parks, beaches, and gardens – asking parents to bring in materials from home, recycling in the setting, and joining recycling centres.

Open-ended materials encourage imagination, creativity, and problem-solving skills so learning is richer. It supports children who are constantly conducting experiments, testing ideas, and building their understanding of the world. As children play with the materials, they are exploring what happens, coming up with new ways of manipulating the materials, deciding that one material can symbolise something else and using lots of language. This type of play is open-ended and builds creative thinking. There is the freedom to choose and create with many possibilities. Table 8.1 provides some ideas of loose parts with space to add your own ideas.

 RESEARCH TO EXPLORE

THE THEORY OF 'LOOSE PARTS'

British Architect Simon Nicholson first presented a theory of loose parts in 1972. Loose parts are materials with no specific set of directions, and they can be used alone or together with other materials. They can be moved, carried, combined, redesigned, lined up, taken apart, and put back together in multiple ways. The child (not the adult) determines how the loose parts are used.

When children have access to loose parts, it frees their creativity and imagination to change the world around them in infinite ways. The more flexible the materials in their environment, the greater the level of creativity and inventiveness they express.

Table 8.1 Open-ended loose parts

Stones	Pallets	Plastic gutters	Oven racks	Add your own!
Driftwood	Scarves	Tyres	Bricks	
Stumps	Balls	Plunges	Funnels	
Shells	Ribbons	String	Nuts and bolts	
Sand	Buckets	Seedpods, acorns, pine cones	Hoops	
Bark	Baskets	Tins	Water	
Gravel	Sheets	Wood	Spoons	
Feathers	Crates	Old CD/DVDs	Plastic bottles	
Fabric	Blankets	Cylinders	Reels	
Straw	Boxes	Lids	Trays	
Twigs	Wire	Pipes	Glass pebbles	
Branches	Pebbles	Cartons and tubs	Pegs	
Logs	Leaves	Egg boxes	Corks	
Chalk	Cardboard	Pots and pans	Buttons	
Wood	Rope	Bin lids	Lentils	
Cups	Tarpaulins	Garden pots	Beads	
Popsicle sticks	Beads	Tubes	Spoons	

The great outdoors

Some of my earliest and happiest memories are of playing outdoors with my siblings. I was one of four children and we spent huge amounts of time outdoors playing, exploring and learning. We learnt about risk taking when our elder brother encouraged us to climb trees. We experimented with 'perfume' making, using petals and leaves from the garden. We mixed earth, water and chopped grass to make 'school dinners' for our dolls, or 'mucky gooey' as we called it! We dug really deep holes, thinking we would eventually arrive in Australia, until our Dad explained how big the world was! We challenged ourselves physically with our 'puffa puffa' races and found ways to resolve our sibling quarrels without normally involving our parents. We adapted our few garden toys to suit our activities; my metal dolls pram hardly ever had a doll in it, normally earth, stones and grass ... it made a great wheelbarrow! We converted the small shed into a whole range of things, but mostly it was a 'lift', taking us and our scooters to the next level of the 'car park' in our shopping game. We explored with little supervision from our parents, discovering things for ourselves and developing independence. Our play was child-led: we were in charge of our own play and it was real and natural.

I remember reading this and totally being thrown back in time with my own siblings. All my time was spent outdoors, climbing trees, making perfume and paint out of leaves and flowers, hiding for hours before someone could find me, and coming home covered in dirt – *what wonderful days!!* One of the reasons I rarely wear skirts is because of my disjointed knees from constantly falling over – joys! Anyway, as well as prompting nostalgia, the great outdoors is where many of us hold precious memories, including children. However, it is also the reality that there are many that have not played outdoors, and much more today due to the safety issues that surround us. This makes it even more important for early years settings to offer this experience as a creative space. After all, Margaret Macmillan (1919, p. 109), who opened the first 'open air' nursery in London for slum children, said it best when she said 'the best kept classroom and the richest cupboard are roofed only by the sky'.

The EYFS does not separate the outdoor environment from the indoor; it is known as the 'learning environment' and is based on the understanding that children flow indoors and outdoors throughout the day, utilising both spaces. However, the outdoors is a different space altogether, and is not about offering outside what you do inside, something many adults tell me, and many I have observed to do. After all, where is the creativity in that? Being outdoors offers opportunities for doing things in different ways and on a different scale than when indoors. We already know that being outdoors has a positive impact on children's sense of well-being and health and helps all aspects of children's development. Children have first-hand contact with weather, seasons, and the natural world. It is here they can have the freedom to explore, use their senses, and be physically active and exuberant, and of course shout at the top of their lungs! 'To feel one's life in every limb'! (Macmillan, 1919, p. 109).

The outdoors offers endless possibilities and is about challenge and enjoyment. Often it is noted as much richer than the indoors (Moyles, 2005) and a dynamic living space (Tovey, 2007), one where there is 'a chance to learn, not only by hearing and seeing, but also by tasting, smelling, touching and feeling' (Mirrahimi et al., 2011, p. 395). It is where the possibilities are endless. When developing an outdoor creative space for learning, *experiences*, rather than equipment, are important. Children should have the opportunity to use things in different and adaptive ways. Children can learn to make decisions, solve problems, and grow in confidence in their own abilities, and they need plenty of time to investigate their outdoor spaces purposefully. They will make predictions about what may happen based on their previous play experiences indoors and outside the setting and need to test out these ideas and theories – all part of the creativity process, which they may not be able to do indoors. One way to understand the outdoors as a different creative space in its own right is through the renowned Scandinavian approach of 'forest schools'.

Forest schools

Frulitsliv, which means open air culture, is a way of life in Scandinavian countries and is very much embedded in their early years education. The term 'forest schools' is actually a made-up English name which was given to the provision in the UK, following what a group of nursery nurses from Bridgwater College, Somerset, saw on a trip to Denmark in 1993. The trip was to view the pre-school system there. In Denmark, there are *skovbørnehaver* (forest kindergartens), *skovegrupper* (forest or wood groups), *naturbørnehaver* (nature kindergartens), and ordinary early years settings that use the outdoor area they have available. There is also *udeskole* (meaning outdoor school) which targets 7- to16-year-olds through compulsory educational activities outside of school on a regular basis.

The Danish started a kindergarten system that included natural environments and opportunities for young children to develop and learn outdoors. From this a more child-centred approach to learning and development evolved (Williams-Siegfredsen, 2011). The forest school concept in the UK was started by the Bridgwater nursery nurses, and today stands as outstanding early years practice. It is an ethos, a way of working with children in an natural outdoor space. It allows children to develop confidence and self-esteem and take risks through hands-on learning experiences in woodlands or natural environments with trees. It is about taking learning out of the setting or classroom and into the great outdoors, no matter what the weather.

AROUND THE WORLD
BRISTOL, UNITED KINGDOM

Following on from the Forest School concept, UK is now embracing '**Beach Schools**', where children get an amazing opportunity to connect with the natural environment of the beach, including pebbles, sand, water, and oozing mud as well as all of the habitats for wild animals.

Beach Schools are a way of giving children in their early years the opportunity to learn and develop in a natural environment, sparking their intrinsic motivations to explore, create, and be curious about the world around them (Holland, 2017).

A vital aspect of forest schools is that practical tasks are linked to the national curriculum and EYFS, and are designed to enhance children's development. Although you must be trained in delivering forest schools in the UK, and there are centres across the UK that can be visited with groups of children, there is no reason why settings cannot adapt their own outdoor spaces to deliver some aspects of the forest ethos. The following creative case study on a school in the UK is one example of outstanding practice.

CREATIVE CASE
BILLY'S GARDEN

Name: Billy   **Role**: Caretaker   **Location**: Mayespark Primary School

As you walk into Mayespark school, you get a sense of someone sitting watching you. When you turn to look, it's Darth Vader! Well, not actually him, but a model created out of recycled materials, sat on a bench acting as a scarecrow. As you navigate towards it, you enter a magical world of nature which the children call 'Billy's garden'. There are flowers growing out of tyres, wellington boots, toasters, kettles, bath tubs, hoovers, and even toilets! Plastic rain gutters filled with dirt are being used as planters. There are raised garden beds, and some at ground level which grow carrots, lettuce, tomatoes and all sorts of organic vegetables that the children maintain and eat. Hula hoops are used as plant climbers, and in some large pots, small worlds have been created in and around the plants for children to engage in.

A pond lies in the middle which is home to tadpoles, frogs, toads, pond snails, fleas, damsel flies, and, if lucky, a newt! Visual images are up so children know what they have found in the pond. A bug city has been created using recycled materials such as bricks, logs, wood, pallets, straws, stones, and old pipes. This houses small insects and bugs which children can discover and explore further. Bird feeders are there to attract the flying visitors into Billy's garden. In the midst of all this is a work bench consisting of pots, shovels, trays, seeds, water hose, wheelbarrows, and much more to assist in children growing and looking after their space. Children also make their own compost, where Billy has told them that 'the worm eats all that is put into the compost heap and then pooh it out!' 'Eww' is the children's response.

Billy is the caretaker at Mayespark. He has been here for four years now. 'Miss, my old man had a massive greenhouse when I was little,' he tells me, 'but I never took an interest, not at all, and look at me now'. Watching Billy today, you wouldn't think this; he has a natural connection with the outdoors, where his passion is evident. Billy has been gardening for over 17 years now, and he has brought this passion into the school. When he first started at the school, there was a pond, with many bushes not being used to its potential. Billy discussed with the Head Teacher the possibility of raised beds and planters. The Head Teacher supported Billy 'and things just happened from there onwards'.

In Billy's garden, children can fully immerse themselves in the natural environment, taking part in a hands-on, engaging experience; they can touch, smell, and listen to their surrounding world. They can be at one with nature, immersing themselves in a sensory experience. The garden allows children to discover insects, foliage, varying seasons, and changeable temperatures. At a young age a child's manipulative skills are developing, and here they enjoy tactile experiences; wet and dry soil, grass, water, and other materials. Through exploring the pond or flower bed children learn about water life such as frogs, fish, and different plant species. The children revel in freedom of movement and in play that is inventive, adventurous, and stimulating. However, their discoveries take their curiosities forward by taking in what is happening around them, and imagining more possibilities – 'poppy flower giving hundreds of seeds! Is that even possible?' They think. They ponder. They feel. They take their time to observe, explore, and become fascinated with the natural world. Children are creating homes for creatures, using everyday items in creative ways i.e. hula hoops that hold up the climbing plants, sticks and stones turned into homes.

The upkeep of such a garden is not easy, either. To keep children engaged continuously, Billy and the staff are always looking for ways to develop and add to it. Billy is a regular visitor to the Royal Horticultural Society and other outdoor areas. Here, he regularly documents, mainly through his phone, images of inspiration and takes them back to show the children and discuss ideas for further creations. At present, the garden is being extended to allow for a wildlife area as children have been observed to hide in this space, or sit and look through books. Billy has voiced that the school leadership is vital in maintaining and developing these spaces and that without the Head Teacher's support, many things would not be possible. Billy is going to use the summer holidays to create a mud kitchen and twig house for the children in the nursery . . . and so the adventure continues.

Developing your outdoor creative space

Outdoor spaces offer an excellent opportunity for play, exploration, and active learning. It should be child-led, and the activities should follow the direction in which children choose to take them. They may decide to work independently, working on developing their own problem-solving skills and creativity, or they may join up with other children and work within groups. This is excellent for children's social development, as they will learn how to collaborate within a group and how to share their ideas and listen to others. The adult's role is to support and guide the children's creative learning. This gives children various opportunities to really develop their imagination and creativity's characteristics when carrying out tasks. There are no limitations, and children are free to let their imaginations, and bodies, run wild as they attempt problem-solving and exploration of their surroundings.

 FACT NOTE

GeekDad (whose name is Jonathan H. Liu) reviews books, toys, gadgets, and software on his online blog for parents. He wrote a column called 'The 5 Best Toys of All Time' (2011) for children:

5) Dirt

4) Cardboard tube

3) String

2) Box

1) Stick! Yes, a stick!

Stick is truly a classic toy; it can take infinite forms and become whatever the child imagines it to be or do.

What do you already have? And what can you do with it? – there is the challenge that some adults work in a range of settings which do not all have a readily accessible outdoor space. Some might have a wide-open green space, wooded areas, and gardens; others may mostly utilise a paved area. The starting point is to consider what outside spaces are available and to assess these – *what are the strengths and weaknesses? What is it that you can utilise and work with?* Those with no, or only a small amount of, outdoor space will need to think about their wider community and identify possible parks or other spaces they may be able to have access to. Getting the whole community involved is important. Parents and local businesses may have skills to share, may be willing to supply materials, or may organise fundraising for specific items, as setting budgets may be limited. This will assist in developing the space.

Be a creative researcher – outdoor developments take time to plan, and adults need persistence, patience, and stamina to turn their plans into reality. Start by being a creative researcher and as well as reviewing how your current space is used, visit other quality outdoor spaces, including those with limited spaces, and see what inspirations you can bring back. This includes visits to provisions that offer the forest school ethos. Document what you see through images, notes, and voice notes and bring back to share with the setting. In the Explore section at the end of this chapter, you will find ideas and inspiration for tweaking, changing, or even transforming your outdoor space.

 IDEA
POTION LAB!

Why not set up a potion station or laboratory outdoors where children can stir, squirt, mash, and whisk!

The experiences – to develop a creative space outdoors, adults need to start by thinking about the types of experiences that they wish to offer children, and consider how they will organise space to accommodate these. For example, climbing (this can be trees too!), space to just run, wheeled equipment such as bikes, quiet areas for children to reflect, places to hide in, wild areas, and gardening areas. It is not just about setting up the space with a few bikes and wheeling equipment from indoors to out. Thought needs to be applied for creative learning to happen. Physical play is not just about riding bikes and climbing a frame; what about small ladders to climb trees, or chasing each other, using a hula hoop, or playing ball? It is about allowing children to utilise the space they have and to come up with their own ideas. It is where children can use their imagination, create problem-solving strategies, and be resourceful.

 IDEA
MINI BEAST HOTEL

Create a multi-storey hotel that's full of all sorts of natural materials, such as old bricks, bark, pine cones, wood, sand, soil, logs, and much more. This will provide hidey-holes for creatures galore.

Resources and tools – *tubes, ropes, and twigs . . . oh my! Shovels, buckets, and straws . . . yes!! Pine cones, cardboard, and rocks . . . can it be done?!* The outdoor space should be set in a way where children can explore and get the necessary resources and tools they need. Your outdoor play space will foster creative play if you include 'loose parts,' or open-ended play materials, that children can use, such as recycled cardboard boxes, crates, PVC pipes, milk cartons, and dirt and sticks! When thinking about resources and tools to enable children to learn outdoors, think of what is available naturally for the loose parts. For example, for imaginative play, making dens in hedges, trees, or with an old blanket and washing up line. Props could be in the form of brooms, dustbin lids, sticks, and old clothes. Messy play can be with mud pies or using sticks and stones to create dams in puddles left overnight by the rain. Construction play can be with sticks, stones, logs, boxes, bricks, and anything else the children want to bring to it. Games such as hide and seek, hopscotch, or those mentioned in the creative idea of bringing back the past can do wonders for physical development.

 IDEA

BRING BACK THE PAST!

Why not put up a list of outdoor games which adults can choose at every session and play with the children? This keeps children engaged as well as the adults. Add your own creative twist to it:

- Tug of war – rope needed, two teams created to tug over a line drawn on the ground

- Blind man's bluff – blindfold needed. One child blindfolded and is to chase other children and tag them

- Jump on a rope – skipping rope needed

- Potato and spoon race – potato and spoon needed! Create a start and finish and allow children to race one another

- Capture the flag – flags needed, placed high encouraging children to run and grab

- Land and water – these are instructions children follow when you say a certain word. Water means jump forward. Sea means jump forward twice. Land means jump back. Mountains mean jump back twice. Hill means one step to the right. Lake means one step to the left

- Hopscotch – chalk needed

- Simon says

- What's the time, Mr Wolf? – clock needed to hang around the child who plays the wolf

RESEARCH TO EXPLORE
DEN-MAKING

Canning (2010) conducted a small-scale research examining den-making in three different settings in the UK. The research concluded that successful outdoor play offers flexible opportunities where children engage in imaginative and creative play, develop their communication skills, and build relationships with other children and adults.

For this reason, think about your own garden and where you keep the tools you need to do the gardening, clean up, put up a hanging basket, DIY, or just relax. If you have children, how do you accommodate for their play within the garden? Using this experience may assist you in how you view the settings outdoor space. As adults, we probably have a shed of some kind in the back of the garden; *can a similar concept be available in the children's outdoor space, so that tools within this are at their disposal?* This provision can then be opened daily to allow children free access, without really having the burden of 'setting up'.

Think inclusive practice – it is important to consider the needs of individual children in any creative space you plan. Some children, especially those with disabilities or special needs, may have difficulties in the outdoor space. You can make adaptations for these children just like you would indoors. You can adjust the materials and spaces (install a wheelchair-accessible swing, install railings, lower or raise gardening plots) to best fit their needs. Talk to relevant adults, including parents, to know what modifications may be necessary. Also, as outdoor spaces can be a place for 'letting loose' and for children to use their louder voices, make sure you have calming spaces available outside.

Creative learning does not just happen, and vital to this is the development, quality, and richness of creative spaces. Creative spaces are where children's curiosities, ideas, and discoveries are cultivated, and where creativity's characteristics flourish. *Children really get to know the environment if they can dig it, beat it, swat it, lift it, push it, join it, combine different things with it. This is what adults call creative activity . . . a process of imagination and environment working together* (Moore, 1996, p. 76).

Next steps

 REFLECT

Think of your setting and immediate learning environment. Are there ways in which you might adapt what you have to help create creative spaces that excite curiosity and stimulate imagination? What if you took the learning elsewhere?

What ideas do you have for extending the resources available to you and your children? Are there materials that are inexpensive or free that can be used and adapted to encourage your children to also invent and adapt? Could children invent, design, and make their own?

 EXPLORE

Duffy, C. (2014) A case study of movement and physical development affordances of outdoor play. MA Research module. Birmingham City University. Available at: www. crec.co.uk/research-paper-archive/2014-016.pdf

Mirrahimi, S. et al. (2011) The Impact of Natural Environment on learning, social and emotional intelligence: www.sciencedirect.com/science/article/pii/S1877705811029900

Irving, H. (2012) Nature Deficit Disorder in *The Early Years Foundation Stage Forum*: http://eyfs.info/articles.html/general/nature-deficit-disorder-r136/

■ An article on how children are not receiving the outdoor experiences that they should.

Community Playthings: www.communityplaythings.co.uk/learning-library/articles

■ A number of articles to assist in planning and implementing your creative spaces, both indoors and outdoors:

Outdoor inspiration resources

■ Bristol Beach Schools: www.facebook.com/bristolbeachschools/?hc_ref=SEARCH

■ Children and Nature Network (2016): www.childrenandnature.org/

■ Developing School Grounds and Outdoor Spaces: http://creativestarlearning. co.uk/c/developing-school-grounds-outdoor-spaces/

■ Minibeast Hotel: ww2.rspb.org.uk/get-involved/activities/give-nature-a-home-in-your-garden/garden-activities/build-a-bug-hotel/

■ Potion Station: http://learninglady.co.uk/learning-outdoors-a-potion-station

■ The National Trust (2016) 50 Things to do before you're 11 ¾ Project: www. nationaltrust.org.uk/50-things-to-do

Tech tools

■ Classroom Architect: allows you to interactively design your space with ready-made icons: http://classroom.4teachers.org/

■ Dropmark: a collaborative sharing tool, where images and ideas can be uploaded for the team to share and comment on: www.dropmark.com/

■ Project Timeline: an app to plan all the milestones and time allocation to develop your spaces, or anything else you take on: https://educationstore.microsoft.com/en-gb/store/details/project-timeline/9wzdncrfjb2k

 # Creative approaches

 THINK

What learning experiences or circumstances allow children to become more creative?

What are some of the ways adults can foster creativity through their approaches?

CHAPTER FOCUS

■ Exploring the meaning of creative approaches

■ Offering a varied creative diet to children

■ Exploration of various creative approaches including creative connections, creative sparks and hooks, role-play and creative dramatics, the project approach, and the use of technology and creative partnerships

We all know that the old notion of education where the children are sitting quietly and neatly in their seats, while the adult is up front pouring pearls of wisdom and knowledge into their brains no longer exists. Instead, the adult's role has changed from the traditional 'imparter of knowledge' to that of a facilitator and coach. It is also fact that children in the early years are very curious, eager to learn, and willing to do whatever it takes, providing the climate is right, and their interest in the learning experience is captured. Creative adults not only allow children, but encourage and require them, to take responsibility for much more of their learning than ever before. So, once you have mastered your creative space, it is what unfolds inside of it which is the key to stimulating and nurturing creativity. This chapter supports you to adopt creative approaches in teaching and learning, together with what you have learnt throughout the book, to embed into your early years practice.

What are creative approaches?

All Our Futures (1999, p. 89) advises that teaching creatively is about 'using *imaginative approaches* to making learning more interesting and effective'. It further goes on to state that 'teaching should fire interests and motivate learning'. The focus, then, is on the learning and the ways in which creativity can ensure progression and make it more effective. *What is an approach?* An approach is a way of viewing teaching and learning. It can be informed by the setting's vision and the adult's beliefs and ideas about the nature of learning, and how this is then translated into the teaching context. Underlying creative approaches is a view of what creativity is, how it can be stimulated, and how it can engage children in learning experiences. An approach gives rise to methods, techniques, and strategies for how to teach content creatively and support children's creative learning. Creative approaches, then, are creativity-rich sessions, activities, lessons, experiences, processes, and practices that the adult, and setting, plan and deliver within the creative spaces. All of these allow creativity's characteristics to be applied, practiced, and mastered by the children.

 **CONNECT**

What teaching strategies do adults use? What makes them 'creative approaches'?

The use of time, rich resource materials, the creative space, the climate, planning, and the curriculum are all a part of creative approaches; it is through these that they are implemented. And so is the uniqueness of each child, what they bring to the process, and how they approach their learning, alongside the mess, the noise, the freedom, and the fun! It is also worth noting that certain approaches may foster greater creativity than others, and the adult needs to make decisions regarding which approaches may encourage or discourage creativity through being flexible with them, testing them, and adapting them according to what is unfolding. Creative approaches are also not just about a series of activities or lessons, but about an entire experience; it is an interplay between the child's surroundings, relationships, and experiences (Evangelou et al., 2009, p. 23). The aim is to make what is being taught what it should be – immensely interesting!

A varied creative diet approach

The goal of creative approaches is to offer children a 'varied diet', which consists of inputs, processes, and resources provided by the creative adult. This variety helps promote an atmosphere of expectancy – *'I wonder what will happen today?'* – rather than the feeling of 'expectations' – *'oh, here we go again!'* Of course, when one diets, to be successful, there are certain guidelines that need conforming to; a varied diet for creative approaches is the same.

Guidance for the varied diet

- **Slow and steady wins the race** – diets require you to take one step at a time to see a change or difference. It is the same with creative approaches. Think about your approaches, what you want to offer the children and why, plan it, make changes slowly, go back to it, make further changes, and so on. Don't try to do too much too soon. Let your interactions with the children within the creative space guide you to take the necessary steps to embed creativity in all aspects.

- **Think about clear boundaries** – creative approaches can give rise to enthusiasm and lots of energy (I wouldn't expect it any other way!). So, think about how you will respond to disruption by not letting your emotions lead the way. Ensure you have the 'with-it-ness' – an awareness of what is going on in all areas of your setting – and having a quick response to actual and possible disruptions. It's a 'nip in the bud' approach that stops over-enthusiastic behaviour escalating. *How will you communicate this to the children?*

- **Ensure sensitivity and gentleness** – this is sensitivity to the child's current state of where they are in their learning and development in the present. His or her level of communicative ability and immediate interests – and sensitivity to the meaning the child is endeavouring to communicate (Fisher, 2013, p. 16). This makes the environment safe for the children to explore and engage with what is happening around them, without feeling pressured or intimidated. *How will you communicate this to the children?*

⚲ FACT NOTE

Michael Rosen, an English children's novelist and poet, has said that:

> Whenever I work with people – no matter what their age – I try to run a checklist through my mind: are these people **investigating, discovering, inventing and cooperating** ? They don't have to be doing all four all the time, but is this event, this process, this 'workshop' involving at least one of these? In an ideal moment, it'll be all four. What can I do to increase the amount of whichever one of the four is not happening here? In my experience, things start to happen when all four-take place in a group of people.
>
> (Rosen, 2010, p. 11)

How can you apply all four to your creative spaces and approaches?

DISCUSS

With peers/colleagues how they ensure inclusion within their approaches.

- **Ensure inclusion** – approaches need to ensure that they are accessible and relevant to the children. Those who are dual language learners should be able to demonstrate their abilities, skills, and knowledge, in any language, including their home language. Strong practical and sensory elements are needed to engage those children with special educational needs – *how will you ensure equality of access to your creative approaches?* Practitioners need to know their children in order to best adapt their creative approaches to them. It is about listening to children in their various forms. Goodwin (2008; Goodwin and Edwards, 2009) provides a cycle of listening and responding to children who do not communicate using words, so that it enables an organic child-centred experience. It is provided for the many differing inclusion needs of young children, and a valuable resource to incorporate into practice.

- **Positive relationships** – the EYFS guides in the understanding that children learn to be strong and independent through positive relationships (DfE, 2017, p. 6). Practitioners need to think about the style of relationship they have with their children. Think about what type of relationships you want to develop; could it almost be a creative partnership? Your relationship will, of course, depend on the group, but a balance is needed. Mutually respectful reciprocal relationships are the key. This is where the children are viewed as people in the present, and where they are given a voice in their learning. Creative adults then take part as co-learners in the relationship, and show children creative assurance by building on unexpected contributions and enquiries from them – the teachable moments! By taking the ideas and interests that children initiate; the adult supports and extends learning possibilities in order to build on their real-world understandings and creative experiences.

- **Don't choose content over process!** The content is what you want children to learn, but the process is the way to make it happen. Creative approaches focus more on the process of teaching and learning because the content builds and unfolds through it, integrating the aims and activities naturally – *where are creativity's characteristics embedded in the process of your approaches?* The idea is to merge the content that the practitioner wants to teach with the interests of the children. Within this, the use of time must be considered because it is important to provide children lots of time to explore materials and pursue their ideas. This includes time to think about how to plan, design, construct, experiment, and revise ideas – all vital to the creative process. Creativity's characteristics will be stimulated and exhibited more as children have the time to do so. Don't forget to build in time to talk ideas over with other people – both adults and children.

RESEARCH TO EXPLORE
MULTIMODAL APPROACHES

Gunther Kress (2009) pioneered multimodal approaches for representing and expressing ideas. Multimodality is a theory which looks at the many different modes that people use to communicate with each other and to express themselves.

A mode is generally defined as a communication channel. Examples of modes are writing, gesture, posture, gaze, font choice and colour, images, video, painting, dancing, and even the interactions between them.

How can you use multimodality in the creative approaches you provide?

■ **Be imaginative** – *All Our Futures* advocates the use of imaginative approaches. An early years practitioner who is imaginative with their approaches can do wonders in the setting. Being imaginative allows you to explore and create new things, activities, and experiences through new ideas. This is essential to stimulate interest, add excitement, and teach what you want more effectively. It is about engaging the children. Being imaginative in your approaches will encourage children to do the same. By being imaginative, the sessions, activities, lessons, experiences, and practices will have surprises and elements of fun! Use the approaches in Chapter 4 to assist you in using a dose of imagination to liven up learning.

■ **Creative approaches focus on experiential learning** – the process of learning through holistic experiences (discussed in Chapter 6). Knowledge, skills, and understanding are developed through an active approach which consists of first-hand practical experiences because children learn by doing. However, what is vital with experiential learning is that the focus must be on children's involvement with the learning materials through their imagination, their senses, what they know and can do, play, exploration and investigation, dialogue and collaboration, and their use of creativity's characteristics. These must underpin all creative approaches that the practitioner devises and implements, and in how they respond to children, with rich materials and spaces set up for the experiences to take form.

■ **Ensure a variety of experiences** – this requires links to the local community and cultures, where adults can draw on the knowledge and experiences out there to embed into their approaches. Activities such as trips, celebrating holidays and activities of multi-cultural nature and encouraging children to bring visitors to the setting enhance the creative process. The more varied experiences children have in their lives, the wider the range of creative expression. The more personal experiences children have with people and situations outside of their own environment, the more material they can draw on to incorporate into their learning, play, and creativity. Our challenge is to try not to be intimidated by the variety and diversity of creative expression in our settings.

ACTIVITY

Take a trip to explore a different culture or community other than yours.

What can you identify and bring back as a varied experience for children?

- **Creative conversations** – this is about talking less and facilitating more. A language-rich environment is necessary for children, but there is a huge difference between talking *at* them and talking *to* them. It is about developing creative conversations which are language-rich and dialogic. Meaningful dialogues between children, as well as between practitioners and children, are created to support thinking, learning, engagement, and imagination. By making questioning a part of daily exchange, it will lead to a dialogic culture, but also give rise to the cognitive dance. The creative adult should also be pondering and reflecting on issues in conversations in an open and interested manner, which encourages children to do the same.

- **Reward creative ideas, practices, and processes** – we often reward behaviours such as walking quietly, keeping hands to self, raising hand before speaking, sitting still in a chair. *Do we stand back and ask why?* Surely these are expected behaviours of how one conducts themselves? What about promoting 'had an original idea', 'created a new game outdoors', 'made up a story', 'solved problem for a friend', 'invented something from a common object', or 'came up with a brilliant idea in how to solve the blockage in the water tray'? The creative adult needs to praise creative expression by the children as part of their approaches, because it is this that will encourage children to give more creative responses to take forward.

- **Embed quality creative breaks** – one of the most significant findings of educational research is that health practices greatly facilitate learning. Learners who move around, practice proper breathing, and take breaks to stretch and unwind consistently do better. The same is said for the creative process: when children's well-being is looked after, their involvement is high. Laevers (1993, 1994) describes children whose well-being is high as if they are 'standing on firm ground'. 'When involvement in high, the child is in a "state of flow". When these two situations concur simultaneously, "deep level learning" is happening'

(Laevers, 1993, p. 60). This does not simply mean sending children outdoors for 'play time', but rather more beneficial creative breaks. One way to enhance creative learning is by bringing health practices into the setting. Whether its Tai Chi, Chi Kung, Yoga, Pilates, Brain Gym or whatever you create, they must be adaptable to any child, relatively easy to do, and above all should be fun. *How can you incorporate this into your routines?*

 RESEARCH TO EXPLORE
EXPERIENTIAL EDUCATION SCALES (EXE)

Originating in Flanders and the Netherlands, EXE, otherwise known as 'wellbeing and involvement scales', can be used to explore the context, process, and outcomes of approaches for children (Laevers, 2015).

It is formally measured by a scale reflecting children's well-being (feeling at ease, being spontaneous and free from emotional tensions) and involvement (being intensely engaged, a necessary condition for deep learning and involvement).

■ **Extend creative approaches beyond the setting into the home and community** – the result of interactions with significant others in their family and their community at large complements children's learning (Rogoff, 1990). There are renowned benefits of engaging parents by breaking down home/setting barriers which then impact on children's dispositions, attitudes, and motivation to learn. When setting children learning to engage with in the home, creative adults do so to make this more applicable to the lives of the children, to their daily experiences, to the things that matter to them, and to enable interactions amongst the family and community. Therefore, a creative approach is to make every homework a field trip, a research junket, or a personalised piece of work. As a creative adult, an essential part of our roles is to discover how to hook the spirit of the learner to what is being taught. This won't happen unless we bring the learning out of the setting and into the child's own life, and engage parents to understand the role of creativity in learning through it, but not through a work sheet.

The creative approaches

You! – *what approach are you going to take in the setting to teach creatively and promote creative learning? What will you do when finding those 'teachable moments', those moments of creative expression?* Jackson (2014) has stated that there are three types of approaches that adults use to promote development and provide support in learning:

■ 'Sage on the stage' – a knowledge transmitter

■ 'Guide on the side' – a facilitator

■ 'Meddler in the middle' – an involved co-learner/co-producer in the learning process

All these approaches are relevant and can be used to aid in creative learning and development, but the promotion of children's creativity is best served by adults who are 'meddlers' and 'guides' – *what are the teaching and learning contexts in which you are able to meddle or facilitate? Are there more opportunities for meddling?* Creative adults act as facilitators, scaffolding, empowering, and enabling children. They have an ability to take stock of a situation, to know when to move and when to stay still (Rinaldi, 2005). They explore and learn with the children as co-learners, asking open-ended questions and encouraging children to do the same. Through these approaches, creative adults have activity/lesson ideas, which are not rigid, and they are found to be actively listening to children and responding to them by getting involved and building on what they are saying and doing.

 ACTION RESEARCH

Observe a couple of early years adults in the setting. Make notes on when they used the approach of:

■ Sage on the stage

■ Guide on the side

■ Meddler in the middle

Was it appropriate for what was happening? How were the roles being used to nurture creativity?

Approaches which provide opportunities for creative connections between children – this happens in a collaborate environment, and builds positive relationships amongst children, not just between the adult and child as advocated by the EYFS. Sometimes, it is exciting to just get the children together and do some team building; after all, this is what happens in the adult's world of work!

Many children in reception are placed in different groups for literacy and math, often with children in a neighbouring reception classroom. These children spend almost an hour together and may come away not knowing each other's names, as the session focuses heavily on content. Children need time to know each other as learning is a shared experience, and one that flourishes in positive relationships with each other.

(EYFS Teacher)

CONNECT

How do you and your setting facilitate creative connections amongst children?

A setting should be a collaborative environment where children work together to support each other's learning. Here, it is about facilitating children to connect with each other, where they are interested in each other, support each other, and work together. It is where creativity thrives through sharing what they are doing and giving voice to their thoughts and ideas. A great way to set the tone is with some fun collaborating exercises.

> My favourite is a simple team task that can take an hour or even two! I set out big and small marshmallows and some raw spaghetti, divide the children into groups of four, and ask them to build the tallest freestanding tower. Once the children have the supplies and an understanding of what you expect, sit back and watch the creativity explode!
>
> (Early years practitioner)

Approaches embed children's creative sparks! – sparks are 'things, phenomena, conversations – anything that provokes deeper thought' (Seitz, 2006, p. 2). Sparks are what trigger a child (and adults!) to want to know more and to investigate it further. It can be as simple as finding a pebble in one's shoe, grabbing an idea or story line from a book, or finding something in the outdoor area. Young children have these 'sparks of interest' all day long, and a part of the creative adult's role should be to observe and capture these sparks to then take forward in their creative approaches.

Consider the nut bolt practice story. It is obvious that Angela's spark-led interest around her discovery led her to explore and engage in many areas of learning. This could have been enhanced even further with the provision of clipboards, papers, and pencils so that the recording of checked trikes could take place and thus allow literacy and mathematical learning and development to take place. The nut bolt led to many questions, and thinking about the possibilities of where it might have come from. Through it, Angela investigates, explores, and ponders. Her thoughts lead her to realise that there are trikes that are currently being used and that she cannot investigate them. She problem solves by stopping the trikes through road signs – *can you connect further creativity's characteristics to Angela's story?*

To avoid the burden of trying to meet each creative spark religiously (which is impossible!), use the four-point approach below to assist you in filtering them. This can provide for effective planning by assessing the creative possibilities that can be attached to them as and when they come along:

1) A spark may be acknowledged with a comment or question – a response as part of a teachable moment.

2) A spark may be acknowledged by the provision of resources and materials to extend on what is happening – a response as part of a teachable moment.

3) A spark may be noted down or filed away for possible future use – to use in planning creative approaches.

4) A spark becomes the start of a bigger project or investigation in which children and adults work together to further explore it – the devising of inquiry-based projects.

! STORY FROM PRACTICE
THE NUT BOLT

During outdoor play, 4-year-old Angela discovers a loose metal nut about half an inch in diameter. She shows the nut to the practitioner.

Angela: Look what I found. It looks just like the big one on our workbench.

Practitioner: Yes, it sure does, Angela. It's called a nut.

Angela: I wonder where it came from.

Practitioner: Where do you think it may have come from?

Angela: Well, it is the same as the ones in the workbench inside.

Practitioner: This nut looks very similar to the nuts and bolts inside. I think this nut might be bigger than the nuts and bolts we have inside.

Angela: Maybe it came off of something out here.

Practitioner: Where do you think it is from?

Angela: Umm, I don't know – something out here.

Practitioner: Maybe you should check.

Angela: Okay.

Holding the nut tight in her fist, Angela walks around, stopping to examine the play equipment, the tables, the parked trikes, and anything else she thinks might have a missing nut. She can find only bolts with nuts on the trikes. She spies a large 'stop' sign, puts her special treasure in her pocket so other children cannot see it, and sets up a roadblock for the busy trike riders so she can check the nuts and bolts on their trikes. Edmund stops and asks her what she is doing, and she explains. Edmund says he needs to see the nut. When Angela shows it to him, he gets off his trike and starts helping her inspect the other trikes. They eventually find the one that is missing the nut. Other children are curious and crowd around.

Approaches use creative hooks – think back to your most memorable learning experiences, the courses you enjoyed, and the educators/facilitators you found most effective. How did they start their classes or workshop sessions? How did they greet you when you came into their session? Chances are they intentionally planned to draw you into the learning experience; this is what a hook is! Where children present their sparks during the day, in creative approaches, adults identify a 'hook' to engage children in the creative learning process. Much like provocations, discussed in Chapter 8, a hook is powerful in creative learning, and when done right, children can 'spark' an idea through their responses and take their creative learning forward. What is the hook that you intend to use to capture children's interest and curiosity?

Creative hooks involve children in the experiences to then help them transition positively throughout the creative space in the process of their learning. Children can make positive connections with their peers, explore or review learning materials, create a context around the teaching, and, most importantly, shift their focus to the here and now through the hook that creative adults provide. Find a hook! Engage children from the moment they walk in through the door. A hook can be objects, postcards, images, quotes, a task, conversations, a scenario like how the aliens crash landed in the lunch hall, and so on. Children are drawn in by colourful, novel, or intriguing objects, whether they are tools, old toys, or items found in nature. Children often share and reflect more readily when they attach their thoughts and feelings to an item that can be touched and shown to a group during discussion. Brain research also suggests that using metaphors, pictures, symbols, and concrete items helps children cement experiences and transfer learning to everyday life and future learning (Willis, 2006, 2010).

! STORY FROM PRACTICE

I carry skeins of wool and foam balls in the trunk of my car and use them to make massive diagrams on the floor, to symbolise interactions and dynamics between people, animals, objects, to make whatever images I require in the moment. I have also used found objects, forests, fire (though not in the forest), living sculptures of people, fruit of various kinds, stones, wood, eggs, Star Wars action figures, postcards, live cats, images of Curious George, and so on. You get the idea: more interesting (or more bizarre) equals more effective in hooking the children.

Approaches encourage children to 'play with ideas' – creative thinking takes time to develop, and children in the early years need to be encouraged to do so in visible forms. This is so that they can see the value of it through how the adult encourages it. Through approaches, children should be able to generate ideas and have the opportunity to utilise their surroundings to play and tinker with them. Adults encourage the children to come up with ideas, and support them to take their ideas forward in their play. When it comes to being creative and coming up with new and fresh ideas, children are experts. But, in order to harness and hone their creative juices, the cognitive tool set of an adult is vital through the approaches used and, of course, through those teachable moments when they spot children having an idea.

Adults need to provide children with a way to capture their ideas on a daily basis. When a new idea pops into our heads, we jot it down immediately; something similar is needed for children. It is a creative habit we are allowing children to establish by saying you can have these ideas, they are awesome ideas, and they are ideas that matter. Indulge children in 'what if?' or 'why not?' questions as a springboard to inquiry and new ideas. Inviting children to consider 'What if?' encourages investigation, inquiry, and artistry to explore new possibilities and ways of thinking (Kwek, 2011). Approaches need to build upon children's existing ideas with effective questioning to encourage children to share their trains of thought. Observing children and watching their ideas unfold 'in the moment' is crucial, especially with those children whose language is limited – *how can you turn these ideas into 'teachable moments'? – how can this be achieved?*

⚲ FACT NOTE

Edwin Land (1909–1991) was an inventor who studied chemistry. On holiday, he took a photograph of his 3-year-old daughter. She asked why she could not see the result straight away and she kept asking 'why not?' Land pondered this question and an idea formed in his mind. He went on to develop the Polaroid camera. *The many possibilities when asking 'why not?'!*

Approaches allow children their own planning opportunities – many creative experiences require planning on part of the creative adult. Planning is also a part of children's creative learning. For children, planning is choice with intention. That is, the child begins with a specific goal or purpose in mind that results in the choice they make (Epstein, 2003) to achieve it. Engaging children in planning encourages them to identify their goals and consider the options for achieving them. For example, they might consider what they will do, where they will do it, what materials they will use, who they will do it with, how long it will take, and whether they will need help. Planning in this way will involve decisions on actions, predicting interactions, recognising problems, proposing solutions, and anticipating consequences and reactions – all a part of the creative process!

Start by making planning a part of the day. It can take place at the same time every day, say after morning greeting or circle time. You can plan with children in small groups or pairs, as well as individually, making sure each child gets to express his or her intentions. In fact, children benefit from planning in small groups because the thoughts and elaborations of others often 'spark' their own ideas, and plant creative seeds.

- When planning, make sure children can see all that is available in their creative spaces. Visibility is important for younger planners whose mental representations are limited. You can always tour the room when planning – *what do we have? What can be used? How can it be used?*

- Ask children open-ended questions to seek genuine information about their intentions and how they plan to carry them out. '*How will you build your tower?*' will elicit more detail than '*Will you use the big blocks?*'

- Listen to children, not just to their words, but to gestures and body language, too. You will learn about their ability to anticipate and think about the details of their plans. Then you can choose the most appropriate support strategies to help them elaborate their ideas and consider the options for implementing them.

- Don't reject or offer children an alternative to their plans. This defeats the whole purpose of encouraging them to express their own intentions and the creative process.

- Encourage children to elaborate throughout the process by helping them to extend their ideas. Encourage them to give details about where they will work, the materials they intend to use, the sequence of their activities, and the outcomes they expect to achieve.

- Record children's plans; this will give them the message that their ideas are valuable. Label things, take dictation when children describe their intentions, write the child's name on the plan, get the older children to write their own and possibly their ideas. Use photography and videos to capture plans. Recording in this way will let children elaborate on their ideas, and review their documented plans as they reflect on their experiences and compare their intentions with the actual outcomes.

I use the concept of thought bubbles with children for planning learning. These are real balloons blown up as it has to be visible for young children. I get the children to think about the activity, and how they will attempt it. We then use symbols and words to draw on the balloon. At the end, we review by popping those met, and add another if a new approach was used.

(Nursery Nurse)

It is vital to understand that when we plan as adults and have our intentions of what we expect children to learn, these are so different from what children think they are learning. For example, I planned an activity of baking soda and dyes. I wanted children to see what happened to the soda when it reacted to the dye. However, when speaking to a 4-year-old, he told me he was learning what colours were created as they mixed. Children have their own learning intentions that need to be recognised.

(Senior Practitioner)

DISCUSS

With peers/colleagues how they provide children with opportunities to plan their learning.

Approaches embed effective questioning skills – which extend creative and critical thinking by giving rise to the cognitive dance. Children need practitioners to encourage them to share their ideas, contemplate possibilities, and help them document what is learnt. Questioning approaches have to be creative and effective for this purpose. Asking simply yes or no questions can stifle responses. When you ask questions that only produce rote answers, such as 'what colour is the cube?' you don't get any information about what the children know or think. Therefore, questions should be about collecting details of children's creative learning and pondering on the possibilities. This can be done through open-ended questions that encourage more than one response or idea. Children will be prompted to think about what they know, what they may want to know, or be wondering about. Harle and Trudeau (2006) provide some effective questions to spark thinking and responses to help children to ponder:

CONNECT

How effectively is 'questioning' used in your setting to encourage creative thinking?

Questions to spark reflection:	Responses to Ponder:
What do you know about . . .?	Let's try your idea and see what happens.
What do you want to know about . . .?	I've been thinking . . .
What ideas do you want share with others?	Let's see if we can . . .
How can we use this?	Let's find out if any friends might be able to help.
What other ways can we use this?	How interesting; you made . . . by . . .
How might this work?	This didn't work for me. I'm wondering what else might work.
What might happen if . . .?	You look like you are really thinking about . . .
What do you remember about . . .?	I've never thought about it like that. That's an interesting way.

RESEARCH TO EXPLORE
FIVE TYPES OF INEFFECTIVE QUESTIONING

Many adults question children in a way that confuses their thinking or suppresses their responses. A study by Napell (1978) introduced five types of questions that do this and thus are ineffective in children's learning. They still seem relevant even today:

1) The *dead end* question

2) The *chameleon* question

3) The question with a *programmed answer*

4) The *put down* question

5) The *fuzzy* question

Research and find out what these all mean!

The use of questioning in children's reflection is also vital to facilitate connections in their learning. Thinking out loud with children will let them hear and see you using visible reflection, such as 'I was thinking I might want to mix some paint with the sand. I'm wondering what will happen'. Thinking out loud will assist children in learning to verbalise and organise their thoughts. The use of photographs of experiences, drawings, paintings, children's creations, and mark-making can be used for reflection, where children can have conversations around it with the adults (sustained shared thinking), capturing comments and adding to it as written documentation. These can then later be displayed to show the connection of learning and reflection for children to further explore.

Approaches embed problem-solving – creativity is often regarded as surfacing when one is faced with a problem which they then solve. Children love to problem solve. They just don't want to do it in a math worksheet most of the time. They'll always come up with creative ways to solve problems if you give them time, the space, and the experiences to do so. In trying to build a tower earlier, children can use knowledge from math and physics in explaining why certain plans would or would not work. Observing them will give visibility to their trial and error techniques. Solid communication skills and planning are needed to be successful in the task. In fact, all the skills that children have picked up in the setting, not forgetting creativity's characteristics, can be seen when you give them a problem, and time to solve it. Adults need to use this approach to create difficult problems for children that need solving – easy problems are boring! It is essential to remember that this approach is not about presenting children with pre-planned problems and designated solutions, because this shortcuts creativity

(Starko, 2014, p. 202). It is approaches where you can brainstorm multiple solutions to problems together.

 OBSERVE

A child in your setting. When and how are they using problem-solving? How does the adult facilitate?

Approaches embed problem finding – of course, creativity is not just confined to solving a problem, but also about going out there and *finding* one. There needs to be an emphasis on the formulation of problems just as important as the resolution of them. Starko (2014, p. 50) emphasises this approach through group problem finding opportunities. Children can explore their surroundings to find a problem which can then be facilitated by the creative adult for children to solve through the ideas they may have. Starko advises giving children roles that they are in to help them:

■ **Inventors** – find situations where an invention is needed to solve a problem

■ **Visual artists** – find inspiration for a new work of art

■ **Musicians** – find sounds that might be combined to create something

■ **Playwrights** –: look around for characters or situations for role-play

■ **Naturalists** – exploring the outdoors through the plants, trees, bugs etc.

 CONNECT

What other roles can children take on to problem find?

Approaches utilise role-play – no surprise here as children in the early years are always playing differing roles according to what they have experienced and the knowledge they hold. However, sometimes this type of play is not utilised effectively in learning. Role-play is a technique that allows children to explore realistic situations by interacting with other children and adults in a managed way to develop experience, and to trial different strategies in a supported environment. Depending on the intention of the activity, children might be playing a role similar to their own (or one in the future), or could play the opposite part of a conversation or interaction. Both options provide the possibility for significant learning, with the former allowing experience to be gained and the latter encouraging children to develop an understanding of the situation from the 'opposite' point of view. Children are able to think aloud, ponder, and question whilst in-role, something they may not be able to do so readily in whole group discussions. *How can the creative approach of role-play be used to deliver creative teaching and learning?*

 RESEARCH TO EXPLORE

MANTLE OF THE EXPERT

A dramatic-inquiry based approach to teaching and learning invented and developed by Professor Dorothy Heathcote in the 1980s. The big idea is that the children do all their work as if they are an imagined group of experts. They might be scientists in a laboratory or archaeologists excavating a tomb, or a rescue team at the scene of a disaster. They might be running a removal company, or a factory, or a shop, or a space station. Through activities and tasks, the children gradually take on problems and challenges from the above encounter and come up with new ideas and possibilities (Taylor, 2016).

Approaches which use creative dramatics – this is where children can explore ideas with their bodies as well as their minds. Creative dramatics allow children to explore a situation physically in an effort to find and express creative ideas (Starko, 2014, p. 184). Where role-play enables children to take on realistic roles, creative dramatics moves into the imaginary, into the fantasy; children become melting snow, walls of a building, a rubber band, or a lion's tail. Young children actively use their bodies better than adults and are always engaging their senses; this form of approach engages their natural active learning trait. Some examples of this approach can be children pretending to be puppets, pulled by strings that are attached to their bodies. Children can be animals and imitate their movements and mannerisms to learn about them. Children walk in a place under a variety of circumstances: through the jungle, on hot sand, in a flooded town. *How can you use creative dramatics in your approaches?* This approach is especially accessible to the very young, and those children whose communication and language may be limited.

Creativity is best served through the project approach – this is inquiry-based learning, which merges the requirements of teaching with children's ideas to form a project. According to Katz and Chard (1989, p. 5), projects need not be all of the curriculum, but they complement play, on the one hand, and learning, on the other. Projects promote in-depth understanding and cover a wide range of relevant subtopics and areas of learning. For this reason, they usually take several weeks to complete – and sometimes much longer, dependent on the age and interests of the children. A whole unit of learning can be delivered over several weeks.

Rather than offering immediate answers to the questions children ask, early years practitioners provide experiences through which children can discover the answers themselves through inquiry. The beauty of creative projects is the unpredictability; you of course need a basic framework for it (see Explore), but it needs to be flexible and manageable by shaping the development of what is being investigated. Practitioners guide the children through the process from the beginning to the conclusion. This is the vital bit – it is not the end, but a conclusion, because from a conclusion, another creative adventure begins!

> If the children wonder what shoes are made of or how are they made, the adult may arrange a field visit where the answer to these questions can be provided by an expert, in this case a shoe factory, the shoe repair man's shop, or a shoe store. Children also consult secondary sources of information such as books and the internet in the setting and with their parents at home.
>
> (EYFS Coordinator)

The project approach presents many opportunities for young children's ideas to be valued, their creativity to be encouraged, their interests to be nurtured, and their learning needs to be met. Through project work, children can not only improve their understanding of the world around them, but can also strengthen their dispositions to go on learning creatively for the rest of their lives (Katz and Chard, 1989, p. 5). Projects or inquiries can emerge from the questions children raise, sparks that are observed, and planning discussions that take place, with teaching content planned into it. They encourage children to think, question, ponder, and be challenged. Through them, children are able to make connections and see relationships, speculate, pursue, act, and discuss, as well as apply and master creative skills and characteristics.

Within projects, children should also be given impossible tasks/activities to inquire about or investigate. This is where problem-finding and -solving come in. Adults need to find them in what they intend to teach and use them, and then watch learning unfold mystery with wonder, where 'that's not possible!' turns into the many possibilities that even the adult may not have thought of. For example, children are asked to spend their weekend spotting a multi-coloured car on the streets – *is that even possible?* This will encourage outdoor learning, watching cars go by, changing locations to see if it can be spotted anywhere else. *What possibilities could the children come up with?* What about asking children 'if dogs can talk?' Adults need to design or embed challenges into their practice and creative spaces for which there are no single right answers, but which do not penalise children if they are not successful in finding one. Remember, its's about the process and stimulating creativity!

Projects and inquiries that stem directly from the children are individual to them; there is higher engagement and motivation as it is fired from the child's interest. Children are excited to explore different passions and present their discoveries in ways that are comfortable to them. It provides a stronger understanding of the material, because children are given the chance to explore and present in ways that are meaningful to them. By working in a mode in which they are most comfortable, they can explore the information more fully, but it is the creative adult's role to find them and facilitate for them.

> I had a child build a boat with his grandfather this year. He spent time in the setting looking at books on boats and cutting them out from a magazine and sticking them in a book I provided. He was so engaged that I don't think he realised that he was actually learning. He improved on skills by working on something creative that mattered to him.
>
> (Nursery teacher)

Approaches use many kinds of technological tools effectively – during their learning experiences, children often ask a lot of questions; they want to know more and more, and they will seek the possibility of trying things for themselves and exploring them in a direct way. To broaden the many possibilities in children's learning, the combination of technology and creativity is key to providing immersive experiences that children need. It is not about providing an iPad or screen for children to click through a series of images. It is about meaningful creative engagement, through apps for the children and other digital technology for the practitioner to use in their approaches. When adults use technological devices to integrate their activities, say, with sounds, projected images, lights, and so much more, they offer an imaginative environment for children, almost magical, where positive engagement is guaranteed. Children become more engaged, the understanding process in their minds is boosted, and they begin making links and connections among concepts they are receiving in a more tangible form.

 OBSERVE

Your setting. How are technological tools being used to engage children?

Technological tools, when used effectively, can enhance children's experiences; for example, interactive storybooks bring a whole new dimension to storytelling. It has also been shown that when books are consumed digitally, boys respond better and are more likely to engage in reading for pleasure as a result (Picton, 2014, p. 5). Steve Jobs once said: 'The best way to create value in the 21st century is to connect creativity with technology' (Issacson, 2012). And when this happens inside the setting, it means that practitioners are preparing children for their future in the most significant way. The idea is to use tools of technology as creativity triggers that help children develop creative thinking and other essential skills.

The Literacy Trust provides six engagement features to assist adults in exploring apps for children to use. These are 'Fun', 'Playing together', 'Interactive', 'Loads to do', 'Creative', and 'Make it your own' (Literacy Trust, 2016). There are, however, a growing number of apps that meet or exceed those recommended:

- **Lots of fun** – the app is fun and makes children feel included and empowered through the response of the screen, e.g. touches/tapping/swiping etc.

- **Play together** – the app allows the child to play with others, either in person or virtually.

- **Interactive** – the app has goals and rules and gives clear feedback or encouragement when the child engages with it. These goals and rules can be adjusted to suit the child.

- **Loads to do** – the app gives children different activities, characters, and stories to be involved with.

- **Creative** – the app lets children use their imagination, make new stories, or change what is happening.

- **Make it your own** – the app can be changed to relate to the child, i.e. adding voices or pictures or by creating their own characters.

 RESEARCH TO EXPLORE

USE OF APPS

Marsh et al. (2015) conducted a co-produced study in collaboration between academics at the Universities of Sheffield and Edinburgh, the BBC (CBeebies), a primary school, and children's media companies. It explored play and creativity in pre-schoolers' use of apps. The findings were presented as a report for early years practitioners. The study explores tablet access, use, competence, favourites, interactions, and experiences.

Approaches make good use of and encourage creative partnerships – this refers to outside organisations that can assist and support creative approaches. Think artists, storytellers, sculptors, dancers, photographers, den makers, bakers, architects, engineers, web designers, and much more. There has been an increasing emphasis on the creative industries working in collaboration within early years education, not necessarily all about art, but for the engagement and learning opportunities provided through their creative processes. It is about thinking, problem-solving, inventing and reinventing, and flexing imaginative muscles (Creative Partnerships, 2007). It is where children can make connections across the areas of learning and between the setting and the wider world. Combining teaching skills with the perspective of an external partner can activate the intellect, emotions, and imagination; this is a dynamic model for learning for creativity (ibid). Not only this: it also builds the confidence and skills of practitioners in combining creative modes within early years practice,

In the UK, a creative learning programme took place between 2009 and 2010 in ten early years settings, collaborating with Creative Practitioners. This was the term used to describe the arts and cultural professionals who offered a creative intervention through their relationships with the early years practitioner, teachers, parents, and children. The settings collaborated in a network, which was established to enable all practitioners to share their thinking and practice, explore creative ways to build more meaningful early learning environments, and learn about opportunities to nurture children's creativity within early years pedagogy (CapeUK, 2011). A more recent collaboration was undertaken by Culture Shift through their project titled Open Sesame: unlocking creativity in early years between 2010 and 2016 (Halsted, 2017). Predominantly through the use of project work, the rich creative learning opportunities that children engaged with through these projects advocate the role of creativity in children's education. The confidence and skills of early years practitioners grew; at the same time, they learned how to build an understanding and integrate creative approaches into the curriculum and, also, dealing with 'academic' expectations from parents versus the importance of creative play were apparent – *how can you tap into creative partnerships to embed in your approaches?*

 AROUND THE WORLD
NORWAY

The Cultural Rucksack is Norway's flagship arts and culture programme, which supports tours by artists, performers, etc. to Norway's schools. It is interested in how Creative Partnership programmes engage schools, adults, children, and parents to ensure a more lasting impact. Professionals within performing arts, visual arts, music, film, literature, and cultural heritage create initiatives and programmes, with targets to the curriculum, to collaborate on with the schools (Christophersen and Breivik, 2013).

Next steps

 REFLECT

Identify a child, or group of children's, sparks. Then, taking the project approach, plan a project to carry the spark forward. The project must include:

■ Opportunities for creative connections amongst the children

■ Planning opportunities for the children in how they will approach the project

- The use of creative hooks

- Opportunities for children to play with their ideas and generate more through effective questioning

- Problem finding and solving

- Role-play and/or creative dramatics

- The use of technology

- Elements drawn from creative disciplines, i.e. artists, storytellers etc.

Remember the possibilities!

 EXPLORE

A Beginner's Guide to Mantle of the Expert by Tim Taylor: www.beginnersguide tomantleoftheexpert.co.uk/

- To support in the use of role-play and creative dramatics.

Get Teaching Creatively: www.creativeteachingsite.com/

- Articles, ideas, and information to inspire creative teaching.

Project Planning Journal: www.tcpress.com/filebin/PDFs/ProjectPlanningJournal.pdf

- An introduction on how to plan and use projects in your approaches.

Earlyarts UK Pocket Guide: 10 Great Techniques to Make Your Teaching More Creative: https://earlyarts.co.uk/ten-great-techniques

- Creativity guide for adults.

Wallis, C. (2017) How Seeing and Using Gestures Make Ideas More Memorable in *MindShift*: ww2.kqed.org/mindshift/2017/10/25/how-seeing-and-using-gestures-make-ideas-more-memorable/

- Article on the use of body language in children's creative learning approaches.

Lindqvist, G. (2007) The dramatic and narrative patterns of play in *European Early Childhood Education Research Journal*, Volume 11, 2003 – Issue 1, pp 69–78: www.tandfonline.com/doi/abs/10.1080/13502930385209071

- The use of narratives to stimulate children's play and, in turn, creativity.

McLeod, N., Wright, D., McCall, K. and Fujii, M. (2017) Visual rhythms: facilitating young children's creative engagement at Tate Liverpool in *European Early Childhood Education Research Journal*, Volume 25, 2017 – Issue 6: www.tandfonline.com/doi/full/10.10 80/1350293X.2017.1380888

■ A paper on creative engagement of a group of 3- and 4-year-old children at Tate Liverpool Art Gallery and how this was facilitated.

Terreni, L. (2015) Young children's learning in art museums: a review of New Zealand and international literature in *European Early Childhood Education Research Journal*, Volume 23, 2015-Issue 5, pp 720–742: www.tandfonline.com/doi/full/10.1080/1350 293X.2015.1104049

■ The benefits of art museums for young children.

CapeUK (2011) *A Journey into Creative Learning: one small step for early years one giant leap for children*: file:///C:/Users/User/Documents/CapeUK-PDF-lo-res.pdf

■ Case studies on creative partnerships in early years settings.

Cre8us: https://workingwithartists.wordpress.com/how-to-do-it/case-studies-the-practitioners-stories/

■ Case studies of creative practitioners working with setting and schools.

Tech tools

■ Google's Arts and Culture Projects and Virtual Tours: www.google.com/intl/en/culturalinstitute/worldwonders

■ International Children's Digital Library: http://en.childrenslibrary.org

■ Creative tools in story building, animations, art, and much more: https://askatech teacher.com/2014/04/17/do-you-miss-kerpoof-try-these-alternatives/

■ Prezi – web-based presentation tool: https://prezi.com/

■ Glogster – multimedia poster creations: http://edu.glogster.com/

■ Scratch – create stories, games and animations: https://scratch.mit.edu/

■ Audacity – free open source digital audio editor and recording software: www. audacityteam.org/

■ Padlet – create boards, web pages etc: https://padlet.com/

■ Visual word cloud apps: www.wordclouds.com/ and www.wordle.net/ and www. tagxedo.com/

10 Creative inquiry and reflection

🗯 THINK

What do you need to think about when considering reflection as a creative learning tool?

🔍 CHAPTER FOCUS

■ Exploring and understanding the role of creative professional inquiry (CPI)

■ Understanding reflection, reflexivity, and reflective practice in the early years

■ The various reflective opportunities available

■ Exploring the concept of 'thinking'

■ Creative reflective practice and their approaches

Reflection on practice is a much-embedded mantra in education and a vital aspect of working with young children. In many ways, it is regarded as the cornerstone of early years practice (Reed and Canning, 2010; Paige-Smith and Craft, 2011). As an adult in early years education, you will be advised to 'be reflective' in your day-to-day practice, with the intention of enabling a deeper understanding of children's creative learning and development as well as your own. You will reflect on your practice and approaches in a variety of ways, not only to improve but also to build on what is already of quality. Developing creativity also requires you to think and reflect on what is happening around you, on your experiences in teaching and learning, and on the children. The aim of this is to devise actions that will assist you to develop and improve your creative skills and approaches in what you offer. This chapter seeks to take a more creative tactic to reflection. It offers creative approaches beyond the norm of cognitive reflective models that can enhance adult self-awareness for teaching creatively and creative learning.

Creative professional inquiry

It is agreed that all early years practitioners must be knowledgeable in child development, research, and best practices in order to take on a more effective role in children's learning. Regardless of what qualifications they may hold, practitioners will need to continually develop their professional skills to keep up to date with the specialism of early years. There is always something new to learn, or understand, in the continual changing landscape of education. Continuing professional development (CPD) opportunities are important for this purpose. It is where one can track and document the skills, knowledge, and experiences that they gain both formally and informally as they work, beyond any initial training and formal qualifications. CPD can be achieved through short courses, training programmes, regulated training events by local authorities, and opportunities provided by the setting or schools one is employed at. The idea is to experience, learn, and then apply into early years practice. However, waiting to attend short course and workshops is not the only way to develop professionally and creatively.

Early years practitioners should always be looking towards 'continual professional inquiry' (CPI) (Mincemoyer, 2013). Inquiry requires you to continually, through varied sources, explore, investigate, examine, probe, search, scrutinise and study early years, and other areas and disciplines that contribute, to develop your practices and approaches in teaching creatively and creative learning. This encourages the practitioner to be a researcher. CPI can be achieved through reading, searching, reflecting, and continued dialogue with other early years professionals, and beyond. By reading publications, articles, books, and professional blogs and websites, practitioners can gain knowledge and ideas that they can immediately apply to their work. Continuous inquiry of this sort is a process of discovery for the creative adult to do their job well, and leads to confidence; when adults feel good about what they learn and accomplish, this develops their professional creative confidence. There are many actions that you can take to build CPI in your role, and even lives:

Start with acknowledging your value as a creative adult: *what are you proud of? What are your strengths? What feedback do you get about your work and from whom? What do the children think of you? Who are you as a creative adult? What impact are you making?* Determining the answers to these questions, as experienced or training adults, will help build a focus for inquiry – *where are you going? And what you need to do to get there?*

You don't know everything, so always look to continually build your expertise and skills. You could start by making a list of topics that will help you attain new skills as well as build on existing skills in teaching and learning.

ACTION RESEARCH

Conduct a survey at your place of work or training. How do the adults here develop and maintain their CPI?

What have you learnt that you can build on and develop?

Creativity, of course, will be at the top of the list! *What do you want to know more of? What do you struggle with? What are you curious about? What are you passionate about?* It is then about identifying how you will go about this – who or what will assist? Use the approaches discussed in Chapter 4 to assist you.

Education is an everchanging landscape and is unpredictable in many ways. Changes at any level affect the way we carry out our professional roles, and therefore attaining information and current research and thinking in our fields is vital. Start by thinking about finding at least three resources that can be used for this purpose. An easier way is to locate a professional early years body or organisation that can offer information and resources, and that keeps up to date with changes for the early years on a regular basis – *where can you find them?*

Reflect and communicate with other early years professionals. Start by listing three professional peers you can communicate with. *What might you share? How and where can you share ideas? What will you do with the information and ideas gathered from this communication?* Consider joining early years groups, blogs, forums, or professional organisations. Think beyond your tribe!

Professional planning also assists in inquiry. This planning requires you to plan about you – *describe your most important professional goals? How do you plan to achieve them?* By answering these questions, you set into motion actions in terms of how to go about achieving them.

 ACTIVITY

See if you can develop a professional plan that will help you in mapping out your CPI.

How creative can you be with it?

Early years practitioners spend a lot of time experimenting and trying out new resources, techniques, strategies, processes, and knowledge in their roles. Potentially, every teaching and learning experience will mean that they are going through a period of trying something new. Sometimes it works, sometimes it doesn't. Becoming used to making mistakes, trying things differently, and allowing for surprises is key to successful creative solutions in early years practice. As educators, we know and understand that we need to experiment widely in order for our ideas and practices to mature. What is much more difficult to do is to make critical decisions about what has worked best and why. Without being able to *reflect* on what we do as part of our CPI, it is difficult to move forward, and in turn move the children forward.

 **CONNECT**

What strategies do you currently use for reflection? And why?

The curse of reflective models

A very central role of CPI is 'reflection'. Early years practitioners can be said to be reflecting all the time; they reflect in children's daily diaries that they keep, when chatting to parents, through planning, through observations, and mostly when they react and respond to children in their play by building on what they are doing and saying. However, there is a dilemma, on the one hand, where there is the increasing requirement to be 'up to date' in our work, building it upon sound, research-based evidence and other forms of standards and requirements set down for us; whilst at the same time, there is an expectation of being 'reflective' about how we go about our day-to-day practice. Practitioners often can sleepwalk their way through the demands of their working day. Teaching itself sometimes becomes robotic, but so does the use of reflective models designed to aid in reflective practice. This is because they are more cognitive models that ask us to compartmentalise our thinking into stages, when we know by now that creative thinking is not linear. Reflection then ends up being applied 'blandly, mechanically and in unthinking ways' (Finlay, 2008, p. 1). Figure 10.1 provides three well-known cognitive models of reflection.

Methods for reflection vary setting to setting. Practitioners may have personal reflective log books which are reviewed regularly, or in many cases may not. Reflection can also take place in a team during staff meetings. The EYFS is also used as a starting point for reflection. By using the cognitive models in Figure 10.1, the production of a narrative (picture with words) is a technique familiar with practitioners through their reflective diaries, reflective journals, or logs. It is something that is also encouraged when undertaking a formal qualification. However, writing in this way requires discipline to be able to dedicate time to doing so. It is the analysis where practitioners fall short in these processes. Unwittingly or not, reflective models have become mechanistic tools, complete with cycles and action plans, and very often are a burden on the creative adult. We should be writing to self-illuminate and explore the process (Bolton, 2014), but somehow end up creating products in the form of action plans and checklists.

Schön (1991) presented the concept of **'reflection in action'** and **'reflection on action'**, and coined the term **'the reflective practitioner'**. Schön's theory is that there are two types of reflection, one during and the other after an activity or event.

Reflection in action	Reflection on action
• Experiencing • Thinking on your feet • Thinking about what to do next • Acting straight away	• Thinking about something that has happened • Thinking what you would do differently next time • Taking your time

Kolb's Learning Cycle (1984) has four elements of a loop which you can start at any point, though normally you start with an experience:

1) Experience–*doing it*
2) Observations and reflections–*reviewing and reflecting on the experience*
3) Development of ideas–*learning from the experience*
4) Testing ideas in practice–*planning, trying out what you have learned*

Gibb's Reflective Cycle (1988) has six distinctive stages, leading from a description of the event/experience through to conclusions and consideration for future events:

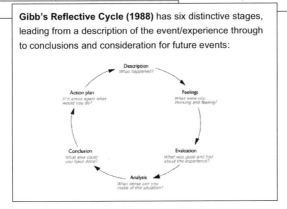

Figure 10.1 Reflective models

 **CONNECT**

Think back to when you were, or are, studying. How were you taught to 'be reflective'?

Understanding reflection and reflective practice

It is necessary for practitioners to understand what the role of reflection is in their professional practice. This will then lead to the importance, and necessity, of it in underpinning our roles and practice. Too often being reflective just becomes a 'thing to do' and we are not really trained into understanding it, or how to go about approaching it according to how we best learn. It is only through understanding reflective practice that adults will know how it impacts on and benefits them, the setting, and the children.

Reflection is a state of mind, an ongoing constitute of practice (Bolton, 2009, p. 4). Reflecting requires one to think. To be able to do this requires one to experience something, think about what happened, learn from the experience, and then apply this to their practice. This is then known as 'reflective practice'. Bolton (2014) dissects the terms associated with reflection to make it easier to understand, and when they are used:

- **Reflection** – is 'focused thinking' which we use in specific situations or relationships. An example of this can be to think about why children do not use the outdoor grass area and avoid it. Or why a particular investigative activity worked well in engaging the children. This is a specific situation. It enables us in finding routes through difficulties, dilemmas, and decision-making. It can celebrate and endorse success, giving strategies for working out how we made things go right, so we can do it again.

- **Reflexivity** – this is 'self-critical thinking' upon our own actions, thoughts, hopes, fears, role, values, and assumptions, with the aim of gaining insight into them. It is a way of self-questioning without knowing where it will lead – for example, the values we may hold about the role of creativity in children's learning. An important aspect of any reflective practice is self-awareness. By stepping back and considering our own perspectives, questioning why we think what we do, and being open to our own prejudices and assumptions, we can have a better understanding of our reactions.

- **Reflective practice** – concerns our work and the areas of experience which impinge on it. Our work is early years practice, and the experiences are what we face on a day-to-day basis, leading to 'reflection' and 'reflexivity'. It is the reflective processes that we can use to focus our thinking and self-questioning in the domains of our practice. Finlay (2008) describes this as 'recapturing practice experiences and mulling them over critically, in order to gain new understandings and so to improve future practice' (p. 1).

Of course, this book is, after all, about creativity, so I have a fourth element to add to Bolton's much needed insight into reflection; an amalgamation, yet again, of the above:

- **Creative reflective practice** – this is 'focused' and 'self-critical thinking' on early years practice, and all the areas and relationships underpinning and surrounding it. It is achieved through the use of 'creative reflective approaches'.

Fishing for reflective opportunities

To be able to settle on a creative approach for reflection that works best is one of the most difficult things to do. It is difficult because there is no right or wrong, and there is no 'one size fits all' approach, as we have learnt with creativity. A wealth of experience is needed that allows creative adults to compare, contrast, evaluate, and take forward. If you think about learning, it can be frustrating to see children opt for the obvious choice or pass on incredible explorations that they overlook, and as practitioners we help guide them back to it so that they can gain a quality learning experience. *So, why can't creative adults do the same for quality creative teaching?* It is possible to practice creative reflective approaches so that they become an inherent part of what we do. However, we do not need to limit ourselves to the tools that are already out there; after all, *where is the creativity in that?* It is about developing your own model of reflective practice that informs your work.

 DISCUSS

With peers/colleagues what other opportunities for reflection exist.

Knowing on what to reflect on in our professional roles is not always straight-forward. Therefore, before exploring creative approaches to assist with reflection, the starting point is to understand what opportunities for reflection and reflexivity arise from various situations in practice. This will enable one to create a logical pathway to categorise practice situations and experiences into groups for better reflection. However, note that this is not set in stone; the creative adult should forever be fishing for opportunities to reflect and how to go about doing so. The following opportunities are suggested, where the word 'practice' means even if you are a student in training:

1) An aspect of practice that did not work well – reflection here will help to consider what might be done differently in the future.

2) An aspect of practice that has exceeded expectations and worked well – this is so that one can identify what exactly worked well, the contributing factors to it, and what can continue or be developed further.

3) On a child or group of children – we are forever doing this in the early years, but this reflection requires you to really focus on who the children are and how you and your setting or school are impacting on them as a whole and developing their creative potential.

4) Reflect on a question or questions in order to challenge our thinking – this is so that one can consider different perspectives and examine underlying beliefs, attitudes, and values that guide our thoughts and actions, and in turn our practice. Examples of such questions may be:

- *Social context. What are our circumstances? Where are we located?*

- *Values and identity. Who are we? Who do we want the children to be or become? Where are we going?*

- **Relationships.** *How are we getting on together? What types of relationships do we have? With each other? With the children? With myself?*

- **Learning.** *How can we understand children's creative learning and development? Do we encourage and facilitate creativity's characteristics?*

- **Curriculum.** *How do we develop children's knowledge and understanding through the characteristics of learning? Do we encourage and facilitate creativity?*

- **Planning.** *How are we implementing the EYFS curriculum? Do we encourage and facilitate creativity?*

- **Organisation.** *How are we managing the environment and developing creative spaces? Do we encourage and facilitate creativity?*

- **Behaviour.** *How are we promoting positive social and emotional behaviour? How are we nurturing creative behaviours?*

- **Communication.** *What are its characteristics? Do we encourage and facilitate creativity through it?*

- **Teaching.** *How are we developing our strategies, our approaches? Do we encourage and facilitate creativity?*

- **Assessment.** *How are we monitoring children's learning, progress, talents, and achievements? How are we assessing creativity's characteristics and informing what we do with it?*

- **Inclusion.** *How are we achieving this?*

 **CONNECT**

Out of the four opportunities suggested here, which require 'reflection' and which require 'reflexivity'?

It's all in the thinking

Once you establish the differing opportunities for reflection, reflective practice is then about *how do I do it? And with what do I do it?* Thinking is the beginning and the very core of any reflective practice: *to think about thinking.* It is this that needs to be done well in order to enhance quality for young creative children, and our own professional creative practice. Very often our brain is crammed and congested with all sorts of information and we do not think as well as we can. Further, descriptive writing as a means of reflection can provide mental blocks. In order to understand reflective approaches as a learning tool, practitioners need to explore 'how they think' through adopting a creative 'thinking approach' to practice in which they have a conversation with themselves. Through their self-awareness, they think about what they do and, with assistance from others, they are able to re-consider their practice and think about refining or changing aspects of how they approach their role. O'Connor and Diggins (2002, p. 9) best describe this process as taking the time to 'stop, think and change'.

Here, I will draw on the business world again and the creative work of Ron von Oech (1998). Van Oech provides a list of all the types of ways one could think (by the way, he 'thinked' them!):

Logical thinking	Mythical thinking
Conceptual thinking	Poetic thinking
Analytical thinking	Non-verbal thinking
Primitive thinking	Analogical thinking
Critical thinking	Lyrical thinking
Foolish thinking	Practical thinking
Convergent thinking	Divergent thinking
Weird thinking	Ambiguous thinking
Reflective thinking	Constructive thinking
Visual thinking	Thinking about thinking
Symbolic thinking	Surreal thinking
Digital thinking	Concrete thinking
Metaphorical thinking	Fantasy thinking

He then categorised them into two types of thinking: 'soft' thinking and 'hard' thinking. Soft thinking, he explains, has many soft characteristics; it is metaphorical, approximate, humorous, playful, and capable of dealing with contradictions. Hard thinking, on the other hand, tends to be more logical, precise, exact, specific, and consistent, a bit like the requirements of the cognitive models in Figure 10.1. Soft thinking tries to find similarities and connections amongst things, while hard thinking focuses on their differences. Within the reflective process, soft and hard thinking can be utilised imaginatively and practically. In the imaginative process, you generate and play with ideas. In the practical process, you evaluate and execute them.

 **CONNECT**

What do each of these types of thinking involve? Which ones do you consider soft or hard?

In the imaginative process, you ask questions such as *what if? Why not? What rules can we break to achieve this? What assumptions do we have that we can drop? How about if we looked at this backwards? Or as a parent/child or student? Is there something we don't know that needs exploring? Something we've missed?* It is about thinking something different. In the practical process, we ask questions such as *is this outcome any good? Do we have the resources to implement it? What about timing? Finance? Who can help us? What will be the consequences of not reaching the objective? How will it impact the children, the parents, my colleagues, the setting as a whole?* It is about doing something with what we have learnt. Both types of thinking play an important role in the creative reflection process; they are combinatorial. We want the unlimited possibilities to then narrow to the specific in terms of how to use what we have learnt through the process of reflection. It is the *approaches* that we use for reflection that allow us to use both thinking processes for a better creative outcome.

Creative reflection approaches

I remember telling a group of MA students that they would not be writing an essay for their assessment this term but, instead, creating posters to make their learning visible. The gasps and horrified looks I received could have left holes in me. This is because the traditional model of higher education assessment is essay-based, encouraging conformity and linear methods, which many students end up getting used to. Models for reflection can also encourage conformity and linear reflection, and we know by now that in creativity, linear has no place! So, to access creative approaches to reflection, adults need to be receptive to it. It is about coming out of their comfort zone and stepping into the unknown by enhancing the possibilities and freeing the imagination! Reflection, then, becomes an adventurous journey where the outcome is unknown.

 RESEARCH TO EXPLORE
CREATIVE REFLECTION, CREATIVE PRACTICE: EXPRESSING THE INEXPRESSIBLE

This research explores the concept and practices of creative reflection developed in a teacher education programme to enhance the model of reflective practice. It discusses creative methodologies for engaging adults individually and collectively in identifying and expanding their creativity practices (Tracey, 2007).

The notion of 'creative reflection' extends beyond the use of cognitive methods by exploring the aesthetic nature of it and how thinking and thoughts can be represented, say, through imagery, objects, stories, music, poetry, and imaginative experiences, rather than just being reliant solely upon written text. It is about different forms of thinking (focused, reflexivity, soft, and hard) and ideas that make reflection visible as we do with visible learning for children. It is vital to remember that the end point of reflection may not be a resolution of an issue, but attainment of a better understanding of the situation in which one finds themselves and their practice. Reflective experiences and learning become new understandings, or the identification of new questions which may be raised about practice and self. Reflection may be individual or collective; it may take place in pairs or small groups in a collaborative environment. Group reflections work best as they are about the 'nurturing of collaborative dialogue' (Siraj-Blatchford and Manni, 2007, p. 17), which encourages a more quality approach to the work that we do.

What makes a great day? Early years practitioners have a lot to think about: curriculum, child development, assessments, observation, documentation, standards, regulations, parents, professional development, activity plans, materials and resources, activities (and the list can go on!). They must also think about snack time, lunch time, sleep time, nappy time, allergies, accidents, clean up time, story time, checklists, and tomorrow (and this list could go on, too!). That is a whole load of thinking, I hear you say. Thinking about what makes for a great day might seem impractical amongst all this, but exploring this approach is worthwhile. Each of us values individual aspects of our profession, but in stressful, busy times, these can be difficult to recognise and acknowledge.

Feeling good about what we do is important. Thinking about what makes a great day can help creative adults recognise what they find positive and how they are positive, and see how it affects their work. This can be achieved through writing a few lines about what makes a great day or cutting out images from newspapers and magazines to represent your thoughts. What about using lyrical, poetic, or metaphorical thinking by Van Oech to describe your day? Once done, talk it through with a peer or colleague to gain the utmost maximum from this reflection – the key question is *what can you take away from it?* Discussions will explore why the positive experience matters, how they were accomplished, and what worked well, in order to develop new insights and creative practices as well as self-awareness of what you perceive to be a positive day in the early years context.

 ACTIVITY

What if you were asked to simply describe what makes a great day?

Think about what makes an enjoyable day for you. Without over-thinking, devise your own approach to answer this.

Write to learn in six minutes – writing should be enjoyable, without the constraints of compartmentalising your thoughts. It is about writing to learn; you learn from it. Bolton (2014) suggests a simple exercise to get into the habit of writing and to really enjoy it, and it only takes six minutes!

- Take a clean page or new screen.

- Allow yourself to write whatever comes in whatever order for about six minutes.

- This is completely private writing, so it doesn't matter if it wanders or jumps about: our minds do naturally. One of these jumps might be inspired.

- Allow yourself not to worry about punctuation, spelling, continuity, or form (these can be sorted out later if necessary). The only thing that matters is that you write whatever is in your mind at that time.

This has three functions; it can:

1) Get you started putting words on the page. Nothing is more off-putting to any writer, however experienced, than the blank page/screen.

2) Help to lay to one side current pressing concerns (Things Which Need to Be Done) until later. Listing these things can help with this.

3) Capture inspirations lurking at the back of your mind which otherwise might never be expressed.

The idea is to enjoy this as a story narrative writing process, which then eventually you build upon to make more focused to practice. Eventually you can use the six-minute approach on writing your thoughts on an image of children at play, or the environment, or your own recording of observations, and of course, six minutes to write your immediate thoughts around your own creativity.

Close your eyes and imagine – this approach can best be done in a group by asking practitioners to close their eyes and imagine something for practice or training. Yes, it may take a little time; however, the power of closed eyes in reflection should not be underestimated. Start with something simple like imagining an ideal outdoor space for children's creative learning: *what would you like in it? What should the children be able to do in it? What can be the challenges? and how can you overcome them? Imagine the children and what they are doing and saying?* As the thoughts and ideas flow, a member of the group can capture the key words from the discussion on post-it notes, which can then be viewed together and further ideas explored. It is about thinking up the many possibilities (the imaginative process) and then filtering those that can be turned into reality (the practical process) – the key question is *what can you take away from it?* Try soft and hard thinking types as you do.

Images, quotations, and music! – images can be used as metaphors to represent feelings, emotions, and predicaments which may or may not be contextualised through a narrative approach to reflection. As adults, when we come across images, or read a quote, or even hear a certain piece of music, it not only evokes memories, but gets us thinking about why we relate to it so much – reflection! This can be applied to professional reflection, too. The use of, say, children's photographs of learning can trigger interpretations and dialogue by creative adults about what is going on and how it has impacted learning or not. Recordings of adults in practice can allow reflexive conversations. Quotes which resonate with practice can be explored, i.e. the creative adult is the child who survived: *what does this say about our own practice with children? How can we ensure creativity not only survives, but thrives?* Think about choosing a theme: teaching, learning, talking, play, imagination, investigation, and creativity. Then, explore images, quotes, or music pieces relevant to that theme. This approach recognises the differing perspectives practitioners may have about the themes and helps them unravel assumptions or values they hold against them or for them. *Why does this image represent how you view play? How does this piece of music or rhythm define creativity for you?* This makes for further delightful debate and dialogue – the key question is *what can you take away from it?*

AROUND THE WORLD
TORONTO, CANADA

The Origami Chatterbox – Martin (2016) devised an approach that uses enabling questions as a way of contributing to collaborative workplace cultures. Originally for the Nursing and Midwifery practice, it is a questioning tool aimed at enhancing adult reflective learning through play. The tool is an origami 'chatterbox', which is a square of paper folded into a boxlike structure that fits over the thumb and index finger of each hand. The use of questions and questioning through the chatterbox was key, and this experience led to deeper reflections on the role of play in adult learning and reflection.

IDEA

Record it! If you're not one to write or doodle, why not think about recording your reflections? It's a simple conversation with yourself which you can play back and think about what it means to you and your professional inquiry and practice.

Playful questioning – the use of *effective* questioning enables the provocation of adult memories of particular children they work with, and reveals internal dialogues of their responses to those children, or on any aspect of practice. This approach supports critical thinking. Yet again, a playful creative approach to this can be used. There are four levels of questions that can be used by undertaking roles of a 'Robot', 'Detective', 'Judge', or 'Inventor'.

Robot (sets the facts):

- Who, what, where, when.

- What happened first, second, third?

- Who are the individuals, the environment, and the problem?

Detective (explores why):

- Why?

- What caused . . .?

- What do you predict?

- What does it mean?

- Why do you think . . .?

Judge (focuses on finding answers):

- What things did (child, adult, you etc.) do that were . . .?

- Do you think . . .?

- Would you agree that . . .?

- In your opinion . . .?

- Do you agree with the (child, adult, you etc.)? Why? Or why not?

- How did you feel about the part where . . .?

- Would it be better if . . .?

- How do you know . . .?

Inventor (moves what is learnt forward creatively):

- How would you . . .?

- Were you ever . . .?

- What would you do if . . .?

- If you were . . . had . . .?

 IDEA

Role play! Explore the *Six Thinking Hats* system designed by Edward de Bono (1985), which describes a tool for group discussion and individual thinking involving six coloured hats. Then, create the six hats in different styles and colours. Wear them to use with a group to discuss a theme in teaching and learning. Start with creativity!

Using metaphors – metaphors convey experiences and understanding in another, indirect, form by giving a situation or relationship the name of another one (Lakoff and Johnson, 1980). The whole human system of concepts is defined and structured metaphorically (ibid.). A key enabler of the use of metaphor is the link between the personal and professional self and that insights lead to changes in behaviour and professional practice (Schwind et al., 2012). Metaphors connect two very different meanings through the similarities they have. For example, an early years professional saw themselves as a clarinet and the insight is that they can sometimes step back and allow others to play. Such an insight could only come from this metaphorical reflection that enables them to understand their practice in relation to something else, which then leads to opening up to insights. The beauty of metaphors is that they can be used in any of the approaches discussed in this chapter and beyond.

 RESEARCH TO EXPLORE

USING LEGO TO TRIGGER REFLECTION

Brown (2017) is a lecturer in Education and encourages students in teacher training to use LEGO® and other visualisations to create physical metaphors as triggers for reflection. Students are asked to picture a river from source to mouth and to consider its natural and man-made features, such as rapids, waterfalls, meanders, tributaries, bridges, stepping stones, etc. Students then map their learning experiences onto the river, creating their personal 'River of Learning'. Challenges and enablers in student learning become more meaningful and detailed.

To enable adults in exploring this as a technique, I normally ask them to identify an item which they feel they are most like as a teacher, student, parent, etc., and why? An item can be an animal, object, material, absolutely anything. Or, I ask them to go get an item from their surroundings to represent it. The responses are fascinating and I share some below:

- *I am a scale! I am always trying to balance time to get everything done. There is sometimes so much to do in my setting that it's about finding that balance.*

- *I am a sponge! I am always seeking knowledge, reading and absorbing good practice to make my practice better. However sometimes I get soggy due to over-load and the busy environment!*

■ *I am a slinky! I am flexible and keep going really fast with lots of ideas, however I am so fast at times that other practitioners can't keep up!*

■ *I am a beaver! Always busy doing everything, however once I get in there, it has to be finished, I follow it through to the end!*

■ *I am a treasure basket! I hold various knowledge and skill bases about practice with children, and all my colleagues come to me where I share them out.*

■ *I am a binocular! I am always trying to keep an eye on everything around me and what happens in all parts of my setting. I zone in on everything!*

(Mohammed, 2013)

Reflective play – a major characteristic in the creativity process is also a concept that can be used in creative reflection. 'Play isn't the enemy of learning, it's learning's partner. Play is like fertilizer for brain growth. It's crazy not to use it' (Brown, 2010, p. 101). The idea is to use materials, resources, objects, props, and whatever else you can involve in play to represent your thinking and then discuss with practitioners. This is best achieved in small groups as the dialogue is critical to the approach. The idea behind play resources is that they can be moved as your thinking takes shape and your discussion plants further creative seeds. Working with props lets you think about your practice; as you manipulate the concrete forms, it gives rise to visible thinking and a narrative for exploration. Thinking then becomes symbolic, metaphorical, and analogical – *which other thinking types are at play?* One practitioner, for example, used scarves to form a circle and then Russian dolls were placed on the outskirts – these were the children that were not engaging with the learning offered. The practitioner discussed why this could be and how she wanted to move them from the outskirts into the inner circle; the remaining group responded with critical questions. Creative hooks for these children were discussed in depth. This was a powerful approach in discussing inclusion. Using their hands gives adults the opportunity to clarify thoughts or feelings, and to see the situation in a new light. Having an image or physical object to represent and discuss enables communication and connection with others more directly, too (Gauntlett, 2011, p. 4).

Creative mind-mapping – humans have a tendency to think in multi-dimensional ways – that is, with lots of thoughts occurring simultaneously, triggering further ideas. Rather than attempting to record thoughts in the traditional sequential, linear fashion, i.e. writing these down as lists or paragraphs, creative adults can do so by collecting, recording, and organising ideas graphically using a visual diagram such as a mind map. Mind map refers to a diagram that has a branch or root-like structure radiating from a central image or word on the page, and which uses lines and colours to show relationships, groupings, and connections between words, ideas, and images. A mind map helps with thinking clearly and ensures that a range of possibilities is considered; this encourages thinking outside the box!

FACT NOTE

Anthony Peter 'Tony' Buzan is an English author and educational consultant. He popularised the idea of mental literacy, and developed a powerful graphic technique for thinking which provides a universal key to unlocking the potential of the brain. It harnesses the full range of cortical skills – word, image, number, logic, rhythm, colour, and spatial awareness – in a single, uniquely powerful manner. In so doing, it gives you the freedom to roam the infinite expanses of your brain. He called it 'mind-mapping'.

Start with a central image around creativity on either portrait or landscape paper; the paper can be as big as you want! The image can represent any theme in practice. Use curved lines to add main branches to the centre and then connect these to smaller branches; use single words and images; add colours as you go along. Creative mind-mapping is not just about sticking to the official mind-maps; it can be a tree diagram, spider diagram, or even just a splurge of thoughts on paper, as long as it documents a range of ideas and possibilities connected to the theme you are reflecting on – *what do you do with the thought processes through this?* Below are some further creative tips to gain the maximum from this approach:

- Take a photograph to put in the middle as a main concept.

- Use coloured areas to contain text.

- Draw pictures, symbols, or doodles to illustrate ideas visually.

- Play with words, overlay them, make some bold, others light to emphasise them. You could create a collage of words using cuttings from a newspaper or magazine.

- Collage torn images, textures, and surfaces together to represent your reflective theme. This can provide a creative base upon which to write and doodle further ideas.

- You can mind-map on small pieces of paper, post-it notes, and cardboard and then layer them into one form. This way the pieces can be moved around and added to as you advance in your reflective thought processes.

- If you feel the pressure, a simple form of mind-mapping will do by using text with circles and dots; after all, it's what works for you and your creative reflection!

- Use a pin board as a base to capture images, texts, and materials by pinning them, and use string as arrows to connect the different parts together.

- Use a large-scale image to hand write ideas and create an entire mind map or thought bubble upon it.

■ Create a mind map online using free mind map software, apps, or any other digital drawing tool.

■ Follow the idea of a 'mood board'!

 IDEA

Art journaling is a visual diary – it's record keeping combined with creativity! It's a place to record your thoughts, memories, and emotions through images, art, and words.

Why not start one?

Reflective stories – as stated in previous chapters, storytelling comes naturally to us; we do it all the time. Stories help us make sense of ourselves and our world (Bolton, 2009). We tell and re-tell them, both minor and major, to colleagues, students, loved ones, strangers, and children. Stories engage feelings, and these are evident throughout any reflective processes. *Learning Stories* (2012) is a concept derived from the work of New Zealand educators Margaret Carr and Wendy Lee. A 'learning story' is a record of what the adult has seen a child (or group of children) doing or saying. The written story may be as short as one paragraph or one page or longer. It is usually focused on a specific incident or episode, but it may also be a snapshot of a child's activities over a specific amount of time (e.g. 10 minutes). It may focus on a group activity and be a learning story about an activity that the children did together, such as visiting a fire station or going on a walk. It only becomes a 'learning' story when the adult adds his/her interpretation of the child's competencies and dispositions toward learning (such as curiosity and creativity). The learning story generally is formulated by the adult to highlight what the child can do and is doing rather than what they can't do. A collection of learning stories is commonly called a 'portfolio'. A portfolio is similar to the traditional photograph album, but it is more than an album as it includes the written story behind the images and may include comments and reflections from the child, family, and other adults. The physical form of the portfolio may be a book or folder. Alternatively, the video, voice, and images may be loaded directly into an online e-portfolio.

Taking this concept, another method of creative reflection approach can be mastered through the practitioner creating their own 'reflective stories'. With the use of images, photographs, videos, voice recordings, and narratives that read as a story, practitioners can form creative stories which they can then share amongst their colleagues and other early years professionals, or keep private. As an early years practitioner, you need to find an approach that works best for you and your learning style to create the stories. You may keep a notebook with inserts of your stories and images. You may choose to create a blog around your stories or a Facebook page, or even an online e-portfolio. You may choose to create story boards based more on images, with the writing reduced to captions or one liners. It's how it suits you and your reflective approach. Writing the story should not be time consuming, either, as you can write a paragraph, up to a page, or whatever you can in six minutes! If you choose to keep stories electronically, you may record voiceovers for your stories. Always share your stories, as in this way they become more powerful in your professional inquiry, confidence, practice, and in turn creativity.

Next steps

 REFLECT

Try some of the creative approaches for reflection in this chapter on your own or within your team.

■ What have you learnt about yourself, your practice, the children, your colleagues, and the role of creativity within it?

■ What other creative approaches can you come up with?

■ How can you encourage the concept of reflection with children through the use of sustained shared thinking?

 EXPLORE

Borkett, P. (2014) Understanding and Developing Reflective Practice in *The Early Years Foundation Stage Forum (EYFS)*: http://eyfs.info/articles.html/teaching-and-learning/understanding-and-developing-reflective-practice-r165/

■ An insight into how you can change practice as a result of reflection.

Paige-Smith, Alice and Craft, Anna eds. (2011). *Developing Reflective Practice in the Early Years* (2nd ed.). Berkshire: McGraw Hill, Open University Press: www.mheducation.co.uk/openup/chapters/9780335222773.pdf

■ Chapter 1 What does it mean to reflect on our practice?

Gauntlett, David (2015), 'The LEGO System as a tool for thinking, creativity, and changing the world', in *Making Media Studies: The Creativity Turn in Media and Communications Studies*, New York: Peter Lang. Available at: http://davidgauntlett.com/complete-list-of-publications/

■ A chapter exploring LEGO as a reflective thinking tool.

Early Childhood Studies Blogspot (2007) on reflective practice: http://earlychildhood studies.blogspot.co.uk/2009/01/reflective-practice.html

■ A blog post highlighting the key quotes from literature around reflection and reflective practice.

Reflective Writing Experiences (Bolton, 2014): https://study.sagepub.com/bolton/ student-resources/reflective-writing-experiences

■ A selection of shared reflective writing experiences from a range of professionals working in Healthcare and Education.

Read to Learn. Write to Learn (Bolton, 2014): http://live-sagecompanion.pantheonsite. io/sites/default/files/Read%20to%20Learn%20Write%20to%20Learn%20Exercises.pdf

■ Series of exercises encouraging to write in six minutes – do these, they are awesome!

Edward de Bono's Six Thinking Hats: www.debonogroup.com/six_thinking_hats.php

■ For the six hats role-play idea within this chapter.

What is Art Journaling? Websites to get you started.

■ Tangie Baxter & Co: https://shoptangiebaxter.com/pages/what-is-art-journaling includes an app to download

■ Daisy Yellow: https://daisyyellowart.com/aj101/

Tech tools

Create your own reflective blog:

■ Blogger: www.blogger.com/about/?r=1-null_user

■ Wordpress: https://wordpress.com/learn-more/?v=blog

■ How to choose the best blog: https://blogbasics.com/free-blog-sites/

Mindmeister: an online mind-mapping tool: www.mindmeister.com and Coggle: http:// coggle.it/?lang=en-GB

Appendix: Work tools

The Appendix contains the following work tools, as referred to throughout the book. These resources may be photocopied for re-use.

Work Tool 1   Creativity's characteristics
Work Tool 2   CoETL play and exploration profile
Work Tool 3   CoETL active learning profile
Work Tool 4   CoETL creating and thinking critically profile
Work Tool 5   Creative profile
Work Tool 6   30-day photography challenge
Work Tool 7   Creative thinking tools
Work Tool 8   Planning prompts

Work Tool 1 Creativity's characteristics

What children do	Creative thinking	Creative attitudes	Creative behaviours
Taking joy and interest in what they are doing.	Use of imagination – what if? Why not? What might be?	Enthusiasm in what they do.	Being active in their learning.
Communicating – through talking, listening, mark-making, pictures, and much more.	Wondering.	Wanting to know more.	Concentrating – maintaining focus on their activity for a period of time.
Showing particular interests and pursuing them.	Daydreaming.	Showing determination.	Seeking challenge.
Playing – let's try.	Different ways of knowing – physical, feeling, imagination.	Perseverance – sticking with difficulties and challenges.	Showing a can-do attitude.
Playing with something familiar and what they know.	Constructing and using knowledge in what they do or say.	Flexible – trying alternatives or different approaches.	Being fearless and experimenting.
Exploring and experimenting with materials, objects, ideas, language.	Perceive things in new ways by pretending objects are things from their experiences.	Resilience – overcoming difficulties.	Playing, exploring, investigating.
Investigating objects, materials, the environment, activities, etc. by using all senses	Questioning – what? Why? How? Asking unusual questions.	Learning from mistakes.	Being curious – about objects, events, people, experiences.
Discovering and making connections through play and experimentation.	Problem-solving – using strategies and solutions.	Practising and repeating.	High levels of energy and fascination.
Describing – what they are doing, what they have done, what they want to do.	Problem-finding – using strategies and solutions.	Making compromises in what they do.	Adventurous – up for a challenge.
Illustrating – through drawings, construction, hand gestures, body language, and much more.	Various processes of mental representation through schemas.	Coping well with uncertainty.	Various forms of self-expression.

What children do	Creative thinking	Creative attitudes	Creative behaviours
Developing techniques, practising, and mastering them – what are these? And how do the children do this?	Thinking of ideas.	Being proud of how they accomplished something.	Representing their experiences in play.
Generating ideas in response to stimuli – having, pursuing, testing, and developing them – note the process.	Showing independence of thought – discovering things for themselves.	Be inspired by an object, a person, an experience, a song, a story, a feeling.	Taking on a role in their play.
Applying known skills and knowledge in different situations.	Planning, making decisions about how to approach a task, solve a problem and reach a goal.	**Add your own**	Dealing with frustrations.
Making connections and seeing relationships.	Changing strategies as needed.		Showing confidence in what they do.
Unpicking connections to make sense of them.	Reflecting and reviewing through sustained shared thinking.		Following through what they do.
Making unusual associations or connections between seemingly unrelated things, objects, or thoughts.	Becoming aware of something through the senses.		Risk taking.
Collaborating and connecting with adults and other children. Working together and making friends.	Predicting what might happen.		Being aware and observant.
Responding to ideas, questions, tasks, or problems in surprising ways.	Recording – whatever form this may take, i.e. mark-making.		Showing satisfaction in meeting their own goals.

(Continued)

What children do	Creative thinking	Creative attitudes	Creative behaviours
Reinterpreting what they know and can do and applying it in their learning in other areas.	**Add your own**		Experiencing emotions – this can be through imaginative play, stories, attempting a task.
Adapting and modifying what they do.			Resourcefulness – knowing where to look for what they need.
Using trial and error.			Imitating what they see in order to make sense of it and then try another way.
Paying attention to details.			**Add your own**
Finding patterns, including new and hidden ones.			
Making comparisons in their experiences.			
Following a line of inquiry – self-initiated or adult-led.			
Add your own			
		The CoETL from Development Matters 2012	

Work Tool 2 CoETL play and exploration profile

Finding out and exploring

Prompts	What are children saying/doing/learning?	How are practitioners supporting, facilitating, and interacting?
• What areas/activities is the child drawn to? • Do they prefer to work in a group/alone? • Do they initiate activities/experiences themselves or join in existing ones? • Do they think aloud describing what they do? • How do they use resources? • How does the child use their senses when exploring and discovering?		

Using what they know in their play

Prompts	What are children saying/doing/learning?	How are practitioners supporting, facilitating, and interacting?
• In play, do they draw on experiences from the home/outside the setting? • Do they act out situations in the role-play/home area? • Are they confident in finding the tools, materials, and resources they need for their ideas?		

Being willing to have a go

Prompts	What are children saying/doing/learning?	How are practitioners supporting, facilitating, and interacting?
• Levels of persistence – do they give up at first hurdle or keep trying? • Are they eager to try new ideas or do they stay with what they are familiar with? • Are they able to talk about/review what they have done? Even if it has not worked? • Do they work best with continual support or prefer to get on with activities themselves?		

Work Tool 3 CoETL active learning profile

Being involved and concentrating

Prompts	What are children saying/doing/learning?	How are practitioners supporting, facilitating, and interacting?
• Can the child concentrate? How do you know this? • Do they concentrate better on self-chosen or adult-led activities? • Does the child keep focused on a self-initiated activity for a long period of time? Is this at any activity or always at a particular activity/area in the environment? • Does the child show high levels of energy, fascination, motivation? In what way? • Are they concentrating and involved in the activity without being distracted? Any examples? • What is the child easily distracted by (i.e. other children, toys, noise)? • Does the child show attention to detail and care with what they are doing? • Can the child sit and listen when others are talking? • Do they demonstrate concentration through silence or thinking aloud?		

Keeping on trying

Prompts	What are children saying/doing/learning?	How are practitioners supporting, facilitating, and interacting?
• Does the child show persistence – not giving up even if it means starting again? • Do they ask for help/support if they need it? Or does it have to be offered? • Do they discuss solutions for challenges with other children or adults, or work through things themselves?		

Enjoying achieving what they set out to do

Prompts	What are children saying/doing/learning?	How are practitioners supporting, facilitating, and interacting?
• Is there a sense of satisfaction and pride when they have completed an activity? Do they want to show/tell people? • Do they relish challenges and continually try to make things better? • Do they evaluate themselves and try different things as a result? • Are they 'intrinsically motivated' – achieving things for themselves as opposed to adult praise?		

Work Tool 4 CoETL creating and thinking critically profile

Having their own ideas:

Prompts	What are children saying/doing/learning?	How are practitioners supporting, facilitating, and interacting?
• Does the child try something different rather than follow what someone else has done? • Do they address a problem with an idea/strategy? • What new ideas have they formed? • Do they retain independence by not asking for support even if it takes longer to achieve the outcome?		

Using what they already know to learn new things

Prompts	What are children saying/doing/learning?	How are practitioners supporting, facilitating, and interacting?
• Do children understand patterns and predictability of events? • Do children talk about/explain how what they are doing links to previous knowledge or learning? • Do they draw upon knowledge or experiences not immediately related to their activity?		

Choosing ways to do things and finding new ways

Prompts	What are children saying/doing/learning?	How are practitioners supporting, facilitating, and interacting?
• Are they confident in using a 'trial and error' approach and talking about why some things do or do not work? • Do children choose different ways of approaching activities/experiences and adapting them if it does not work? • How does the child plan and make decisions about how to approach a particular learning experience? • Does the child think about what they are doing? How?		

Work Tool 5 Creative profile

The following questions are designed for you to interrogate your values and beliefs when it comes to creativity in teaching. Be honest with your answers, and be brave enough to share with peers/colleagues to gain a perspective on your thoughts. Why not copy for multiple people to gather their thoughts?

In a learning situation, what makes you come alive?	What can you remember about being taught in school? What worked for you? What didn't work for you?
Notes:	Notes:

When are you most creative?	Who helped or hindered your creativity?
Notes:	Notes:

What is your **theory** of creativity?	Ask a few of your friends or colleagues to describe their ideas of creativity. What did you find?
Notes:	Notes:

Consider the various adults you have come across that work with children. Which do you consider most creative and why?	What has formed this perception?
Notes:	Notes:

Which 'creative blocks' do you struggle with most?	What solutions have worked for you?
Notes:	Notes:

How do adults come up with creative teaching ideas?	What do they do when they are planning?
Notes:	Notes:

Work Tool 6 30-day photography challenge

This task is intended to help you develop a '**creative eye**' through the use of photography. No need for expensive equipment – just use your phone! Go on, get 'eye-sy'!

	What to photograph	✓ Progress	Notes
Day 1	Self portrait		
Day 2	What you wore		
Day 3	Clouds		
Day 4	Something green		
Day 5	After dark		
Day 6	Obsession		
Day 7	Changes to come		
Day 8	Routine		
Day 9	Someone you love		
Day 10	Childhood memory		
Day 11	Something blue		
Day 12	Sunset		
Day 13	Cannot live without		
Day 14	Eyes		
Day 15	Silhouette		
Day 16	A good habit		
Day 17	Technology		
Day 18	Your shoes		
Day 19	Something you want		
Day 20	In my bag		
Day 21	Faceless self-portrait		
Day 22	Inspirational		
Day 23	Patterns		
Day 24	Animal		
Day 25	Strangers		
Day 26	Close-up		
Day 27	Celebration		
Day 28	Flowers		
Day 29	Black and white		
Day 30	Self portrait		

Reflect on the task:

- *How did it unfold?*
- *What were the difficulties/challenges?*
- *What have you learnt about yourself during this task?*
- *How can you use some of your photography collection in teaching?*

Work Tool 7 Creative thinking tools

Thinking tool	What it means	Note how you use this tool
Observing	Observation goes beyond the visual; it involves all the senses. The mind must be trained to observe, and the skill of observation has to be practiced.	
Imaging	Imaging is to imagine the look, smell, sound, touch, or taste of something without it being physically present in front of you. It is also imaging something in your mind, and either creating something, solving a problem, or inventing and experimenting before you start to do it physically.	
Abstracting	To really look at something, to take time to dissect it and view it from many different angles and perspectives. It shows hidden connections between things.	
Recognising patterns	Recognising patterns in language, dance, mathematics, the environment, and much more. By recognising patterns, we start to form connections between things and understand them in deeper ways. It is the first step to forming them.	
Forming patterns	Forming patterns is juxtaposing one element or operation with another in a consistent way. You combine elements in new and often unexpected ways.	
Analogising	An analogy is the relationship, function, or even characteristic similar between two seemingly different things. You can form an analogy between a house and a nest. They are both types of homes, different things, but it's their function that makes them analogous to each other.	
Body thinking	Awareness through the body before it gets to the mind. Body thinking is when you use your muscles, physical tension, or touch in order to think or create. Body thinking can also imagine touch, movement, or body tension as easily as another person can imagine a scene from a book or the melody of a favourite song.	

Thinking tool	What it means	Note how you use this tool
Empathising	Related to body thinking, it is about losing yourself in what you are studying, researching, seeing. You see the world through other people's eyes. Play-act. Familiarise yourself with your subject or subject of others. For example, becoming a dancer to experience movement for children.	
Dimensional thinking	Moving from 2D to 3D or vice versa, like when we create a sculpture out of a picture we've seen. **Mapping** – transforming information provided in one set of dimensions to another set, like when we create a globe from an atlas. **Scaling** – altering the proportions of an object or process within one set of dimensions, like when we use blocks to create a tower.	
Modelling	This is creating and playing with model-making before creating it for real. It gives a concrete and visual form to our thoughts to then take it further.	
Playing	Tinkering with things, playing with possibilities, mental skills, whether it is practice, symbolic, or game play. It provides a fun and risk-free means of seeing from a fresh perspective, learning without constraint, exploring without fear. Play transforms knowledge and builds understanding as new worlds, personas, games, activities, and experiences are created.	
Transforming	Involves transforming ideas from one language of communication into another. To transform something is to define a problem using one set of thinking tools, investigate it with another set of tools, and then express a solution using another set. For example, you might imagine what a fictional world might look like, then create a small-scale model of the world, and then finally write a novel about that world.	

(Continued)

Thinking tool	What it means	Note how you use this tool
Synthesising	Sensory impressions, feeling, knowledge, memories, ideas, images, and so on come together in a multimodal, unified way that allows us to see the 'whole' – to make sense of the world. You synthesise what you know and do through the other 12 tools to create an experience.	

Work Tool 8 Planning prompts

Planning headings	Prompt
Learning intention/outcome	• *What do you want the children to be learning?* • *Which is the knowledge?* • *Which is the understanding?* • *Which is the skill?* • *Which creativity's characteristics will children have an opportunity to demonstrate?*
The EYFS areas covered	• *Which areas are being covered and how? – **the cross-curricular approach***
Prior learning	• ***What have the children learnt previously which will be useful in this activity/lesson?*** • *How will children make the connection?*
Success criteria	• *How will you know if the children reached the intended outcome? What will tell you?* • ***How will the children demonstrate what they have achieved?***
The activity/lesson	• ***Where will the activity be taking place?*** • ***What will the children be doing?*** • ***What will the adult be doing?*** • ***Timings to ensure effectiveness*** • ***What creative teaching and learning approaches will be used?***
Resources	• *What will be needed to successfully carry out this activity/lesson?* • *Who will be responsible to ensure that it is in place? Budgets/funding?* • *Can you recycle resources? Who outside the setting can assist?*
Vocabulary	• *What are the key terms associated with this activity/lesson that children need to know?* • *How will you explain these terms?* • *What are the key questions that will be answered?*
Target children	• *Are there any children that will be targeted specifically? Why? And how?*
Differentiation	• *How will you ensure that **all** children can access the activity/lesson?*
Assessment	• *How will you know that the children have achieved what you planned for (observation, written work etc.)?* • *How will you gather and record this?* • *What else did children demonstrate which was not planned for? How could you use this?*

(Continued)

Planning headings	Prompt
Evaluation	• Were teaching and learning targets met? • What went well? How do you know? • What didn't go well? How will you use this knowledge for next time? • Were there some children that did not engage? Why? What will you do? • What about those that excelled? What did you learn about them?
Next steps	• How will you use the above for your next planning session?

References

Ananiadou, K., and Claro, M. (2009) *21st Century Skills and Competences for New Millennium Learners in OECD Countries*. OECD Education Working Papers, No. 41, OECD Publishing, Paris. Available at: http://dx.doi.org/10.1787/218525261154

Ang, L. (ed.) (2014) *The Early Years Curriculum: The UK Context and Beyond*. Oxon: Routledge.

Arthur, L., Beecher, B., Death, E., Dockett, S., and Farmer, S. (2008) *Programming and Planning in Early Childhood Settings* (4th ed.). Melbourne: Thomson.

Ashiabi, G.S. (2007) Play in the Preschool Classroom: Its Socioemotional Significance and the Teacher's Role in Play. *Early Childhood Education Journal*, Vol. 35, pp. 199–207.

Avogadro, E. (2016) in A New Age of Culture: The Digitisation of Arts and Heritage. *A Report from The Economist Intelligence Unit*. Available at: http://newageofculture.eiu. com/Google_%20A%20New%20Age%20of%20Culture_final.pdf

Banaji, S., Burn, A., and Buckingham, D. (2010) The Rhetoric's of Creativity. *Arts Council England*. Available at: www.creativitycultureeducation.org/wp-content/uploads/rhetorics-of-creativity-2nd-edition-87.pdf Accessed: 16th February 2017.

Barnes, J. (2011) *Cross-Curricular Learning 3–14*. London: Sage.

Barras, C. (2014) Can You Learn to Be Creative? *BBC Futures*. Available at: http://www.bbc. com/future/story/20140314-learn-to-be-creative Accessed: 5th May 2017.

Beetlestone, F. (1998) *Learning in the Early Years: Creative Development*. Leamington Spa: Scholastic.

Beghetto, R.A. (2013) *Killing Ideas Softly? The Promise and Perils of Creativity in the Classroom*. Charlotte, NC: Information Age Press.

Be Open (2017) A Review of Policy, Provision and Excellence in Arts Teaching Across Secondary Education in Europe. *Be Open Foundation*. Available at: http://beopenfuture. com/all-projects/research/a-review-of-policy-provision-and-excellence-in-arts-teaching-across-secondary-education-in-europe/ Accessed: May 2017.

Bergen, D. (ed.) (1998) *Play as a Medium for Learning and Development*. Olney, MD: Association for Childhood Education International.

Bodrova, E., and Leong, D.J. (2005) Uniquely Preschool: What Research Tells Us about the Ways Young Children Learn. *Educational Leadership*, Vol. 63, No. 1, pp. 44–47.

Bolton, G. (2014) *Reflective Practice: Writing and Professional Development* (4th ed.). London: Sage Publications.

Bolton, G. (2009) Write to Learn: Reflective Practice Writing. *InnovAiT: Education and Inspiration for General Practice: Sage Journal*, Vol. 2, No. 12, pp. 752–754. Available at: http://journals.sagepub.com/doi/abs/10.1093/innovait/inp105

Bramwell et al. (2011) *Creative Teachers*. Available at: http://spectrum.library.concordia.ca/974917/1/Creative_Teachersfinal.pdf

Bronson, P., and Merryman, A. (2010) The Creativity Crisis. *Newsweek Magazine*. Available at: www.thedailybeast.com/newsweek/2010/07/10/the-creativity-crisis.html

Brown, N. (2017) Everything Is Awesome? Using LEGO ® to Trigger Reflection in Higher Education. *Higher Education Academy*. Available at: www.heacademy.ac.uk/blog/everything-awesome-using-lego%C2%AE-trigger-reflection-higher-education Accessed: 23rd September 2017.

Brown, S. (2010) *Play: How It Shapes the Brain, Opens the Imagination, and Invigorates the Soul*. London: Avery, Penguin.

Bruce, T. (2004) *Cultivating Creativity in Babies, Toddlers and Young Children*. London: Hodder and Stoughton Educational.

Brunton, P., and Thornton, L. (2013) Good Practice in Early Years Observation and Assessment. *Optimus Education*. Available at: http://my.optimus-education.com/good-practice-early-years-observation-and-assessment Accessed: 13th September 2017.

Canning, N. (2010) The Influence of the Outdoor Environment: Den-Making in Three Different Contexts. *European Early Childhood Education Research Journal*, Vol. 18, No. 4. Available at: www.tandfonline.com/doi/full/10.1080/1350293X.2010.525961 Accessed: 23rd March 2017.

CapeUK (2011) *A Journey into Creative Learning: One Small Step for Early Years One Giant Leap for Children*. Available at: file:///C:/Users/User/Documents/CapeUK-PDF-lo-res.pdf Accessed: 24th December 2017.

Carr, M., and Lee, W. (2012) *Learning Stories: Constructing Learner Identities in Early Education*. London: Sage Publications.

Carr, M. (2001). *Assessment in Early Childhood Settings: Learning Stories*. London: Paul Chapman.

Christophersen, C., and Breivik, J.K. (2013) *Den kulturelle skolesekken* [The Cultural Rucksack]. Oslo: Arts Council Norway.

Clary,R. (2017) *How to Stop Using Pre-Planned Topics and Plan from Children's Interests: Right from the Start*. Available at: https://rachelmcclary.com/tag/in-the-moment-planning/ Accessed: 13th August 2017.

Constantinides, M. (2015) Creating Creative Teachers. In Maley, A. and Peachey, N. (eds.) *Creativity in the English Language Classroom*. London: British Council.

Cook, C., Goodman, N.D., and Schulz, L.E. (2011) Where Science Starts: Spontaneous Experiments in Preschoolers' Exploratory Play. *Cognition*, Vol. 120, No. 3, pp. 341–349. http://doi.org/10.1016/j.cognition.2011.03.003

Cook, G. (2000) *Language Play, Language Learning*. Maidenhead, UK: Open University Press.

Craft, A. (2011) Creativity and Early Years Settings. In Paige-Smith, A. and Craft, A. (eds.) *Developing Reflective Practice in the Early Years* (2nd ed.). Buckingham: Open University Press.

Craft, A. (2010) Deconstruction or Reconstruction? In Tims, C. (ed.) *Born Creative*. London: Demos.

Craft, A. (2005) *Creativity in Schools: Tensions and Dilemmas*. Abingdon: Routledge.

Craft, A. (2003) The Limits to Creativity in Education: Dilemmas for the Educator. *British Journal of Educational Studies*, Vol. 51, No. 2, pp. 113–127.

Craft, A. (2001) Little c Creativity. In Craft, A., Jefferey, B. and Leibling, M. (eds.) *Creativity in Education*. London: Continuum.

Craft, A. (2000) *Creativity across the Primary Curriculum*. London: Routledge.

Craft, A. (1999) Creative Development in the Early Years: Implications of Policy and Practice. *The Curriculum Journal*, Vol. 10, No. 1, pp. 135–150.

• Craft et al
= 2001 d 2007.

Craft, A. (1998) UK Educator Perspectives on Creativity. *Journal of Creative Behavior*, Vol. 32, No. 4, pp. 244–257.

Craft, A. (1996) Nourishing Educator Creativity: A Holistic Approach to CPD. *British Journal of In-Service Education*, Vol. 22, No. 3, pp. 309–322.

Craft, A., and Hall, E. (2015) Changes in the Landscape for Creativity in Education. In Wilson, A. (ed.) *Creativity in Primary Education* (3rd ed.). London: Learning Matters, Sage Publications.

Creative Little Scientists (CLS) (2015) *Creativity in Science and Mathematics Education for Young Children*. Available at: www.creative-little-scientists.eu Accessed: 5th July 2017.

Creative Partnerships (2007) *Building Creative Partnerships: A Handbook for Schools*. London: Art Council England.

Cremin, T., Burnard, P., and Craft, A. (2006) Pedagogy and Possibility Thinking in the Early Years. *Thinking Skills and Creativity*, Vol. 1, No. 2, pp. 108–119.

Csikszentmihayli, M. (1997) *Finding Flow: The Psychology of Engagement with Everyday Life*. New York: Harper Collins.

Curtis, D. and Carter, M. (2015) *Designs for Living and Learning: Transforming Early Childhood Environments*. (2nd Ed). St Paul: Redleaf Press.

Davis, P. (2017) How Children Develop a Sense of Humour. *The Conversation*. Available at: https://theconversation.com/how-children-develop-a-sense-of-humour-77028 Accessed: 7th September 2017.

De Bono, E. (1985) *Six Thinking Hats*. New York: Little Brown and Company.

Department for Children, Schools and Families (2009) *Learning, Playing and Interacting Good practice in the Early Years Foundation Stage*. Nottingham: DCSF Publications.

Department for Children, Schools and Families (2008) *Effective Practice: Observation, Assessment and Planning*. Nottingham: DCSF Publications.

Department for Children, Schools and Families (2007a) *Effective Practice: Characteristics of Effective Learning: Playing and Exploring*. Nottingham: DCSF Publications.

Department for Children, Schools and Families (2007b) *Effective Practice: Characteristics of Effective Learning: Creating and Thinking Critically*. Nottingham: DCSF Publications.

Department for Education (DfE) (2017) *Statutory Framework for the Early Years Foundation Stage (EYFS)*. Available at: www.gov.uk/government/publications/early-years-foundation-stage-framework-2

Department for Education (DfE) (2006) *Roberts Review: Nurturing Creativity in Young People: A Report to Government to Inform Future Policy*. London: DfE.

Dodge, D.T., Heroman, C., Berke, K., Bickart, T., Colker, L., Jones, C., Copley, J., and Dighe, J. (2010) *The Creative Curriculum for Preschool* (5th ed.). Bethesda, MD: Teaching Strategies, Inc.

Driscoll, P. (2012) *The Primary Curriculum: A Creative Approach*. Thousand Oaks, CA: Sage Publications, p. 236.

Duffy, B. (2006) *Supporting Creativity and Imagination in the Early Years*. Maidenhead, UK: Open University Press.

The Early Childhood Pedagogies Collaboratory (2017) *Educators, in Collaboration with Others, Foster Ethical Pedagogies*. Available at: www.earlychildhoodcollaboratory.net/ Accessed: 21st October 2017.

Early Education (2012) *Development Matters in the Early Years Foundation Stage (EYFS)*. London: Early Education.

Education Scotland. (2013) *Creativity Across Learning: 3–18*. Livingston: Education Scotland.

Edwards, C. P. (2002). Three Approaches from Europe: Waldorf, Montessori and Reggio Emilia. *Early Childhood Research and Practice*, Vol. 4, No.1. Retrieved from http://ecrp.uiuc.edu/v4n1/edwards.html

Edwards, C. (1993). Partner, Nurturer, and Guide: The Roles of the Reggio Teacher in Action. In Edwards, C., Gandini, L. and Forman, G. (Eds.), *The Hundred Languages of Children: The Reggio Emilia Approach to Early Childhood Education* (pp. 151–169). Norwood, NJ: Ablex.

Egan, K. (2008) Introduction. In Judson, G. (ed.) *Teaching 360: Effective Learning through the Imagination*. Rotterdam: Sense Publishers.

Ephgrave, A. (2017) Planning Next Steps in the Moment. *The Early Years Foundation Stage Forum (EYFS)*. Available at: http://eyfs.info/articles/_/teaching-and-learning/planning-next-steps-in-the-moment-r217# Accessed: 30th December 2017.

Epstein, A.S. (2003) How Planning and Reflection Develops Young Children's Thinking Skills. *Beyond the Journal*. Available at: http://journal.naeyc.org/btj/200309/Planning&Reflection.pdf Accessed: 22nd August 2017.

Epstein, R. (1996) *Cognition, Creativity and Behaviour*. Westport, CT: Praeger.

Evangelou, M., Sylva, K., Kyriacou, M., Wild, M., and Glenny, G. (2009) *Early Years Learning and Development Literature Review*. London: DCSF.

Ferguson, K. (2012) Embrace the Remix at *TedGlobal*. Available at: https://www.ted.com/talks/kirby_ferguson_embrace_the_remix. Accessed: 14th February 2017.

Finlay, L. (2008) *Reflecting on 'Reflective Practice'*. A discussion paper prepared for PBPL CETL (www.open.ac.uk/pbpl) Paper 52.

Fisher, J. (2013) *Starting from the Child: Teaching and Learning in the Foundation Stage* (4th ed.). Maidenhead: Open University Press.

Fleer, M. (2015) A Cultural-Historical View of Child Development: Key Concepts for Going Beyond a Universal View of the Child. *Asia-Pacific Journal of Research in Early Childhood Education*, Vol. 9, No. 1, January 2015, pp. 19–37.

Fryer, M. (1996) *Creative Teaching and Learning*. London: Paul Chapman Publishing.

Fumoto, H., Robson, S., Greenfield, S., and Hargreaves, D.J. (2012) *Young Children's Creative Thinking*. London: Sage Publications.

Gardner, H. (2007) *Five Minds in the Future*. Boston: Harvard Business School Press.

Gauntlett, D. (2011) *Making Is Connecting: The Social Meaning of Creativity, from DIY and Knitting to YouTube and Web2.0*. Cambridge: Polity Press.

Gauntlett, D., Whitebread, D., Wolbers, T., Weckstrom, C., and Thomsen, B.S. (2011) *The Future of Learning*. The Lego Foundation. Available at: www.legofoundation.com/nl-nl/research-and-learning/foundation-research Accessed: 18th August 2017.

Gelman, S.A. (2009) Learning from Others: Children's Construction of Concepts. *Annual Review of Psychology*, Vol. 60, pp. 115–140. Available at: www.ncbi.nlm.nih.gov/pmc/articles/PMC2829654/

Gonzalez, J. (2013) *Find Your Marigold: The One Essential Rule for New Teachers*. Kentucky: Cult of Pedagogy.

Goodwin, M. (2008) *Listening and Responding to People Who Do Not Communicate Using Words*. Available at: info@disabilitydice.co.uk

Goodwin, M., and Edwards, C. (2009) I'm Creative Too in PMLD Link Bulletin. Vol. 21, No. 1, Issue 62. Available at: www.pmldlink.org.uk/wp-content/uploads/2015/09/PMLD-Link-Issue-62.pdf

Goouch, K. (2008) Understanding Playful Pedagogies, Play Narratives and Play Spaces. *Early Years: An International Journal of Research and Development*, Vol. 28, No. 1, pp. 93–102.

Gray, P. (2013) *Free to Learn: Why Unleashing the Instinct to Play Will Make our Children Happier, More Self-Reliant, and Better Students for Life*. New York, NY: Basic Books.

Griffith, M. (2014) Encouraging Imagination and Creativity in the Teaching Profession. *European Educational Research Journal*, Vol. 13, No. 1.

Hallet, E. (2016) *Early Years Practice: For Educators and Teachers*. London: Sage Publications.

Halsted, C. (2017) *Open Sesame Unlocking Creativity in Early Years: Evaluation Report.* Culture Shift. Available at: www.cultureshift.org.uk/wp-content/uploads/2014/12/OpenSesame_Evaluation_FINAL.pdf Accessed: 31st August 2017.

Hamilton, D. (2014) *Towards a Theory of Schooling.* Oxon: Routledge.

Harle, A.Z., and Trudeau, K. (2006) Using Reflection to Increase Children's Learning in Kindergarten. *Young Children*, Vol. 61, No. 4, pp. 101–104. Available at: https://eric.ed.gov/?id=EJ751400 Accessed: 9th November 2017.

Haughton, C., and Ellis, C. (2016) Play in the Early Years. In Palaiologou, I. (ed.) *The Early Years Foundation Stage: Theory and Practice* (3rd ed.). London: Sage Publications.

Hendy, L., and Toon, L. (2001) *Supporting Drama and Imaginative Play in the Early Years.* Buckingham: Open University Press.

Hirsh-Pasek, K., Golinkoff, R., Berk, L., and Singer, D. (2009) *A Mandate for Playful Learning in Preschool: Presenting the Evidence.* New York: Oxford University Press.

HMSO (2006) *Leitch Review of Skills: Prosperity for all in the Global Economy – World Class Skills Final Report.* Norwich: HMSO. Available at: www.gov.uk/government/publications/prosperity-for-all-in-the-global-economy-world-class-skills-final-report Accessed: 13th April 2017.

Hodgman, L. (2011) *Enabling Environments in the Early Years: Making Provision for High Quality and Challenging Learning Experiences in Early Years Settings.* London: Practical Preschool Books.

Holland, C. (2017) What Are the Benefits of Beach Schools? *First Discoverers.* Available at: www.firstdiscoverers.co.uk/benefits-beach-schools/ Accessed: 18th August 2017.

Huberman, M. (1995) Networks That Alter Teaching: Conceptualisations, Exchanges and Experiments. *Teacher and Teaching: Theory and Practice*, Vol. 1, No. 2, pp. 193–211.

Hughes, B. (2011) *Evolutionary Playwork* (2nd ed.). Abingdon, UK: Routledge.

Hughes, B. (2006) *Playtypes: Speculations and Possibilities.* London: Centre for Playwork Education and Training.

Hughes, B. (2002) *A Playworker's Taxonomy of Play Types* (2nd ed.). London: Playlink.

Huizinga, J. (1970) *Homo Ludens': A Study of the Play Element Culture.* London: Maurice Temple Smith.

Hunt, T. (2015) *Creative Schools Review – We Need to Call Time on Exam-Factory Education.* Available at: www.theguardian.com/books/2015/apr/23/creative-schools-revolutionising-education-from-the-ground-up-ken-robinson-lou-aronica-review Accessed: 21st October 2016.

Hutchin, V. (2013) *Effective Provision in the Early Years Foundation Stage: An Essential Guide.* Berkshire: Open University Press.

Ingledew, J. (2016) *How to Have Great Ideas: A Guide to Creative Thinking.* London: Lawrence King Publishing.

Issacson, W. (2012) The Real Leadership Lessons of Steve Jobs. *Harvard Business Review.* Available at: https://hbr.org/2012/04/the-real-leadership-lessons-of-steve-jobs Accessed: 9th April 2017.

Isbell, R.T., and Raines, S.C. (2013) *Creativity and the Arts with Young Children.* (3rd ed.). Belmont, CA: Wadsworth, Cengage Learning.

Jackson, N.J. (2014) Developing Students' Creativity through a Higher Education. In Xie, A. and Lei, L. (eds.) *International Symposium on 'The Cultivation of Creativity in University Students'* (pp. 8–28). Macao: Macao Polytechnic Institute.

Jeffrey, B., and Woods, P. (2003) *The Creative School: A Framework for Success, Quality and Effectiveness.* London: Routledge/Falmer.

Johnston, J., Nahmad-Williams, L., Oates, R. and Wood, V. (2018) *Early Childhood Studies: Principles and Practice.* (2nd ed.). Oxon: Routledge.

Jones, E. (2012) The Emergence of Emergent Curriculum. *Young Children (NAEYC)*, March 2012, pp. 66–68.

Joubert, M. M. (2001) The Art of Creative Teaching: NACCCE and Beyond. In A. Craft, B. Jeffrey and M. Leibling, eds. *Creativity in Education*. London: Continuum, 17–34.

Kagan, S. (2012) *Starting Well: Benchmarking Early Education Across the World*. London: The Economist Intelligence Unit.

Kangas, J. (2016) Enhancing Children's Participation in Early Childhood Education through the Participatory Pedagogy. *Department of Teacher Education, Faculty of Behavioral Science, University of Helsinki*. Available at: https://helda.helsinki.fi/bitstream/handle/10138/159547/enhancin.pdf?sequence=1

Katz, L.G., and Chard, S.C. (2000) *Engaging Children's Minds: The Project Approach*. New Jersey: Ablex Publishing Cooperation.

Katz, L.G., and Chard, S.C. (1989) *Engaging Children's Minds: The Project Approach*. Norwood, NJ: Ablex. (ERIC Document No. ED407074).

Katz, L.G., and Helm, J.H. (2011) *Young Investigators: The Project Approach in the Early Years*. New York: Teachers College, Columbia University.

Keenan, S.F., and Mishra, P. (2016) Profiling Scholars of Creativity: Practicing the Process with Dr. Michele Root-Bernstein. *TechTrends*, Vol. 60, pp. 200–203. doi: 10.1007/s11528-016-0055-2

Kessler, R. (2000) *The Soul of Education: Helping Students Find Connection, Compassion and Character at School*. Alexandria, VA: Association for Supervision and Curriculum Development.

Khoo, I. (2015) Finland Education Does Away with 'Subjects'. *The Huffington Post: Canada*. Available at: www.huffingtonpost.ca/2015/04/24/finland-education-subjects_n_7021048.html Accessed: 8th April 2017.

Kinos, J., Robertson, L., Nancy Barbour, N., and Pukk, M. (2016) Child-Initiated Pedagogies: Moving Toward Democratically Appropriate Practices in Finland, England, Estonia, and the United States. *Childhood Journal*, Vol. 92, No. 5, pp. 345–357. Available at: www.tandfonline.com/doi/abs/10.1080/00094056.2016.1226107 Accessed: 23rd March 2017.

Koster, J.B. (2012) *Growing Artists: Teaching the Arts to Young Children* (5th ed.). Belmont, CA: Wadsworth Cengage Learning.

Kousoulas, F. (2010) The Interplay of Creative Behavior, Divergent Thinking, and Knowledge Base in Students' Creative Expression during Learning Activity. *Creativity Research Journal*, Vol. 22, No. 4, pp. 387–396.

Kress, G. (2009) *Multimodality: A Social Semiotic Approach to Contemporary Communication*. London: Routledge.

Kuchner, J.F. (1991, May) *The Humour of Young Children*. Paper presented at the Meeting of the National Association for the Education of Young Children, Washington, DC.

Kudryavtsev, V.T. (2011) The Phenomenon of Child Creativity. *International Journal of Early Years Education*, Vol. 19, No. 1, pp. 45–53.

Kwek, S.H. (2011) *Innovation in the Classroom: Design Thinking for 21st Century Learning*. (Master's thesis). Available at: www.stanford.edu/group/redlab/cgibin/publications_resources.php

Laevers, F. (2015) Making Care and Education More Effective through Wellbeing and Involvement: An Introduction to Experiential Education. In *Centre for Experiential Education*. Belgium: University of Leuven.

Laevers, F. (Red.) (1994) *The Leuven Involvement Scale for Young Children: Manual and Video. Experiential Education Series, No. 1*. Leuven: Centre for Experiential Education, 44p.

Laevers, F. (1993) Deep Level Learning: An Exemplary Application on the Area of Physical Knowledge. *European Early Childhood Research Journal*, Vol. 1, pp. 53–68.

Lakoff, G., and Johnson, M. (1980) *Metaphors We Live by*. Chicago: University of Chicago Press.

Land, G., and Jarman, B. (1998) *Breakpoint and Beyond: Mastering the Future Today*. Scottsdale, AZ: Leadership 2000 Inc.

Langston, A., and Abbott, L. (2005) Quality Matters. In Abbott, L. and Langston, A. (eds.) *Birth to Three Matters: Supporting the Framework of Effective Practice*. Maidenhead: Open University Press.

Lave, J., and Wenger, E. (1991) *Situated Learning: Legitimate Peripheral Participation*. Cambridge: Cambridge University Press.

Lear, J. (2015) *Guerrilla Teaching: Revolutionary Tactics for Teachers on the Ground, in Real Classrooms, Working with Real Children, Trying to Make a Real Difference*. Wales: Independent Thinking Press.

Leong, D.J., and Bodrova, E. (2012) Assessing and Scaffolding Make-Believe Play. *Young Children, NAEYC*. Available at: www.naeyc.org/files/yc/file/201201/Leong_Make_Believe_Play_Jan2012.pdf Accessed: 8th September 2017.

Le Guin, U.K. (2017) *No Time to Spare: Thinking about what Matters*. New York: Houghton Mifflin Harcourt Publishing Company.

Lin, Y.-S. (2011) Fostering Creativity through Education – a Conceptual Framework of Creative Pedagogy. *Creative Education*, Vol. 2, No. 3, pp. 149–155.

Literacy Trust (2016) *How to Choose Apps*. Available at: http://literacyapps.literacytrust.org.uk/how-to-choose-apps Accessed: 14th October 2016.

Liu, J.H. (2011) The 5 Best Toys of All Time. *Wired.com*. Available at: www.wired.com/geekdad/2011/01/the-5-best-toys-of-all-time/all/1

Loizou, E. (2005) Humour: A Different Kind of Play. *European Early Childhood Education Research Journal*, Vol. 13, No. 2, pp. 97–109. https://doi.org/10.1080/13502930585209701

Lombardi, J. (2013) Providing a Path to Early Success: Securing the Foundation for Learning. In *Early Childhood Matters*. Netherlands: Bernard van Leer Foundation.

Loughton, T. and Teather, S. (2010) Creating Conditions: Trusted Professional and Targeted Resources for Creativity in the Early Years. In Tims, C. (ed.) *Born Creative*. London: Demos.

MacDonald, M. (2007) Developmental Theory and Post-Modern Thinking in Early Childhood Education. *Canadian Children*, Vol. 32, No. 2, pp. 7–10.

McMillan, M. (1919) *The Nursery School*. London: J.M. Dent and Sons.

Malaguzzi, L. (1998) History, Ideas, and Basic Philosophy: An Interview with Lella Gandini. In Edwards, C., Gandini, L. and Forman, G. (eds.) *The Hundred Languages of Children: The Reggio Emilia Approach – Advanced Reflections* (2nd ed., pp. 49–97). Norwood, NJ: Ablex.

Malaguzzi, L. (1993) History, Ideas, and Basic Philosophy: An Interview with Lella Gandini. In Edwards, C., Gandini, L. and Forman, G. (eds.) *The Hundred Languages of Children: The Reggio Emilia Approach – Advanced Reflections* (2nd ed.). Greenwich, CT: Ablex Publishing.

Marsh, J., Plowman, L., Yamada-Rice, D., Bishop, J.C., Lahmar, J., Scott, F., Davenport, A., Davis, S., French, K., Piras, M., Thornhill, S., Robinson, P., and Winter, P. (2015) *Exploring Play and Creativity in Pre-Schoolers' Use of Apps: Report for Early Years Practitioners*. Available at: www.techandplay.org

Martin, M. (2016) Critical Reflection on Practice: A Reflection on Using Play to Facilitate Learning. *International Practice Development Journal*, Vol. 6, No. 1, p. 7. Available at: www.fons.org/library/journal.aspx Accessed: 1st December 2017.

Marzollo, J., and Lloyd, J. (1974) *Learning through Play*. Sydney: Allen & Unwin.

McCammon, L.A., O'Farrell, L., Saebø, A.B., and Heap, B. (2010) Connecting with Their Inner Beings: An International Survey of Drama/Theatre Teachers' Perceptions of

Creative Teaching and Teaching for Creative Achievement. *Youth Theatre Journal*, Vol. 24, pp. 140–159.

Meador, K.S. (1992) Emerging Rainbows: A Review of the Literature on Creativity. *Journal for the Education of the Gifted*, Vol. 15, No. 2, pp. 163–181.

Mercilliott Hewett, V. (2001) Examining the Reggio Emilia Approach to Early Childhood Education. *Early Childhood Educational Journal*, Vol. 29, No. 2, pp. 95–100.

Michalko, M. (1998) Thinking Like a Genius: Eight Strategies Used by the Supercreative, from Aristotle and Leonardo to Einstein and Edison. *The Futurist*, Vol. 32, No. 4. Available at: www.questia.com/magazine/1G1-20925508/thinking-like-a-genius-eight-strategies-used-by-the Accessed: 8th October 2017.

Mincemoyer, C.C. (2013) *Embracing Professionalism in Better Kid Care Program*. Pennsylvania State University. Available at: www.extension.psu.edu/youth/betterkidcare

Mirrahimi, S., Tawil, N.M., Abdullah, M.S., and Usman, I.M.S. et al. (2011) Developing Conducive Sustainable Outdoor Learning: The Impact of Natural Environment on Learning, Social and Emotional Intelligence. *Procedia Engineering*, Vol. 20, pp. 389–396.

Mohammed, R. (2014) The Challenges of Implementing an Early Years Curriculum: A Practitioner's Perspective. In Ang, L. (ed.) *The Early Years Curriculum: The UK Context and Beyond*. Oxon: Routledge.

Mohammed, R. (2013) Thinking Approaches for the Reflective Professional. *The Early Years Foundation Stage Forum (EYFS)*. Available at: http://eyfs.info/articles.html/general/thinking-approaches-for-the-reflective-professional-r154/

Moore, R. (1996) Compact Nature: The Role of Playing and Learning Gardens on Children's Lives. *Journal of Therapeutic Horticulture*. Vol. 8, pp. 72–82.

Morais, M.F., and Azevedo, I. (2011) What Is a Creative Teacher and What Is a Creative Pupil? Perceptions of Teachers. *Procedia Social and Behavioural Sciences*, Vol. 12, pp. 330–339. Available at: www.sciencedirect.com

Moyles, J. (2005) *The Excellence of Play* (2nd ed.). Maidenhead: Open University Press.

Munns, G., Arthur, L., Downes, T., Gregson, R., Power, A., Sawyer, W., Singh, M., Thistleton-Martin, J. & Steele, F. (2006). Motivation and Engagement of Boys Evidence-based Teaching Practices. Report submitted to the *Commonwealth Department of Education, Science and Training*.

Munns, G., Martin, A. J., & Craven, R. G. (2006) Crossing the Great Divide: The Motivation and Engagement Framework in Action. Proceedings of the Fourth International Biennial SELF Research Conference. Available from: https://www.researchgate.net/publication/228557177_Crossing_the_great_divide_the_motivation_and_engagement_framework_in_action Accessed: March 2 2018.

Napell, S.M. (1978) Using Questions to Enhance Class-Room Learning. *Education*, Vol. 99, No. 2, Winter, p. 188, 10p.

National Advisory Committee on Creative and Cultural Education (1999) *All Our Futures: Creativity, Culture and Education*. London: DFEE.

Nicholson, S. (1972) The Theory of Loose Parts: An Important Principle for Design Methodology. *Studies in Design Education, Craft and Technology*, Vol. 4, No. 2, pp. 5–14.

O'Connor, A., and Diggins, C. (2002) *On Reflection: Reflective Practice for Early Childhood Educators*. Wellington, NZ: Open Mind Publishing.

Office for Standards in Education (Ofsted) (2017) *Bold Beginnings: The Reception Curriculum in a Sample of Good and Outstanding Primary Schools*. Manchester: Ofsted. Available at: www.gov.uk/government/publications/reception-curriculum-in-good-and-outstanding-primary-schools-bold-beginnings

Ornstein, A., and Hunkins, F. (2009) Curriculum Design. In *Curriculum: Foundations, Principles and Issues* (5th ed., pp. 181–206). Boston, MA: Pearson/Allyn and Bacon.

Oxford English Dictionary. Oxford: Oxford University Press. Retrieved from http://www. oxforddictionaries.com/definition/english/curriculumPaige-Smith, A., and Craft, A. (eds.) (2011) *Developing Reflective Practice in the Early Years* (2nd ed.). Maidenhead: Open University Press.

Papatheodorou, T., and Moyles, J. (eds.) (2009) *Learning Together in the Early Years: Exploring Relational Pedagogy.* Oxon: Routledge.

Pascal, C., and Bertram, T. (2017a) *Creativity and Critical Thinking are Central to an Effective Early Years Curriculum and Pedagogy.* BECERA. Available at: www.becera.org.uk

Pascal, C., and Bertram, T. (2017b) *How to Catch a Moonbeam and Pin It Down: Creativity and the Arts in the Early Years.* Birmingham: Amber Publications and Training.

Petrie, P., Boddy, J., Cameron, C., Heptinstall, E., McQuail, S., Simon, A., and Wigfall, V. (2009) Pedagogy – a Holistic, Personal Approach to Work with Children and Young People across Services. In *University of London Thomas Coram Research Unit.* Institute of Education. Available at: http://eprints.ioe.ac.uk/58/1/may_18_09_Ped_BRIEFING_PAPER_JB_PP_.pdf

Picton, I. (2014) *The Impact of Ebooks on the Reading Motivation and Reading Skills of Children and Young People.* London: National Literacy Trust.

Pink, D. (2006) *A Whole New Mind: Why Right-Brainers Will Rule the Future.* New York: Riverhead Books.

Qualifications and Curriculum Authority (2004) *Creativity: Find It! Promote It!* London: QCA.

Querido, R.M. (1987) *Creativity in Education: The Waldorf Approach.* San Francisco: H S Dakin Co.

Reed, M., and Canning, N. (eds.) (2010) *Reflective Practice in the Early Years.* London: Sage Publications.

Riddle, H. (2016) *Everyday Early Childhood Education Advocacy.* Washington, DC: Council for Professional Recognition.

Rinaldi, C. (2005) Documentation and Assessment: What Is the Relationship? In Clark, A., Kjorholt, A. and Moss, P. (eds.) *Beyond Listening: Children's Perspectives on Early Childhood Services.* Bristol: The Policy Press.

Ritchhart, R., Church, M., and Morrison, K. (2011) *Making Thinking Visible: How to Promote Engagement, Understanding, and Independence for All Learners.* San Francisco: Jossey-Bass.

Roberts, P. (2006) *Nurturing Creativity in Young People a Report to Government to Inform Future Policy.* London: DfE.

Robinson, K. (2015) Sir Ken Robinson: Creativity Is in Everything, Especially Teaching. *Mind Shift.* Available at: ww2.kqed.org/mindshift/2015/04/22/sir-ken-robinson-creativity-is-in-everything-especially-teaching/

Robinson, K. (2011) *'Bridge Building' Connecting the Arts and Schools.* London: A New Direction. Available at: www.youtube.com/watch?v=h_2jh3MRjtI&feature=relmfu Accessed: 13th April 2017.

Robinson, K. (2005) *Presentation by Sir Ken Robinson.* Denver, CO: Education Commission of the States. 2005 National Forum of Education Policy. Chairman's Breakfast.

Robinson, K., and Aronica, L. (2015) *Creative Schools: Revolutionizing Education from the Ground Up.* USA: Allen Lane.

Robson, S., and Lowe, V. (2012) Observing Young Children's Creative Thinking: Engagement, Involvement and Persistence. *International Journal of Early Years Education*, Vol. 20, No. 4.

Rogoff, B. (1990) *Apprenticeship in Thinking: Cognitive Development in Social Context.* Oxford: Oxford University Press.

Root-Bernstein, M. (2014) *Inventing Imaginary Worlds: From Childhood Play to Adult Creativity across the Arts and Sciences.* Lanham: Rowman and Littlefield Education.

Root-Bernstein, M. (2012) The Creation of Imaginary Worlds. In Taylor, M. (ed.) *The Oxford Handbook of the Development of Imagination.* Oxford: Oxford University Press.

Root-Bernstein, R., and Root-Bernstein, M. (1999) *Sparks of Genius: The Thirteen Thinking Tools of the World's Most Creative People.* New York: Houghton Mifflin Company.

Rose, J., and Rogers, S. (2012) *The Role of the Adult in Early Years Settings.* Maidenhead: Open University Press.

Rosen, M. (2010) Foreword to Born Creative. In Tims, C. (ed.) *Born Creative.* London: Demos.

Runco, M.A. (ed.) (1996) *Creativity from Childhood through Adulthood: The Developmental Issues.* New Directions for Child Development No. 72. San Francisco, CA: Jossey-Bass.

Russ, S., and Fiorelli, J. (2010) Developmental Approaches to Creativity. In Kaufman, J. and Sternberg, R. (eds.) *The Cambridge Handbook of Creativity* (pp. 233–249). New York: Cambridge University Press.

Russ, S.W., Robins, A.L. and Christiano, B.A. (1999) Pretend Play: Longitudinal Prediction of Creativity and Affect in Fantasy in Children. *Creativity Research Journal,* Vol. 12, pp. 129–139.

Ryhammar, L., and Brolin, C. (1999) Creativity Research: Historical Considerations and Main Lines of Development. *Scandinavian Journal of Educational Research*, Vol. 43, No. 3, pp. 259–273.

Sahlberg, P. (2006). Models of Curriculum Development: International Trends and the Way Forward. In Sahlberg, P. (ed.), *Curriculum Reform and Implementation in the 21st Century: Policies, Perspectives and Implementation* (pp. 108–121). Proceedings of the International Conference on Curriculum Reform and Implementation in the 21st Century. Istanbul, Turkey. Available at: www.pasisahlberg.com/index.php?id=15

Sancisi, L., and Edgington, M. (2015) *Developing High Quality Observation, Assessment and Planning in the Early Years, Made to Measure.* Oxon: Routledge.

Sandbrook, B. (2012) *Music, Education and Creative Learning.* Available at: www.bensandbrook.com/publications Accessed: 24th February 2017.

Sawyer, R.K. (2012). *Explaining Creativity: The Science of Human Innovation.* New York: Oxford University Press.

Sawyer, R.K. (2006). Educating for Innovation. *Thinking Skills and Creativity*, Vol. 1, pp. 41–48.

Schwab, K. (2016) *The Fourth Industrial Revolution: What It Means, How to Respond.* World Economic Forum.

Schwind, J.K., Cameron, D., Franks, J., Graham, C., and Robinson, T. (2012) Engaging in Narrative Reflective Process to Fine Tune Self-as-Instrument-of-Care. *Reflective Practice*, Vol. 13, No. 2, pp. 223–235. doi:10.1080/14623943.2011.626030

Seifter, H., and Buswick, T. (2005, October) Special Edition on Arts-Based Learning for Business. *The Journal of Business Strategy*, Vol. 26, No. 5.

Seitz, H.J. (2006) Innovative Practice. The Plan: Building on Children's Interests. *Beyond the Journal.* Young Children on the Web: Innovative Practice.

Sewell, K. (2015) *Planning the Primary National Curriculum: A Complete Guide for Trainees and Teachers.* London: Learning Matters.

Shaheen, R. (2010) Creativity and Education. *Creative Education*, Vol. 1, No. 3, pp. 166–169. Available at: http://file.scirp.org/Html/3369.html Accessed: 4th October 2016.

Sharp, C. (2004) Developing Young Children's Creativity: What Can We Learn from Research? *Topic*, No. 32. NFER Research Report. Available at: www.nfer.ac.uk/publications/55502 Accessed: 6th July 2017.

Simister, C.J. (2007) *How to Teach Thinking and Learning Skills*. London: Paul Chapman Publishing.

Sinclair, R. (2004). Participation in Practice: Making It Meaningful, Effective and Sustainable. *Children & Society*, Vol. 18, pp. 106–118.

Siraj-Blatchford, I. (2014) Early Childhood Education (ECE). In Maynard, T. and Thomas, N. (eds.) *An Introduction to Early Childhood Studies* (3rd ed.). London: Sage.

Siraj-Blatchford, I., and Manni, L. (2007) *Effective Leadership in the Early Years Sector (the ELEYS Study)*, Issues in Practice Series. London: University of London Institute of Education.

Siraj-Blatchford, I. (2007) Creativity, Communication and Collaboration: The Identification of Pedagogic Progression in Sustained Shared Thinking. *Asia-Pacific Journal of Research in Early Childhood Education*, Vol. 1, No. 2, pp. 3–23.

Smidt, S. (2005) *Observing, Assessing and Planning for Children in the Early Years*. Oxon: Routledge.

Spencer, E., Lucus, B. and Claxton, G. (2012) *Progression in Creativity: Developing New Forms of Assessment*. Newcastle: CCE.

Starko, A.J. (2014) *Creativity in the Classroom: Schools of Curious Delight* (5th ed.). New York: Routledge.

The Sutton Trust (2017) The State of Social Mobility in the UK. *Sutton Trust*. Available at: www.suttontrust.com/wp-content/uploads/2017/07/BCGSocial-Mobility-report-full-version_WEB_FINAL.pdf Accessed: 12th July 2017.

Sylva, K., Melhuish, E., Sammons, P., Siraj-Blatchford, I., and Taggart, B. (2004) *The Effective Provision of Pre-School Education (EPPE Project): Final Report*. London: DfES/ Institute of Education.

Tarr, P. (2004) Consider the Walls: Young Children. *Theory into Practice*, Vol. 59, No. 3, pp. 88–92.

Taylor, T. (2016) *A Beginner's Guide to Mantle of the Expert: A Transformative Approach to Education*. Norwich: Singular Publishing.

Thomas, J. (1999). Nine Barriers to Thinking Creatively. *Women in Business*, Vol. 51, No. 1, p. 14. Available at: http://connection.ebscohost.com/c/articles/1434714/nine-barriers-thinking-creatively Accessed: 21st October 2017.

Thornberg, D. (2014) *From the Campfire to the Holodeck*. San Francisco CA: Jossey-Bass.

Tickell, C. (2011) *The Early Years: Foundations for Life, Health and Learning: An Independent Review on the Early Years Foundation Stage*. London: Department for Education.

Times Higher Education (TES) (2002) Is Imagination More Important than Knowledge? Einstein. Available at: https://www.timeshighereducation.com/features/is-imagination-more-important-than-knowledge-einstein/172613.article Accessed: 21st[t] October 2017.

Tobin, J., Wu, D., and Davidson, D. (1991) *Preschool in Three Cultures: Japan, China and the United States*. Yale: Yale University Press.

Toffler, A. (1970) *Future Shock*. New York: Random House.

Toivanena, T., Halkilahtib, L., and Ruismäkic, H. (2013) Supporting Children's Creativity through Drama. *The European Journal of Social & Behavioural Sciences*. Available at: www.futureacademy.org.uk/files/menu_items/other/ejsbs96.pdf Accessed: 5th December 2017.

Tovey, H. (2007) *Playing Outdoors: Spaces and Places, Risk and Challenge*. Maidenhead: Open University Press.

Tracey, S. (2007) *Creative Reflection, Creative Practice: Expressing the Inexpressible*. Cardiff: University of Wales/ Higher Education Academy.

Ulger, K. (2015) The Structure of Creative Thinking: Visual and Verbal Areas. *Creativity Research Journal*, Vol. 21, No. 1, pp. 53–72.

Veale, F. (2014) *Pedagogical Approaches in Early Years Education.* Conference Paper at South Devon College Inaugural Research Showcase. Available at: www.researchgate.net/publication/303538160_Pedagogical_Approaches_in_Early_Years_Education Accessed: 17th October 2017.

von Oech, R. (1998) *A Whack on the Side of the Head, How You Can Be More Creative.* New York: Warner Books Inc.

Vygotsky, L.S. (2004) Imagination and Creativity in Childhood, (M.E. Sharpe, Trans.). *Journal of Russian and East European Psychology*, Vol. 42, No. 1, pp. 7–97 (Original work published 1967).

Vygotsky, L.S. (1978) *Mind in Society: The Development of Higher Psychological Processes.* Cambridge, MA: Harvard University Press.

Waldron, J. (2017) *The Effective Pre-School, Primary and Secondary Education Project (EPPSE).* Available at: www.ucl.ac.uk/ioe/research/featured-research/effective-pre-school-primary-secondary-education-project Accessed: 4th September 2017.

White, R.E., Prager, E.O., Schaefer, C., Kross, E., Duckworth, A.L., and Carlson, S.C. (2017) The 'Batman Effect': Improving Perseverance in Young Children. *Child Development*, Vol. 88, No. 5, pp. 1563–1571. Available at: http://onlinelibrary.wiley.com/doi/10.1111/cdev.12695/abstract?campaign=woletoc Accessed: 21st November 2017.

Whitebread, D., and Pasternak, D. (2010) Metacognition, Self-Regulation and Meta Knowing. In Littleton, K., Wood, C. and Kleine Staarman, J. (eds.) *International Handbook of Psychology in Education.* Bingley, UK: Emerald.

William, D. (2013) Assessment: The Bridge between Teaching and Learning. *Voices from the Middle*, Vol. 21, No. 2. National Council of Teachers of English.

Williams-Siegfredsen, J. (2011) *Understanding the Danish Forest School Approach.* Oxon: Routledge.

Willis, J. (2006) *Research-Based Strategies to Ignite Student Learning.* Alexandria, VA: ASCD.

Willis, J. (2010) *Learning to Love Math: Teaching Strategies That Change Student Attitudes and Get Results.* Alexandria, VA: ASCD.

Wood, E., and Attfield, J. (2005) *Play, Learning and the Early Childhood Curriculum* (2nd ed.). London: Sage.

Woods, P., and Jefferey, B. (1996) *Teachable Moments: The Art of Creative Teaching in Primary School.* Buckingham: Open University Press.

Woolf, F., and Belloli, J. (2005) Reflect and Review: The Arts and Creativity in Early Years. *Arts Council England.* Available at: http://webarchive.nationalarchives.gov.uk/20160204123634/www.artscouncil.org.uk/advice-and-guidance/browse-advice-and-guidance/reflect-and-review-the-arts-and-creativity-in-early-years

Xanthoudaki, M. (2015) Museums, Innovative Pedagogies and the Twenty-First Century Learner: A Question of Methodology. *Museum and Society*, Vol. 13, No. 2, pp. 247–265. Available at: https://www2.le.ac.uk/departments/museumstudies/museumsociety/documents/volumes/xanthoudaki Accessed: 21st December 2017.

Yānez, L. (2013) Learning from Birth. In *Early Childhood Matters.* Netherlands: Bernard van Leer Foundation.

Index

Note: Page numbers in *italics* indicate figures; **bold** indicates tables.

Printed in Great Britain
by Amazon